THE
BIBLICAL HERITAGE
OF
AMERICAN DEMOCRACY

THE
BIBLICAL HERITAGE
OF
AMERICAN DEMOCRACY

by
ABRAHAM I. KATSH

KTAV PUBLISHING HOUSE, INC.
NEW YORK
1977

Library of Congress Cataloging in Publication Data

Katsh, Abraham Isaac
   The Biblical heritage of American democracy.

   Bibliography: p.
   Includes index.
   1. Bible. O.T.—Influence—United States. 2. United
States—Religion. I. Title.
BS538.7.K37   973.2   76-22468
ISBN 0-87068-488-4

MANUFACTURED IN THE UNITED STATES OF AMERICA

To Estelle
The Joy of my Heart

Table of Contents

Illustrations

Acknowledgments

I wish to express my gratitude to Frank Blisard, who read the manuscript in its early stages and prepared to map of place names of Biblical or Hebrew origin, and to Yvonne Wood and Elinor Johnson for their able assistance in preparing the manuscript for publication. Special thanks are extended to my friends Joseph Handleman, David Rose, Joseph Strauss and William B. Thomas.

I also wish to acknowledge with thanks permissions granted by the various publishers to quote from the following:

1. *Annals of the Jewish Academy of Arts and Sciences,* edited by Hirsch L. Silverman, New York, 1974.
2. *Hebrew Studies,* edited by Israel T. Naamani, Louisville, 1976.
3. *Justice, Justice Shalt Thou Pursue,* edited by Rabbi Ronald B. Sobel and Sidney Wallach, New York, 1975.
4. *The Hebrew Impact on Western Civilization,* edited by Dagobert D. Runes, New York, 1965
5. *The Joseph Papin Festschrifts,* Volumes I & II, Philadelphia, 1972, 1976.
6. *JNF Yearbook,* edited by Leon L. Wolfe, New York, 1976
7. *Halutz V'Maas,* edited by Yaacov Ben-Yoseph. Tel-Aviv, 1976.

Introduction

Even the most cursory study of early American life reveals the extensive influence of the Hebrew Scriptures, the Hebrew language, and the Hebrew spirit. The New World, as an extension of the Old, absorbed much from its cultural roots, and in the process the carefully cultivated European flower of Biblical devotion was transplanted, with appropriate adaptation, to the soil of a new continent. The most familiar example of this passage is that of the Puritans, although they are far from an isolated case. Pilgrims, Quakers, Huguenots, Moravians, the Reformed Church, Mennonites, Mystics, and Pietists were among the numerous groups that came to the New World seeking a haven from religious persecution. In their flight for freedom they turned alike to the Scriptures for inspiration, spiritual strength, and practical guidance in their daily affairs.

Returning to the milieu of these early settlers, the picture that presents itself is that of pioneering men and women proudly and fearlessly carrying their Bibles both in their hands and in their hearts. The Scriptures were read not only in the communal houses of worship but at the family hearths

1

as well, so that the Bible served as the core and basis of domestic worship. Psalms were sung and Biblical proverbs recited in prayer by the colonial family morning and night, every day of the year. Consequently, their very thoughts and feelings were shaped and molded by the distinctively Hebraic spirit of piety and prudence communicated in the Scriptures.

This "Biblical" spirit pervaded even the most mundane and incidental areas of colonial life, dictating not only spiritual affairs but even the very names the colonists chose for their settlements, their offspring, and their household pets. In 1629, for instance, the site previously called Naumkeik was renamed Salem (Hebrew *shalem*), for the settlers read in their Bibles the opening verses of Psalm 76:

In Judah is God known; His name is great in Israel.
In Salem also is His tabernacle, and His dwelling place in Zion.

Then, of course, there is the tale of the Puritan who named his dog "Moreover," because of the revelation in the Book of Judges (7:5) that "Moreover, the dog came and lapped up the water."

These same Hebrew Scriptures continue to exert a formative influence in the world. Many current philosophies, Occidental and Oriental alike, pattern themselves after the philosophy of the Bible, and entire contemporary non-Jewish theologies and religions have their roots in, and derive their authenticity from, the Hebrew Bible. Likewise, the far-reaching effect of Biblical law is evinced by the universal acceptance in the West of the Mosaic Decalogue as the basic moral code of society. There have even been attempts by various gentile nations to emulate the Biblical system of law almost in its entirety: e.g., King Alfred's Code; the many Anglo-Saxon laws that quote the Pentateuch, the Book of Kings, Job, the Psalms, and Proverbs; Calvin's Theocracy; and, of course, the strictures of the Puritans. Particularly during the American colonial period, judges were exhorted to mete out punishment in accordance with the "Law of God," i.e., the laws of the Bible. The eventual cessation of this policy prompted Washington Irving to comment wryly that "New Englanders had seen fit to be governed by the laws of God until they could make better laws for themselves."

Similarly, the influence of the Hebrew Scriptures on Western literature, both as a source of dramatic material and as a model for style, is unmatched by that of any single work ancient or modern. Shakespeare's debt to the Bible, for instance, even when imperfectly measured by his twelve hundred Scriptural references, is profound, as illustrated in the following passage from *Richard II:*

> Which blood, like sacrificing Abel's, cries
> Even from the tongueless caverns of the earth
> To me for justice and rough chastisement.

And no less a stylist than Joseph Addison concludes that "There is a certain coldness and indifference in the phrases of our European languages, when they are compared with Oriental forms of speech; and it happens that the Hebrew idiom runs into the English tongue with a particular grace and beauty."[1] Indeed, the simplicity, brevity, and clarity of Biblical Hebrew is a lasting monument to the poetic genius of ancient Israel. For a statistical comparison, on the level of vocabulary alone, while Shakespeare in his voluminous plays employs at least twenty thousand different words, and Milton in his sprawling epics requires ten thousand, the vast panorama of Biblical thought and emotion is conveyed in "the Hebrew idiom" in little more than six thousand words. This is so because the linguistic economy of Hebrew compacts each word with a wealth of imagery and meaning that the more diffuse modern languages can approximate only by an increased number of words.

This accident of language has given rise to a perennial difficulty in dealing with the Scriptures in the framework of literature. Precisely because of the extreme economy of the

Hebrew language, the Bible is in essence untranslatable. Indeed, some idioms are virtually unintelligible when rendered literally in another language. Hence the constant need for textual revision and improved translation. Such revision, according to the noted theologian P. Marion Simms, generally has three aims: (1) a translated text resembling the original as closely as possible; (2) a more faithful translation based on new knowledge obtained through critical Biblical scholarship; and (3) the elimination of archaisms and obsolete expressions in the language of translation.[2]

Thus, language is a major obstacle to the satisfactory understanding and interpretation of the Bible. What meaning, for instance, has the following English translation for the reader with no knowledge of Hebrew: "And thou shalt call Me Ishi, and shalt call Me no more Baali" (Hos. 2:18)? How is he to know that *Ishi* means "my husband," in deliberate contrast and foil to *Baali,* "my master"? To translate is thus to transform, and repeated translations from one language to another, entailing misinterpretation of words and entire passages, only contribute to the confusion. For example, in the Song of Deborah (Judg. 5:2), one translator interprets the Hebrew text as "when the leaders took the lead in Israel," while another renders "when men let grow their hair in Israel"—in clear violation of the context furnished by the complementary phrase "when the people willingly offered themselves." And so, there is little standardization of meaning or agreement on the appropriate equivalents for the Hebrew words, and the task of reconciling a plethora of translations with the actual meaning of the Hebrew text remains unfinished.

But even when the translation is technically accurate, the emphasis may change in the language of translation. For instance, the same word in English, "ark," is used to denote both the craft (Hebrew *teba*) in which Noah weathered the Deluge and the chest (Hebrew *aron*) that contained the two tablets of the Law, while the Hebrew terms are wholly different both in appearance and in meaning. Similarly, the bewilderment produced by such an anomalous phrase as "voice of the turtle" could have been forestalled by the more accurate rendering of the Hebrew as "voice of the turtledove." A more far-reaching error has resulted in the traditional iconographic representation of a horned Moses: the Hebrew word *qrn* (used in Exodus 34:35 to describe Moses' appearance after his meeting with the Lord face to face) can be understood as either "ray of light" or "horn," depending on the context. In this case it clearly indicates a radiance surrounding the Lawgiver's countenance, not (as the Vulgate has it) that the face of Moses was "horned."

With respect to the language of the Bible, W. L. Roy echoes the sentiments of all scholars when he writes that "the Bible can never be understood, unless through the medium of the language in which it was originally written, and the spirit by which it was dictated. . . . Hebrew is so pregnant and rich in sense that no translation can do it justice."[3] Careful examination of the injustices done to the Scriptural text in the name of translation bears this out. Indeed, it was in reaction to such textual corruption, both accidental and deliberate, that the Protestant reformers undertook to study the Bible in its original language and to attempt improved translations.

Protestant devotion to the Bible is proverbial. Indeed, as Frank Rosenthal has observed,[4] the Protestants based their entire theology and religion on the primacy of the Scriptures. It became their great pedagogical task to prepare for scholars a Latin text of the Bible, corrected on the basis of the Hebrew, and a good vernacular version for the people. These endeavors required a thorough knowledge of Hebrew, as was understood by the Wittenberg Circle and its guiding spirit and bold protagonist, Martin Luther (1483–1545). He wanted to write good German, but he never forgot that the Hebrew text was his ultimate source; and his aim was to convey in idiomatic German the true religious understanding and emotion that illuminates the Hebrew text. The Hebrew Scriptures provided the teachings of holiness, covenant, glory, and mercy. The reformers established these Biblical terms for the Protestants as a basis for their own religious psychology, while avoiding the rabbinic teachings since the Jewish interpretation lacked the idea of Jesus.

The value attached to Hebrew by Christian and Jewish scholars alike is historically attested. But, while devotion to the *leshon ha-qodesh,* or "sacred tongue," is for Jews a matter of religious and cultural integrity, Christian interest in the Hebrew language and literature has been prompted by many motives throughout the Christian era. In the main, however, two factors governing this Christian interest can be determined. Primarily, a knowledge of Hebrew enabled the Christian scholar to better understand the origins of Christianity, through a clearer comprehension of the culture and religion from which the Christian movement emerged and of the Scriptures to which the early Christian literature constantly refers. Moreover, in the crucial religious disputations of the Middle Ages, knowledge of Hebrew enabled the Christian scholars to cite a given text in its primary source, thus rendering them more skillful in the attempted refutations of their Jewish opponents. Martin Luther epitomized this attitude in a later phrase when he said, "I am acquainted with a sufficiency of Hebrew to be able to combat all my enemies, and the knowledge of which, though small, I prize above millions of gold."

In contrast to this proselytizing impulse, however, many Christian humanists through the ages have pursued the study of the Hebrew language and Hebraic learning out of pure academic interest and intellectual curiosity. The history of the Christian attitude toward Hebrew is a story of constant oscillation between two poles. Roger Bacon, for example, felt that all translations of the Bible had become hopelessly corrupt. Ever an advocate of precise and pure thought, Bacon, on more than one occasion, expressed his fondness for the language.

This affection for Hebrew and the Hebrew Bible was the heritage of many of the Christian sects that came to America in the initial stages of its settlement. This was particularly true of the Puritans and the Quakers, both of whom cherished the Hebrew Bible as much for its language and style as for its content. Through this traditional love for the Bible, many classic "Hebraic" values became woven into the fabric of American civilization. One example of this process is the survival and development of the Biblical principle of equality. Forged in the tribal precincts of the Sinai Desert in an era long dead, it survived the passage of nearly three millennia, and became an integral part of our country's heritage as Protestant Christian reformers and their colonial descendants drew freely on the Scriptures for the inspiration and nourishment of their religious and political convictions.

Thus, the very cornerstone of our democracy, the Constitution, has as its central theme the distinct Biblical injunction that all men are equal before the law, irrespective of position. This maxim echoes throughout the Scriptures. In Leviticus 19:15, to cite but one example, the judge is warned: "Thou shalt not respect the person of the poor, nor honour the person of the mighty." Likewise, the oath administered to members of the Supreme Court—"I will administer justice without respect to persons, and do equal right to the poor and to the rich," reflects this same spirit, being nearly a paraphrase of Deuteronomy 1:17: "Ye shall not respect persons in judgement; but ye shall hear the small as well as the great." The fundamental social concept of a corpus of written law, to which all are accountable, as the basis for the body politic can likewise be traced to Hebraic origins. In America, it is the written law which is the method of the Republic, and not the command of one leader or the example of one individual. This was the rule of the Hebrews as well. The "elders" of the people ruled not by any overriding sentiment but by virtue of the law.

Throughout the history of the United States, this theme recurs again and again as men of courage and faith have arisen in times of crisis to renew the Biblical spirit of justice and brotherhood in the hearts of their countrymen. During the "times that tried men's souls," the founders of the Republic both memorialized and invigorated the freedom-loving spirit of the new nation in the famous Liberty Bell inscription, taken from Leviticus 25:10: "Proclaim liberty throughout [all] the land unto all the inhabitants thereof."

England's essential contribution to America was by way of this Biblical spirit, which, if not manifest in the prevailing religious and social philosophy, was readily apparent in the thought and work of contemporary writers. Indeed, whereever men in the West could read, they were sure to be touched by the Hebrew Bible and its spirit—just as they continue to feel its inspiring effect to this day. In illustration of this, I have sought to outline in the coming pages the major contributions of the Hebraic spirit to the English-speaking peoples generally and to the American people in particular. The subsequent chapters accordingly deal with the following topics: (1) the impact of the Hebrew Bible on Western civilization; (2) Biblical and Hebraic influences on the Puritans in the New World; (3) the early popularity of the Hebrew language; (4) the Judaic spirit; (5) legislation and justice; (6) the Biblical background of American legislation; and (7) the effect of the Hebrew Bible on the literature of England and America.

The aim of the present study is to show that the language and message of the Hebrew Bible are very much alive today—to those who are alive to the spirit of the Bible. Both, each through the other, are equally potent forces that, let us hope, will help restore some order and sense of balance in our chaotic age, some peace and tranquility, through Isaiah's message, that the tools of destruction shall be converted into the implements of construction.

Chapter

I

The Impact of the Hebrew Bible on Western Civilization

Although the influence of Hebrew culture on Western civilization is usually recognized by scholars, the great majority of laymen are generally unaware of any such contributions. Of course this influence was not wholly one-sided. As the Jews exerted considerable influence in many spheres on non-Jewish elements, so they in turn were influenced by others.

In the modern world, the most outstanding and easily recognizable link between Hebrew and Western civilization is the Bible. Specifically, the Hebrews were concerned with their Hebrew Bible, all of which they credited as a true account of their own experiences. It was these, and the lessons they derived from them, that the Hebrews passed on to the world. The God of the Hebrews was the God of Righteousness, and the ideals of his spokesmen—Isaiah, Amos, Micah—were those of social justice and compassion. Contrary to Greek or other ancient philosophies, the ideals of the Hebrews were unique in this respect: namely, the moral view of the world was a totality that tolerated no half-measures. One could not accept part of the Hebrew world-view and ignore the rest—there was total interdependence of all concepts of ethics, morality, and the like.

The basis of the Hebrew contribution to the Western world, and of the Bible, was not simply monotheism. The Bible and the Hebrews did more than merely assert the oneness of the Creator; they rather endowed their creeds of faith with a distinct ethical impulse. Thus it was almost inevitable that they destroy the forces of polytheism and the too-human lusts and failings the many gods of the world had spawned. From the start there was a strong moral and ethical tone to the Bible, as opposed to polytheism. Men were inspired to value human life and to respect the sanctity of the home. In the pages of the Bible are found the whole duty of man, the constant outcry of the prophets for peace, the elevation of man to the height of his potentialities.

Despite our current emphasis on science and our ability to "disprove" certain bald statements in the Bible, its precepts and spirit remain as valid today as ever.

It may be said that the triumphs of science have to a great extent been the result of the firm belief in the rationality of the universe, which is one of the primary tenets of the faith of the Hebrew prophets, upon which they based the ethical monotheism that they gave the world. Matthew Arnold, the classic-minded author of *Dover Beach,* finds a more basic explanation for the continued validity of the Bible and man's return to it: "To the Bible men will return; and why? Because they cannot do without it. Because happiness is our being's end and aim, and happiness belongs to the righteous, and righteousness is revealed in the Bible."[1]

Philo Judaeus, the Alexandrian Jewish philosopher (20 B.C.E.–50 C.E.), rightly said that

the laws of Greek legislators are continually subject to

change; the laws of Moses alone remain steady, unmoved, unshaken, stamped as if it were with the seal of nature herself, from the day when they were written to the present day, and will so remain for all time as long as the world endures. Not only Jews but all other people who care for righteousness adopt them. . . . Let all men follow this code and the age of universal peace will come about, the kingdom of God on earth will be established.

The concept of the brotherhood of man and the aspirations of universal peace have become commonplace today in a world so often threatened by war. However, one must always bear in mind that they were uniquely original when first voiced by Moses and the prophets of Israel, in an age when conquest was the lawful right of the strong and war was the ordinary occupation of the state.

The Bible has been put to every conceivable use. The Bible has been translated with varying success (but always with remarkable devotion) into upwards of a thousand languages. It cannot be regarded merely as the dead record of an ancient people. It is an account that has relevance today.

The Hebrews in the desert were a people faced with the difficulties of nature and the liabilities of their weak tribal structure. They were faced with fragmentation, disruption, and even political secession. And yet, despite these and other adversities, they were able to rise above their condition and produce the Bible, the basis of their national and religious identity. The very nature of this process makes the Bible a living literary possession of the world. Time and time again the moral feelings of men have been deepened, strengthened, and even, one might go so far as to say, created, by the Hebrew prophets. Into this account of the welding of a relatively weak federation of tribes into a homogeneous and dynamic entity, one may read the entire story of the transformation of man from his feeble and groping beginnings to his organization and control of vast civilizations. Here are the materials with which man toughened the fiber of his character, emancipated himself from the bondage of idolatry and emptiness, and rose to moral triumph and spiritual excellence.

Despite the almost constant ill-treatment suffered by the Jews, their culture and outlook left a permanent mark wherever it touched. Beginning with their initial exilic period, the original Babylonian captivity (586 B.C.E.), when they were for the first time forcibly exposed to alien influences, through the period of Egypt, the early Samaritans, Ethiopian Africa, Babylonia, Persia, Asia, and down to their wanderings in Christian and Muslim Europe, the Hebrew Bible was carried by the Jewish people wherever they went. The Jews gave the Western world not only a document, but an outlook derived from that document and usages based on it. Their conception of morality, godliness, and ethics left its mark quietly but indelibly. As they moved they carried with them their particular usage of the Scriptures, and so not only transplanted it in ever new and fertile soil, but also strengthened their own ideas about monotheism, morality, and ethics. The fact that these ideas were assimilated throughout the Western world is an indication that they were, of necessity, acquired as an indispensable vehicle in the evolution of Western civilization. To Matthew Arnold the secret of the Jews was that they have discerned the way the world was going, and hence they prevailed.

The early wandering of the Jews brought them to Greece as early as the third century B.C.E. They arrived in Rome and in Italy in the second century B.C.E., and two centuries later they appeared in Spain before the absorption of the Visigoths by the Romans. France saw Jewish settlements before the Franks reached its soil and gave it their name, and the barbarians found Jews living in Hungary, the Balkans, and Southern Russia when they began their incursions.

One need only look at the beginning of Christianity in the Western world to understand the important role played by the Bible and the Hebrews. The dispersion of the Jews throughout the Mediterranean world helped Christianity to take root there and spread. The first centers for proselytizing to which the early Christians came were the synagogues. Although the Judaeo-Christian doctrine was rejected by the Jewish congregations in the Mediterranean world, the Christians soon established their own sectarian synagogues, and the Jewish and Biblical influence was significant.

The influence of the Hebrews can be seen in the very concept of the church as a place of spiritual communion. But beyond that, the actual physical structure of the early churches, as well as their rituals, strongly points to this influence. Worship in much of Europe was directed to the east, namely, to Jerusalem; the stoup for holy water at the church door bears a distinct resemblance to the laver at the synagogue entrance; the light before the high altar was no doubt derived from the perpetual lamp of the Temple and the synagogues; and the early segregation of the sexes has its precedent in Hebraic practices. It is necessary only to mention rituals such as baptism, the communion service, or the use of Psalms in prayer in order to see how the Biblical and Hebraic elements of Christianity extended to the ceremonial practices of the churches.

During the Dark Ages, while most of European culture slept, the Jews, by nature and instinct observant and restless, kept alive and constantly expanded what little knowledge was vouchsafed to them. Jewish learning kept the intellectual spirit alive in an age when authority, and not inquiry, was the dominant factor. This spirit later proved to be of vital importance in the intellectual rebirth of Europe. The Jews, as travelers, merchants, and students of science and learning, did much to promote the exchange of cultures years before the Crusades were to have a similar effect. The era abounds in names that would do honor to any people: Solomon ibn Gabirol, Yehudah Halevi, Maimonides, Rabbi Gershom, Eldad the Danite, and the inveterate traveler Benjamin of Tudela, to name but a few. But this is not the place to deal with the accomplishments of individual men, no matter how worthy they might have been. How can one begin to summarize the importance and consequences of the work of men like Saadia Gaon, Jona Marinus, Maimonides, or Abraham ibn Ezra, the traveler, philosopher, and exegete. Utilizing their brilliant command of languages, they contributed much of the work that subsequently became so important in Christian scholarship.

Indeed, during all of the Middle Ages, Hebrew scholarship flourished among enlightened Latin Christians. As early as the thirteenth century, disputations arose between Hebrew and Christian scholars concerning the exact meaning of the Hebrew text of the Old Testament and other sources. The most famous disputation was in 1240, when a converted Jew, Nicholas Donin, called the attention of the Pope to passages in the Talmud and other Jewish works which were allegedly of an anti-Christian nature. A formal disputation took place that year in Paris. The result of the first great public hearing was what has been called "a vast bonfire of Hebrew books," a preoccupation popular throughout Europe in that period and known so well in more recent times.

But to others, Hebrew writings and Hebrew as a language were something to be treated with respect and diligence. The Hebrew version of the Old Testament, or the Greek translations of the Bible by Jews, Jewish-Christians, or the disciples of the rabbis, served as the bases of the great exegetes of the early church. Such was the case with Origen, Jerome, and Theodore of Mopsuestia. Jerome, when criticized for his interest in Hebrew, said: "Why should I not be permitted to inform Latins of what I have learned from the Hebrews? It is most useful to cross the threshold of the masters and to learn the art directly from the artists."[2]

In effect, there were two major avenues for the transmission of Biblical tradition to Christianity. The first was the Christian study of Jewish sources through translations, and the second was the study of Hebrew sources in the original tongue by Christian scholars who had been taught the language by Jews. These reached such proportions during the Reformation that Hebrew learning became a sign of "enlightenment."

The motives behind the early Christian interest in Hebrew and Hebraic sources are of importance and give the key to their impact. The initial impetus for the study of Hebrew is obvious: in order to study the basis of the Gospels, it was of the utmost importance to study the Hebrew Scriptures in their original language. With the advent of the Jewish-Christian disputations from the thirteenth century onward, a knowledge of Hebrew enabled the Christian scholar to stand his ground with greater facility, since he was able to cite the original sources of his arguments. The element of conversion was also closely linked to this, and the Christian theologian felt he could better prove to the Jew the "error" of his ways if he could bolster his claims with citations in the original tongue.

The early Christian interest in Hebrew also had its origins in the dictates of geography and in medieval Latin psychology. First of all, if a scholar intended to learn Greek, the other major language necessary for medieval scholarship, it was necessary to travel either to Byzantium or to Southern Italy. Hebrew, however, was available from the Jew living in the same town. But even more important was the mystic appeal of Hebrew for the early Christian scholar.[3] Hebrew was thought of as the mother tongue of all languages and the current language of heaven. Thus Hebrew appealed to the emotions, philosophy, and historical sense of the Latin scholar.

An additional factor lending importance to the traditional Jewish sources was the fact that they included linguistic and grammatical material important for textual understanding. The best-known Hebrew scholar to use glossing in the vernacular throughout his works was the eleventh-century exegete Rashi (Rabbi Shlomo ben Yitzhak). His writings were important not only for the technical aids they offered. Most significant is the fact that they were almost entirely incorporated into the works of Nicholas de Lyra, the fourteenth-century Franciscan exegete, upon whom Luther leaned so heavily in his work.[4]

In this manner much of the traditional Jewish interpretation of the Hebrew Bible entered the works of Christian scholars with the appropriate Christian slant. It became commonplace for church scholars to study the Hebrew text of the Scriptures in conjunction with rabbinical commentaries. Beryl Smalley, a noted scholar, is indeed justified in writing that "the Hebrew text was no more separable from its traditional commentaries than the Vulgate was from its *Gloss.*"

Some works which were originally thought to be of purely Christian origin were later proved to be of Jewish authorship. An example of this is the classic *Fons Vitae,* originally ascribed to the Spanish Christian writer Avicebron. Only in the nineteenth century did a famous scholar discover that the writer of this work, a classic for medieval churchmen, had in fact been none other than the famous Hebrew poet Solomon ibn Gabirol.

The tradition of early English churchmen who valued Hebrew is a long one indeed. The Venerable Bede, in his great *De Temporum Ratione,* claims to have based the chronology in his work on the "Hebrew truth" as he found it. Robert Grosseteste, the learned bishop of Lincoln and the mentor and teacher of Roger Bacon, was a pioneer in the field of Hebrew. Bacon himself repeatedly stated that a knowledge of Hebrew was necessary for the proper comprehension of science, theology, and philosophy. Bacon's conviction in this matter was so great that he went so far as to work on a Hebrew grammar. The religious impulse was an important factor influencing Bacon's attitude. Hebrew was the language in which God had originally revealed himself. Bacon felt that the beginnings of knowledge were to be found in the Hebrew writings. From an academic point of view, Bacon was dissatisfied with the previous translations of the Bible. He was a Franciscan monk, and his attitude toward Hebrew was so characteristic of the order as a whole that "when in a thirteenth-or-fourteenth-century manuscript we find any evidence of Hebrew knowledge we may suspect a Franciscan origin."[5]

In time, literary criticism, which was developed for use in

analyzing classical literature, was applied to the Latin Bible. As a result, the influence of Hebraic scholarship increased during the Reformation. In essence, the Reformation was to a great extent the rejection of the Catholic tradition and a return to the Bible. However, the Bible was generally available only in the Catholic version—the Vulgate. Thus a number of German theologians turned to rabbis for assistance. Almost all the leaders of the Reformation were learned Hebraists: Luther, Zwingli, Melanchthon, Tyndale, Servetus, and others.[6] Some religious sects, such as the Hattemists, the Versichorists, and later the Hutchinsonians, even made a knowledge of Hebrew an important tenet of their faith. H. Lowe noted that "it is interesting that Melanchthon often prefixed the Jewish formula 'In the Name of God' or 'With the help of God' to his letters. He also often used to date them with Jewish dates."

As a result of this interest in Hebrew and Hebrew scholarship, there was considerable activity, from the Middle Ages on, in the translation of the Bible from Hebrew into other languages. Several attempts were made to translate from Hebrew into Latin, among them a rare example of the interlinear technique. Some fragments have been found of an Italian version based on the Hebrew. But by far the most interesting are those in Castilian. A number of people, all of them Christian, worked on these translations. One such example had an interesting history. At the end of the fifteenth century, when the Jews were expelled from Spain, they took their native tongue with them to the Eastern Mediterranean. These people then required a Bible, and this was first printed for them in Ferrara in 1553.[7]

The transition from the Dark Ages was in great part due to the scholarship of the Moorish Arabs, "and they were solely indebted to the Jews who interpreted Greek literature to them."[8] The great Hellenic tradition, to all intents and purposes lost to the Western world during the Middle Ages, was preserved and cultivated by the Arabs and was particularly developed in Muslim Spain. Hippocrates, Ptolemy, Aristotle

were all studied and admired in the world of Islam. Although, as was stated above, the original texts were inacces-
sible, their Arabic translations were available. When the
Christian scholars wished to avail themselves of these works,
it was to the Spanish Muslims and to Saadia Gaon and
Maimonides that they turned. It was here that the Jews
served as a bridge between two worlds. The Christian scholars looked to the Jews of their own country, who in turn
could draw on the knowledge of their brethren across the
Pyrenees in Spain.

Hundreds of these translations by the Jews of Europe during the Middle Ages have survived to our day. The thinkers
and writers of Europe quickly accepted and made use of the
Muslim-Hebrew version of Hellenic thought. For example,
Dante's cosmogonic system is, without a doubt, an adaptation of the Hebraic-Arabic conception of the world's origin.
This important cultural and intellectual intercourse also
served as the basis for mathematical study in Europe. One
can say, as well, that medicine, to the extent that modern
science has its origins in the rudimentary gropings of
medieval medicine, is equally in debt to this continuous
transfer of cultural and intellectual heritage.

The three major centers for the Jewish interpretation of
Graeco-Arab scientific thought in the thirteenth century were
Toledo, Naples, and Provence. Provence in particular served
as the meeting ground between Muslim Spain and Christian
France. It was there that Jewish scholars translated Arabic
works into Hebrew for the use of their European co-
religionists, and these works soon found their way into Latin. One need cite only the work of one of the first of the
medieval translators, Faraj ben Salim of Girgenti, who translated *Liber Continens,* an enormous medical compendium by
Rhazes, to convey some idea of the importance of such work.

Another major translator was Moses of Palermo. Having
been taught Latin at the insistence of the king, he set about
translating, into that language, a work (attributed to Hippocrates) on the diseases of horses. It became one of the ear-

liest popular books in the field of veterinary science in Europe.

In addition to the professional Jewish translators, who facilitated the transmission of knowledge between East and West in this manner, there were also many converted Jews who were active in this field. Petrus Alphonsi was one such figure. Perhaps the most important of these was John of Seville, a member of the famous Ibn Daud family, who had been converted to Christianity. The volume of his work was enormous, and its impact was indeed great. His translations included works by Avicenna, Al-Ghazali, and Avicebron. He also was responsible for the introduction of the *Secretum Secretorum* to Europe. This work, attributed to Aristotle, soon became one of the most popular treatises of the Middle Ages. Suffice it to say that it was indeed fortunate for the future development of Europe that their knowledge of Hebrew and Arabic, as well as Latin, enabled the Jews to play the part they did.

Professor George Sarton of Harvard University, the renowned historian of science, asserts that the great cultures of the Muslims and Jews in the so-called Dark Ages were responsible for the preservation of the great cultures of the Greeks and Romans. He maintains that it was they who laid the foundation of modern social structures, and suggests that the modern investigator or student of European civilization would do well to study Arabic and Hebrew instead of Greek and Latin in order the better to understand the medieval sources of the Renaissance and Reformation.[9]

Thus the work, the debt, the perseverance were extraordinary. M. I. Schleiden sums it up as follows:

. . .we find that during the intellectually dark and slothful Middle Ages, the Jews were the preservers of agriculture, of all large industries, the cultivation of silk, dyeing and weaving works. It was they who carried on an international trade which was and ever will be necessary for the well-being of all nations. [They] left no branch of science or learning untouched, ever searching and developing, and at the end of the Middle Ages handing over the results of their long and arduous labors to the nations who were only then commencing to wake up.

The world underwent many changes, and one age followed on the heels of another. The Middle Ages gave way to the Renaissance. This was in turn succeeded by the Age of Enlightenment. But despite the enormous changes that took place, time found the descendants of the ancient Hebrews still adhering to the old truths and to their creed. Industrialization affected them as a people almost not at all. Great individuals rose from amidst their ranks as they had always done in the past. Now we have emerged into the atomic age, and here, too, the basic Hebrew contribution to civilization is apparent. As man has pushed back the horizons of learning, he has sought to apply the principles which for over two thousand years have guided him.

Expression and explanation of this is found in every literature. Very often this entered through the translation by Jews of their liturgies and holy books into the language of their place of residence. Rashi of Troyes, as was mentioned above, was a pioneer in the field of glossing in the vernacular. The Jews of Apulia, Italy, wrote their religious poetry in the dialect of Apulia. This was equally true of Spain, Portugal, and most other European countries, and was bound to leave its traces in the general literature of those countries.

No literature, however, was as deeply and profoundly influenced by the Hebraic spirit and the spirit of the Bible as that of England. Were one to eliminate from English literature whatever it owes to the Bible and Hebraic writings, the remainder would be "barely recognizable." If the medieval miracle play, the forerunner of the modern-day theater, is considered, the influence of the Bible is inescapable. When not dealing with the Passion or the Nativity, this important element of popular medieval religion portrayed the story of Joseph and his brethren, the Deluge, Susannah, the Sacrifice of Isaac, and other incidents of the Bible or the Apocryphal books.

Indeed, the extent of the Bible's influence on English literature is great, and in turn that of English literature throughout the world is inestimable. This corpus of literature is the direct expression of a people that has spread out from its small island to every corner of the world, carrying its own particular institutions and beliefs. Where the English have gone they have taken their literature. As a result, claims Richard Garnett, "should the Bible be erased from the consciousness of those peoples, it would forfeit well-nigh half of its influence over the world."

But the English language has been repaid for this service "by an elevation, a picturesqueness, and an affluence of beautiful sentiments which confers. . .a great advantage over those which, whether from national incompatibility, or the impediments created by sinister interests, have been more or less debarred from this treasury of grandeur."[10]

All modern literatures have borrowed unsparingly from the Scriptures and the subsequent Hebrew literature and commentaries. Indeed, in the case of English literature there has been so thorough an assimilation that the Hebrew patriarchs and prophets often seem to have been rendered into people born on English soil.

As regards the influence of the Bible during the early period in America's northern colonies, the two most important groups were the Puritans and the Pilgrims, who, though closely related in history and origin, nevertheless comprised separate entities.

The Puritans, those stern and devoted self-styled saints, had a great deal to do with the establishment of much that can be called "typically American." What influenced them, therefore, can be said to have later influenced America. Thus it is necessary to investigate the circumstances surrounding their initial development, the factors that molded their thoughts and beliefs, which in turn had such far-reaching effects on the later evolution of America.

John Richard Green, the noted English historian, has said that Puritan England "became the people of a book, and that book was the Bible." There can be no doubt that the most important influence on Puritanism was the Hebrew Bible. The Puritans found there not only history and morality but also a far-reaching theology—the glory of man reflecting and confirming the glory of God. To them, the Book was not a mere narrative of days gone by, but a Scripture-in-Life, meeting their daily needs and aspirations.

It is necessary, however, to first examine the circumstances which gave rise to a situation whereby all the facets of life were so stringently determined by the Hebrew Scriptures. Puritanism in England rose against the background of the destruction of the Spanish Armada in the late sixteenth century, a national delivery from "popishness." This was viewed over fifty years later in the context of the Lord's deliverance of England from Spanish Catholicism. The Puritans felt that this deliverance had historical precedent in the Bible.

Together with the historical setting for the rise of Puritanism, one must consider the moral tenor of England before the rise of this religious movement. Life in England before Cromwell rose to power was crude, and the general moral tone was low. Thus it is easy to understand why the strict and clear commandments of the Hebrew Bible exerted such influence on English reformers. The Bible became their written guide and mentor. The Puritans found in the Hebrew Scriptures a Book of the Wars of the Lord. Their God became the "Lord of Hosts," and they hoped to completely destroy their "Philistine" and "Amalekite" foes. Religious, political, and moral strife coalesced into one, and in this respect the atmosphere of the Bible was recreated. The Bible became a call to individual and national righteousness, and the Puritans accepted its dictates almost literally.

It was in this atmosphere that the Puritans of England, like the Puritans of America, came to identify themselves with the Israelites of old. For every event a precedent was sought, and generally found, in the pages of the Hebrew Scriptures. The revolt of the Puritans was likened to the uprising of the Maccabees, as was the murder of the first duke of Buckingham (1592–1628) to Mattathias' slaying of the king's man. This identification with events and people in the Bible was not confined solely to the Puritans. There were some sects that were even more extreme in this direction, e.g., the Levellers, who claimed descent from the "Jewish race" and felt that their own sufferings were akin to those of "our ancestors in Egypt."

In such an atmosphere, the numerous attempts to establish the Mosaic code as the law of the country under the Puritans are understandable. In outlook, scholarship, and social, religious, and political institutions, the Puritans of England owed the Hebrew Bible a great debt indeed. And after the Puritan movement was extended to the New World, much of this was transferred to new settings.

Puritan narrowness, strictness, and intolerance are proverbial. Yet whether one agrees with this assessment or not, there is very little doubt that there is nothing more valuable, memorable, weighty, or commendable about the Puritans than their religion—and in that area they were almost solely influenced by the Hebrew Bible.

> The whole Old Testament is vital and commanding with examples of the Puritan spirit. . . .They with their more virile temper, their experience of hardship. . .saw in the ancient testament not history only, theology or praise, but the glory of man reflecting and celebrating the glory of God. It was a Scripture in life which smote and stirred their strong emotion. Not merely as to Deborah under the palm-tree, or to Ezekiel by the river of Chebar, was the majesty of the Eternal manifest to them. The whole Hebrew economy bore its radiance, and declared its effect; an economy stern, sublime, working for freedom because binding to God; training men to be careless of the world with its lusts, that they might be champions of the king-

dom unseen. This was the lambent cloud of glory which filled all Puritan temples when the ancient Scriptures were opened within them.[11]

The Puritans found the whole of their religion in the Bible. Their theology was derived from the Scriptures and rooted in its tenets. Originally one of the basic differences between Judaism and Christianity was the fact that the Jews, when compared with Christians, were far more literal in their reading of the commands of the Bible. The Puritans in England and then in America, as well as other reform movements in England, sought to restore the literal acceptance of Mosaic law and based much of their theology on this. This was part of the phenomenon of the return to the Bible. In essence, Puritan strictness had its roots in the Hebrew Testament ideal, and was perhaps an attempt to reestablish society and religion on the Hebrew Scriptures ideal.

This Biblical model is an important factor in much of Calvinist thinking, too. The Bible was such a major element in their religion because "in the Hebrew Bible they found, or thought they found, a divine example of national government, a distinct indication of the laws which men were ordered to follow with visible and immediate punishments attached to disobedience."[12] This was, to a great extent, the attitude to be found in England.

In the long-drawn-out struggle between the Puritans and the High Churchmen for control of church government, organization, and theology, the importance of the Bible is readily apparent. Each side, in an attempt to overcome the other, resorted to the Hebrew Bible for support. Although the following citation of pamphlets published during the course of this conflict may no more than amuse the modern reader, their contents were of great import when published: *Solomon; or, A Treatise Declaring the State of the Kingdom of Israel, as It Was in the Daies of Solomon* (1596); *The Reformation of Religion by Josiah, a Commendable Example for All Princes Professing the Gospel to Follow. . .*(1600); *Historie of Corah, Dothan, and*

Abiram, applied to the Prelacy, Ministerie, and Church Assemblies of England (1609).

However, ecclesiastical rules and tradition were not the major or only elements of Puritan belief. The Hebrew Bible was of great importance as the chief guide for action; it was the basis of the code of morality and ethics. A reading of Puritan sermons shows that their code was based on the concepts and examples of the Scriptures. An example is a sermon by Thomas Playfere, delivered in Elizabethan England. The sermon, "The Pathway to Perfection," not only urged the acceptance of Biblical morality but couched this message in Scriptural expressions and metaphors. "As Solomon ascended six steps to his throne," Playfere expounded, "so must man ascend six steps to perfection." In outlining these steps he stated, "wherefore though thou have conquered kingdoms yet craze not of it as Sennacherib did; though thou has built Babel yet brag not of it as Nebuchadnezzar did; though thou has rich treasures yet show them not as Hezekiah did; though thou hast slain a thousand Philistines yet glory not in it as Samson did; though thou give alms yet blow not a trumpet." So for the Puritans the Hebrew Bible was "the only and the perfect Rule of Faith."

A rare eighteenth-century compendium of New England sermons states the following:

God declares it to be a sinne for the godly to leave the worship of God for the wickednesse of those that come unto it. We knoe that the sinne of the sonnes of Ely was so great, that men abhorred the offerings of the Lorde: but in so doing it is said, that the Lord's people did transgresse, even unto a cry. Surely this truth will not bee easily outfaced; yet some of them to avoid it say, that no marvell of morall wickedness did not pollute the Jewish worship, because God required only ceremoniall cleanness. But how false this is, appears by God's Covenant with *Abraham* where God requires *Sincerity*; by the morall law which was God's covenant: by God's requiring then, truth in the *inward part*; by his injoyning sacrifices for morall transgressions as well as ceremoniall: by his signifying of pollution by morall uncleannesses: and by threatening of morall sinnes, and *abhorring all ceremoniall* service when men sinned morally against God.[13]

The idea of a covenant between man and God warrants investigation. This subtle agreement, capable of so many and such diverse interpretations, is first mentioned in Genesis in the covenant with Abraham. There are numerous other references. Calvinism and Puritanism adopted the concept of the covenant as one of their main tenets of faith. The contract which both God and man entered upon became the motif of their religion and the justification for their acts. The Puritans repeatedly drew on it, referred to it, worked it into their dealings both religious and secular. The first act of the Pilgrim Fathers and the first major Pilgrim document in America, the so-called Mayflower Compact, is a continuation of this concept and refers to it by name. "We whose names are underwritten. . .having undertaken. . .a voyage to plant ye first colony in ye Northerne part of Virginia, do by these presents solemnly and mutually in ye presence of God, and one another, covenant and combine ourselves together into a civill body politick."[14]

The Puritans felt that their church was in actuality a continuation of the covenant between God and the Jews. This theme was hammered out from every pulpit. John Stevens, in a church in New Marlborough, Massachusetts, said: "The Christian Church so called is only a continuation of the Jewish church."[15] With unconscious and unexpected humor, William Brattle drove this point home: "The covenant of grace is the very same now that it was under the Mosaical dispensation. The administration differs but the covenant is the same."

The Puritans of New England built up a body of laws about the covenant, interpreted previously existing laws in terms of it, and derived a great deal of their power from it. ". . .whatever its origins the covenant gave to each congregation an independence which would have been impossible had it been constituted by any superior human authority. It made of it, in the words of Ames and Cotton and other Puritan leaders, a church responsible not to bishops or assemblies or kings, but to God himself."[16] The idea certainly stemmed from a very palpable relationship with the Hebrew Bible.

It should not be assumed from this, however, that the Puritans were the only sect to draw inspiration from the Scriptures, bringing this spirit with them to America. Another important group which was influenced by the Hebrew Bible and later played an important role in the New World was the Quakers. Although opposing Puritanism, Fox, the founder of Quakerism, professed a doctrine of inner light and possessed a sense of divine mission that can be directly traced back to the spirit of the Jewish prophets. Fox regarded the Bible as the infallible word of God and an immutable guide. His attachment to the literal word of the Scriptures, however, was not as great as that of the Puritans.

John Knox and his followers in Scotland were influenced by the Bible and the covenant concept as well. The analogy of the prophets was used to justify their demands for liberty and their rebellion against temporal powers. In general the English and Scottish varieties of Protestantism have or had a Hebraic tint. The dour and hard-hitting Scotch Presbyterians, who came to America in such large numbers between 1730 and 1770, settling in the upland areas some hundred miles inland from the coastal developments, held firmly to their own ideas about the meaning of the covenant. Theirs was an austere life following the principles of John Knox. To them the Bible was law. "They were brought up," writes Frederick Jackson Turner in *The Frontier in American History,* "on the Old Testament, and in the doctrine of government by covenant."

Morality, not ceremony, was the essence here. The accent was always placed on moral conduct rather than on ritual alone. Three-fourths of human life is conduct. "Hebrew

Scriptures deal preeminently with conduct. Their influence, at any rate on the English-speaking portion of our Western civilization, is three times as important as the influence of the Greeks."[17] Powys feels that the Bible is to us what Homer was to the Greeks; that the words of the Bible have become a magic torch that "throws across the passing details of each individual life the undying beauty of the life of humanity."

This leads us to a very important Biblical thread woven into the woof and warp of Puritanism: the Psalms. One might be led to think that the strains of severity and rigidity found in many aspects of Puritanism were so all-pervasive that the Puritan existence was a joyless one. Although at times this impression seems to have validity, the joy and exaltation which the Puritans found in the Psalms greatly counterbalances these elements. The songs of the Puritans were taken almost in toto from the Hebrew Psalter. John Milton, the most famous Puritan poet, spurred by a love of Hebrew which he shared with Cromwell and by a love of the Psalms, began his career as a poet by translating Psalms into English. The Psalms became the songs of the Puritans in the most uplifting moments of prayer and during the most crucial moments of warfare. Cromwell's soldiers sang the Psalms for encouragement before entering battle, and in celebration after victory.

Although Psalm-singing was by no means confined only to the Puritans, it did characterize them. The Puritans found in the Psalms the expression of their hopes, fears, and ideals. Cromwell, in one of his earliest letters, wrote: "Truly then this I find: that He guideth springs in a dry barren wilderness where no water is. I live in Meshec, which they say signifies *prolonging:* in Kedar which signifies *blackness:* yet the Lord forsaketh me not." Thus the phrases of the Psalms and the verses of the Scriptures were part of Cromwell's world outlook, as they were part of the makeup of most Puritans and of Puritanism in general; this was the spirit they took away with them from England and brought to America, their Canaan in the New World.

Chapter

2

Biblical and Hebraic Influences on the Puritans in the New World

The influence of the Hebrew Bible and the Hebraic spirit marks every step of the Puritans' exodus to their Zion in the wilderness of the New World. This was the spirit which led the Pilgrims forth from their native England and which bore them up "on eagles' wings" (Exod. 19:4) throughout their journey. The *élan vital* of the Pilgrim voyage was the profoundly Biblical and thoroughly Hebraic perception of a supernatural orientation to human history, the "same sense of teleology . . . the same demand for cosmic drama" which guided the course of Christian civilization through the centuries.

> The range of their [the Pilgrims'] ideas would have been utterly simple had they not possessed. . .the Bible. This book formed their minds and dominated their characters; its conceptions were their conceptions;. . .the key to the

29

whole enterprise [their westward voyage] was a conviction of the sanctity of covenants and belief in a Providential guidance through the wilderness into a Promised Land.[1]

After fleeing England, the "Separatists" (as the Pilgrims were known to their contemporaries) sojourned in Leyden, Holland. Before long, however, they began to fear that their children might be assimilated into the alien environment; and when in fact their little ones began to speak the strange language of the Dutch, the group decided to resume their voyage to the New Canaan in America without further delay. When this assemblage, the Scrooby Congregation, was ready to depart for the new land, the members fasted in a manner reminiscent of the fasts held by the Israelites before any new and portentous undertaking. The meeting was solemn; their pastor took as his text I Samuel 23:3–4:

> And David's men said unto him: "Behold, we are afraid here in Judah; how much more then if we go to Keilah against the armies of the Philistines?" Then David inquired of the Lord yet again. And the Lord answered him and said: "Arise, go down to Keilah; for I will deliver the Philistines into thy hand."

—"From which text he taught many things aptly, and befitting the present occasion and condition, strengthening them against their fears and perplexities, and encouraging them in their resolution."[2] The Biblical basis for this procedure is manifest; just as the ancient Israelites prayed and fasted before undertaking an uncertain venture, so did the Puritans, in deliberate emulation of their spiritual forebears. Once settled in America, the custom was retained and frequently renewed. Early in 1620, the very year of the Pilgrims' landing in America, a solemn day of prayer was observed; Pastor Robinson spoke, again quoting from I Samuel 23:3–4, by which he strove to allay their fears and strengthen their determination. From the passages selected, it is apparent that the practice of turning to the Bible for encouragement and fortitude in the face of danger and difficulty was far from a haphazard choice. Under the goad of distress the Puritan leaders turned to certain passages customary for solace, in exaltation to certain other well-worn verses. This custom, combining prayer and fasting with Biblical readings on momentous occasions, persisted at least until 1774, when Massachusetts declared a solemn day of prayer and fasting after the passage of the Intolerable Acts by the British Parliament. President Adams likewise called a national day of prayer and fasting during the Napoleonic Wars. The direct link between this custom and the Old Testament–inspired preparation in Holland is indisputable.

The pioneering Pilgrims were soon followed by other Englishmen of their persuasion, impelled to forsake their native land by several factors. Primary, no doubt, was the political and religious persecution they endured under the prevailing ecclesiastical and civil authorities in England; but while much has been made of this libertarian motive by subsequent historians, the fact is often overlooked that the Puritan voyages to America were also part of a commercial enterprise. The Endicott group, for instance, among the first to be sent to New England (1628), was organized and financed entirely by a commercial concern established by English Puritans with the practical aim of turning a profit. Although it is difficult to separate the diverse strands woven into the Puritan effort to found a new society, the various elements should be kept in view when that effort is assessed.

The next major group of Puritan settlers to arrive in New England (1630) was headed by John Winthrop (1588–1649), who brought with him an organized form of government which attempted to fuse diverse political, social, and religious elements. The Massachusetts Bay Colony, founded by Winthrop, was ruled initially by an oligarchy of leading Puritan families, whose natural instrument of rule, since the colony itself was based on Biblical principles and was moved by the Puritan spirit of the Scriptures, was the Holy Bible. The Puritans wholeheartedly believed that it was their special mission to establish in America a society precisely modeled on the precepts of Sacred Scripture. While there is considerable debate over whether the society established in the new colony was in effect a theocracy, the Massachusetts Bay Colony was at the very least a state inspired by, and thoroughly devoted to, the Bible.

The Puritans, in coming to America, felt that they were entering a wilderness ruled by Satan and his attendant forces of idolatry, and they felt it their sacred duty to secure the rule of the Lord God in this latter-day Canaan. Their attitudes and goals were clearly and deliberately based upon analogies from the Old Testament. The Puritans' conviction that they were the Lord's "chosen people" (redivivus), and, as such, partners in a covenant with Him, pervaded every aspect of colonial life, political as well as religious. This had a twofold effect. Primarily, it distinguished them from other Christian sects in the New World; the well-known intolerance of the Massachusetts colony stemmed directly from this fervent belief in their divine selection. Secondly, it reinforced their sense of autonomy from England; the Puritans were certain that they had been led to America at God's express command, and that their successes were the direct result and special sign of His favor, protection, and guidance. This prevailing belief found expression and confirmation in the Synod of 1679, which declared that "the ways of God towards this His people are in many respects like unto His dealings with Israel of old. It was a great and high undertaking of our fathers when they ventured themselves and their little ones upon the rude waves of the vast ocean, that so they might follow the Lord into this land."

This preoccupation with the Bible colored all their activities. The Scriptures were read constantly by the laity, and not simply left to the clergy to study and relate to their new situation in the context of the New World. Such active lay participation and control, in matters which were not the oridinary concern of the lay members of a church, was due primarily to the dominant role which the laity in general played within the larger Puritan religious establishment. But this tendency toward lay control of religious affairs was also not lacking in a clear-cut Jewish precedent. The New England meetinghouse was consciously modeled on the synagogue, serving as the central place of learning as well as the social center of the community. This Hebrew spirit in the colonies had political implications as well. The Puritan practice of restricting political rights to church members was justified by reference to the Hebrew Scriptures; if "worldly" men were electors, wrote John Cotton, they "would as readily set over us magistrates like themselves, such as might hate us according to the curse. Lev. 26:17."[3]

A diverting but illuminating sidelight of this conception of the Bible as a living document is the Puritan proclivity to see in the native American Indians the "ten lost tribes of Israel."

> In 1649, Eliot, the missionary, proclaimed to the world that the Indians were descendants of the Jews. In 1650, Bowman, another missionary, issued an appeal to the English, that they help the Indians in the New World, on the ground that the Indians were descended from Jews. And when Throwgood, in 1650, published his book *Jews in America*, Eliot of Massachusetts immediately made a declaration that the 37th chapter of Ezekiel refers to the Indians. And when, during the same year, there was a high mortality rate due to an epidemic, it was interpreted as a preparation for the coming of the Jews.[4]

This notion, however romantic, is most illustrative of the Puritan attitude, which regarded the Biblical record as more than a mere chronicle of God's revelation to a bygone age, and it provides a striking instance of their characteristic accommodation of the Scriptures to their contemporary environment.

More significantly, however, in their struggle against the forces of nature in the wilderness, the Puritans continually identified themselves with the Children of Israel, as epitomized in Romeo Elton's versified "Life of Roger Williams" (1853):

> Like Israel's host, to exile driven.
> Across the flood the Pilgrims fled;
> Their hands bore up the ark of Heaven,
> And Heaven their trusting footsteps led,
> Till on these savage shores they trod,
> And won the wilderness for God.

When the Puritans, a bitterly persecuted people, reached America, they drew clear analogies between themselves and the Jews of antiquity. They constantly referred to the Hebrew Bible, renewing the similarities to their own experience, so that its philosophy and spirit came to permeate their lives. The severity of the Puritan Sabbath, for instance, was matched only by the prophetic zeal with which it was observed. Also, like Israel of old, the Pilgrims (and their Puritan counterparts) regarded themselves as the elect of God, so that throughout the Revolutionary War they visualized their enemies as Amalekites or Philistines. And in a manner reminiscent of the traditional Jewish recitation of the Haggadah of Passover night, the Pilgrims too memorialized their passage into freedom:

> Ought not, and may not the children of these fathers rightly say, our fathers were Englishmen, which came over this great ocean, and were ready to perish in this wilderness; but they cried unto the Lord; and He heard their voice, and looked on their adversity; Let them therefore praise the Lord, because he is good and his mercy endureth for ever; yea, let them who have been redeemed of the Lord, shew how he hath delivered them from the hand of the oppressor, when they wandered in the desert wilderness out of the way, and found no city to dwell in; both hungry and thirsty, their soul was overwhelmed in them. Let them there[fore] confess before the Lord his

lovingkindness, and his wonderful works before the children of men.[5]

The early settlers of the Massachusetts colony were not only imbued with the spirit of the prophets and with the lessons of the Scriptures, but they also accepted Biblical precepts and commandments literally and applied them vigorously. This uncompromising spirit affected every phase of life in the colony. One early Puritan ordinance, for example, prohibited the public celebration of Christmas Day on pain of a five shillings fine; this seemingly severe measure stemmed from the Puritan fear that the popular manner of making merry would lead to "immoral revelry" incompatible with the Biblical tenor of the Massachusetts colony. At times, colonial leaders even used the Bible to their own advantage, as in the decision to limit the voting franchise to those specified by the church, in justification of which were cited Exodus 16:21 and Deuteronomy 17:15—the former a divine command to Moses to appoint judges from among the Children of Israel, the latter an injunction against appointing a ruler who is an alien.

The Psalms continued to be an indispensable vehicle for the popular expression of the colonists' religious sentiments. The Psalter was deeply rooted in the affections of most English-speaking people from the days of the first Puritans in England. The Psalms, recited as readily in war as in worship, were revered as the deepest expression of their noblest ideals, a perennial source of encouragement and inspiration. Indeed, the first book printed in America was the *Bay Psalm Book:*

THE WHOLE BOOK OF PSALMES Faithfully TRANS-LATED into ENGLISH Metre. WHEREUNTO is prefixed a discourse declaring not only the lawfulness, But also the necessity of the heavenly Ordinance of singing Scripture Psalmes in the Churches of God. . . . Imprinted 1640.

It is significant that the book also contained Hebrew characters. Interspersed throughout were individual unvocalized Hebrew letters, inserted to stress certain linguistic forms of the original text; nor was the appearance of Hebrew script in a Puritan Psalter considered inordinate or inappropriate. If the literary merit of the *Bay Psalm Book* leaves much to be desired, its publication nonetheless demonstrates the vitality of the Psalms to the New England Puritans. The primary intention of the translators was to produce a metrical version of the Psalter which could be set to music, but their lack of lyrical aptitude and training is painfully evident in the product. Richard Mather, in the preface, sought to justify this lack on the grounds that "it hath been one part of our religious care and faithful endeavour to keep close to the text. If, therefore, the verses are not always so smooth and elegant as some may desire or expect, let them consider that God's altar needs not our polishings." Consequently, Tyndale's familiar rendering of the twenty-third Psalm:

> The Lord is my shepherd; I shall not want. He maketh me to lie down in green pastures; he leadeth me beside still waters. He restoreth my soul: he leadeth me in the paths of righteousness for his name's sake. . . .

became in the new version:

> The Lord to me a shepherd is,
>   want therefore shall not I.
> Hee in the folds of tender-grasse
>   doth cause me down to lie:
> To waters calm mee gently leads:
>   restore my soul doth hee:
> He doth in paths of righteousness
>   for his name's sake leads mee.

Once it became evident that the new translation could not compare with the standard version, the Psalms "were committed unto Mr. Dunster, who revised and refined this translation. . .with some assistance from Mr. Richard Lyon."[6] Thus, though this first effort was found wanting to an extent, it nonetheless indicates the ritual importance of the Psalms in the Puritan milieu. Finally, when Isaac Watts's excellent version of the Psalms reached the colonies, it was at once given a widespread hearing, due to the affection in which the "original" was held, and Watts's psalms were soon in use everywhere.

The intensity of the Puritans' psychological identification with the ancient Israelites is further illustrated by the fact that the colonial settlers saw themselves as a new Israel, fighting in a land of wickedness and paganism against the forces of Satan. The lot of Israel became that of the Puritans. If Egypt had been to Israel a "land of bondage," so was England to the Puritans. The Scriptural text was likewise made to accommodate and commemorate their own plight; on the title page of the first edition of *New England's Memorial* appears the Biblical text: "and thou shalt remember all the way the Lord thy God led thee this forty years in the wilderness."

In searching the Scriptures for readings pertinent to their own situation, the Puritans readily discovered the general similarity between themselves and the ancient Israelites, and proceeded to draw from it some very particular conclusions. They firmly believed that the Hebrew prophets were speaking to them as directly as they had spoken to the Israelites. Thus the history of the Israelites as related in the Bible served, according to the ministers of the day, as a mirror in which the Puritans could see their own activities reflected. From the beginning of the enterprise the leaders were conscious of a similarity between New England and the Jews: "Let Israel be the evidence of the Doctrine, and our glass to view our Faces in," said the ministers, while the irreverent Peter Folger threw the idea into satirical verse,

> *New England* they are like the Jews
> As like as like can be.[7]

The Puritans harked back to the Israelites not only in their historical orientation but in their fundamental religious doctrine as well. As mentioned above, in this respect they differed sharply from the majority of traditional Christian theologies. To the Puritans the primary lesson of the Old Testament was that a nation as well as an individual could enter into covenant with God, thereby constraining itself as a body, by its own assent, to obey His laws and directives. The Puritans reasoned that this institution derived its authority directly from the Bible and had its precedent in the history of Israel. In America, furthermore, the concept of the covenant assumed new dimensions. Previously, in England, it had been an important theoretical aspect of their faith; the belief in their party's covenant with God gave the English Puritans collectively the cohesion and fortitude to attempt the imposition of their radical religious ideas on the established Church of England and, during Cromwell's rule, on the country as a whole. And when the monarchy was reestablished, this same belief gave them the strength to endure the retaliation which followed the drastic reversal of their political fortunes. Finally, their belief in a covenant with the Almighty enabled them to face the hazards and hardships of the passage to the New World. But once they reached the colonies, a new factor entered into the matter of the covenant. In this "brave new world," the Puritans enjoyed the unique opportunity to establish a completely new society based solely upon the concept of covenant between God and man. Nor was this a matter to be treated lightly. "If wee keep this covenant," Governor John Winthrop assured his people, "wee shall find that the God of Israell is among us, but if wee deal falsely with our God . . . wee be consumed out of the good land wither wee are going."[8] The covenant concept was thus the bedrock of Puritan religious communities. Accordingly, Puritan congregations customarily contracted a formal covenant immediately upon arriving at their new homesites, usually assembling in an open space (such as an Indian cornfield) to solemnly, as a congregation, join in covenant with the Lord. The Pilgrims in the Mayflower Compact established just such a Biblical type of contract with God as the basis of their society: "We covenant with the Lord and with one another and do bind ourselves in the presence of God to walk together in all His ways, according as he is pleased to reveal himself unto us in His blessed word of truth."

Although there is a striking similarity of form between the covenant drafted by the Pilgrims and those of other Puritan congregations in the New World, Puritan leaders insisted that the origin and basis of their covenant was the Bible and not the Pilgrim colony at Plymouth. Autonomy, so hard won and dearly paid for, was the keynote sounded by the separate communities in America at this stage of national evolution. John Cotton, one of the original leaders of the New England church, firmly maintained that the covenant was inspired solely by the Bible, a conviction shared by Ames and other English Congregationalists: "That we laid aside the Book of Common Prayer, we received from the. . .second commandment and not. . .from the Separatists."[9] Thus the Puritans were certain of the Biblical system they wished to establish in the New World, and they made plain their determination to do so. They came to America not gropingly but with a remarkable fixity of purpose, as seen in the constant reiteration by Puritan leaders of the importance of the covenant and its Biblical precedents. In his election sermon of 1673, for example, Uriah Oakes emphasized the covenant between the Lord and the Children of Israel, and the manner in which the Israelites were led into the Promised Land. When the matter of the covenant was formally discussed during a convention of Puritan ministers at Boston on May 26, 1698, all present, with one exception, confirmed the belief that "under the Old Testament the Church was constituted by a covenant." Because of this concept, the Puritan Church was not ruled by a formal and rigid ecclesiastical hierarchy but derived its direction immediately from God, ruled by His word as revealed in the sacred writings of the Scriptures.

The Bible was, in all circumstances and for all occasions, the ultimate source of knowledge and precedent. It was followed wholeheartedly and with a rigorous literal-mindedness. It belonged, in the Puritan estimation, to the realm of unchangeable, immutable, and ever-valid truth. That the Bible was the inspired word of God was for them a matter of absolute conviction, and, hence, indisputable:

> Then both sides agree that these are the words of God, and the question of faith is concerning the meaning of the words, nothing is an article of faith, or a part of religion but can be proved by reason to be the sense and intention of God. Reason is never to be pretended against the clear sense of the Scripture . . . we do not test the Bible by nature, but nature by the Bible.[10]

Accordingly, failure to abide by the strict reading and literal interpretation of the Scriptures was severely punished:

> If any "Christian," so-called, spoke contemptuously of the Scripture, or the holy penmen thereof, they were to be punished by fine or whipping. Laws were also passed punishing those who violated the Sabbath. . . . One of the most prominent traits was a conscientious adherence to what they believed were the teachings of the Sacred Scriptures. To them the authority of God was most supreme. Believing as they did that the Bible was his revealed will they made that their exclusive guide in matters of faith and practice. Creeds, characters and customs were all tried by this unfailing test, and all was rejected which, in their opinion, did not stand this ordeal. Laws and regulations adopted by them, which, at the present day, are stigmatized as singularities, were in many instances, the legitimate fruits of their strict adherence to the teaching of the Bible.[11]

It is not surprising, therefore, that so many of the official acts and laws of the colonies either referred to or were directly based on the Scriptures; the Puritans derived their early laws from the Bible and justified them through Biblical citations. An instance in which these laws were pursued to the point of tragedy is the now infamous Salem "witch-hunt" of

1691–92, which resulted in the execution of some nineteen people and the arrest of scores of others, among them members of some of the most prominent families in Massachusetts.[12] Cotton Mather, the famed New England minister, only typified the psychology of his age in drawing from the Scriptures the justification for rooting out Satan manifested in human form. In a society so dominated by the Bible, it is not surprising that they should turn to Scripture for direction and justification in all matters of deep concern, whether rational or irrational. Even though this hysterical outbreak was, in essence, a surfacing of their submerged but overriding fear of the supernatural forces of evil, it is most indicative of their deep faith in the word of God that this very fear was based on the Scriptural injunction against witchcraft (Exod. 22:18). The New Testament has likewise been put to such ignoble use, as when Luke 14:23 became the chief authority for the Inquisition. Indeed, the Bible generally has been made to teach whatever man wants it to teach, and too often this method has worked to the detriment of mankind. The Book of Genesis, for instance, was long used to keep woman in her low social position, and the entire Old Testament has throughout history provided a powerful defense of war. One abominable idea which held sway in the South for a long time was the divine institution of the custom of slavery. And almost every advance of science has met with staunch opposition from Biblical purists; for example, people were actually executed for using anesthetics until it was pointed out that God himself used the first anesthesia when he put Adam to sleep in order to remove his rib from which to make woman.[13]

Most of the official acts of the colonies were determined by the Scriptures. One of these, the Connecticut Code of 1650, adopted a near Mosaic form of government. Its fifteen Capital Laws, with Pentateuchal citations and phraseology, are later found in the Massachusetts Code of 1660. The guide of early Connecticut was Thomas Hooker, a man deeply touched by the Bible and its spirit, and called by some "the

founder of American democracy." The influence of the Bible
on Hooker is obvious in nearly everything he said or wrote;
an interesting example is found in a letter (1648) to his old
friend, Governor Winthrop of Massachusetts, on the subject
of liberty under the law: "*Sit liber judex,* as the lawyers speak.
Deuteronomy 17:10–11: Thou shalt observe to do according to
all that they inform, according to the sentence of the law.
Thou shalt seek that Law at his mouth: not ask what his discretion allows, but what the Law requires."[14] In this connection it is worthy of note that the Puritans' incorporation of
the Mosaic code and injunctions from the Old Testament into
their own legal framework was a thoroughgoing and comprehensive procedure. For example, fully half of the statutes
in the code of 1655 for the New Haven colony contained references to or citations from the Old Testament, while only
approximately three percent refer to the New Testament.[15]

Such conscious analogy with the Old Testament was a
regular feature of Puritan thinking in New England. If Israel
had its Pharaoh, the Puritans had their King George III. The
Atlantic Ocean was their Red Sea, America their Promised
Land, and the Founding Fathers their Moses and Joshua.
Such analogies came naturally to a people who so constantly
drew the Hebrew Bible into their lives. Accordingly, the
first settlers in New England called themselves "Christian Israel." Governor William Bradford wrote in his *History of
Plimouth Plantation* that the New World was the place
"whither the Shekinah had guided them through the Sea."
Bradford's classic work itself was called the "Genesis, Exodus
and Joshua of the Colony." Comparisons of the Puritan leaders with the great leaders of ancient Israel, especially Moses
and Joshua, were common. For example, in Cotton Mather's
Magnalia Christi Americana we find the following evaluation of
Massachusetts Governor John Winthrop:

> Accordingly when the *noble design* of carrying a colony of
> chosen people into an *American* wilderness, was by *some*
> eminent persons undertaken, *this* eminent person was, by

the consent of all, *chosen* for the Moses, who must be the leader of so great an undertaking; and indeed nothing but a Mosaic spirit could have carried him through the *temptations* to which either his *farewell* to his *own land,* or his *travel* in a *strange land,* must needs expose a gentleman of his education.[16]

In the same vein, John Cotton's epitaph reads (in part):

> But let this mourning flock be comforted,
> Though Moses be, yet Joshua is not dead;
> I mean renowned Norton; worthy he
> Successor to our Moses is to be.
> O happy Israel in America,
> In such a Moses, such a Joshua.

And Norton's own elegy, penned by Thomas Shepard, extends the Biblical metaphor to the great prophets of later Israel:

> . . . Oh that mine eyes a fountain were of tears!
> I'd day and night in mourning spend my years.
> My father! father! Israel's chariots thou,
> And horsemen wert! Sons of the prophets now.

William Bradford, too, was often called Joshua. After his death, when Thomas Prince had been chosen to succeed him as governor of New Plymouth, it was said of him: "At such a time and when the condition of this colony was such as hath been declared, God was pleased to mind it, even in its low estate, and when he had taken unto himself not only our Moses, but many of the elders and worthies of our Israel, he hath not hitherto left us without a Joshua to lead us in the remaining of our Pilgrimage."[17] Bradford, in his *History of Plimouth Plantation,* had written of their migration and of the joy of their enemies who slandered them "as if that state had been wearie of them, and had rather driven them out (as the heathen historians did faine of Moyses and ye Israelites when they went out of Egipte)." A final illustration of their extreme self-identification with the ancient Israelites appears in a declaration of war against the Indians: "It clearly appears that God calls the colonies to war. The Narrohaiggansetts and their confederates rest on their numbers, weapons and opportunities to do mischeefe, as probably of ould, Asher, Amalek and the Philistines with others did confederate against Israell."

Even in their daily speech, the Puritans frequently employed Biblical expressions and allusions. The famed religious leader, later declared heretic, Anne Hutchinson was to them "a wretched Jezebel"; likewise, a coachman driving recklessly through the roads of the colonies was often called "Jehu."[18] But if the Puritans commemorated the villains of the Hebrew Bible in their popular invective, they cherished its heroes, perpetuating their memory by conferring their venerable names upon their own offspring. So the names of Daniel, Jonathan, Esther, Enoch, Ezra, Rachel, and a host of others were in constant use among the Puritans. Interestingly enough, there was a conspicuous absence of the names of Christian saints; Puritan names seem to have been derived strictly from the Scriptures, particularly from the Hebrew Bible, and especially the great Hebrew heroes, patriarchs, and prophets. Indeed, the more remote the name, e.g., Hephzibah, Shear-yashub, Maher-shalal-hash-baz, the greater the probability of its appearance on the roll of Puritan names.[19]

Names of cities, towns, and settlements likewise derived from Hebraic sources. The names Salem (peace), Bethlehem (house of bread), and countless others bear witness to this phenomenon. For example, the name Nahumkeik, conferred upon the later Salem plantation (original settlement in 1628), was not, as is generally believed, an old Indian place-name, but is clearly of Hebraic origin. The name, argues Cotton Mather, consists of the combination of two Hebrew words, *nahum* ("comfort" or "consolation") and *keik-heq* ("haven"). "And our English not only found in it an Haven of Comfort, but happened also to put an Hebrew name upon it; for they called it *Salem* for the *peace* which they had and hoped in it; and *so it was called* unto this day."[20]

This practice of investing their strange new environment with the more familiar nomenclature of the Bible was widespread in colonial America, and continued for many generations even after the Puritan spirit began to wane. But even in their own day the custom was not peculiar to the Puritans; it was the common and characteristic reaction of settlers who shared the common religious and cultural heritage of Western civilization in the face of a strange and often hostile new environment. But the Pilgrims who founded the Plymouth colony were among the first to choose Biblical names for their settlements. Very often, names were chosen because the implications they carried or the impression they conveyed seemed appropriate to the chosen site. Thus one minister chose the name Rehoboth, meaning "the Lord hath made room." Names such as Goshen, Canaan, or Sharon were probably selected because they suggested rich valleys or lush plains. The town Bozrah very likely owes its name to the suggestion of good pasture land implied by "the sheep of Bozrah" in the Book of Micah. In the case of one town in New Jersey, the first sermon which the rural minister chose to give his new church was based on the text of Joshua 28:1: "And the whole congregation of the children of Israel assembled together at Shiloh, and set up the Tabernacle of the congregation there." Accordingly, the town which grew up around this church came to be known as Shiloh Church. Many early American towns—Bethesda, Bethany, Zion, to mention but a few—received their Biblical names in this way, and the custom continued throughout the country's history. In the mid-nineteenth century, when men looked toward a Utopia on earth, they often turned to the Bible in search of meaningful names for their homes. One Ohio community called itself Zoar because it was written (Gen. 19:23) that when Lot fled from the burning city of Sodom, "the sun was risen upon the earth when Lot entered into Zoar."[21]

This widespread use of Biblical names, however, was not confined to the naming of offspring, cities, and towns; the rugged terrain of the New World filled the early settlers with awe and inspiration. Although a name like Sinai was not used lightly, owing to its intimate association with the Almighty, the names of many other Biblical heights were eventually bestowed upon the great mountains of America. Mount Carmel and Mount Horeb, homes of the prophets, were popular names, as was Mount Nebo, the final resting place of Moses. Names like Mount Ephraim, Mount Gilead, Mount Hermon, Mount Moriah, Mount Pisgah, were all popular as well. Some mountains in the New World were even called Mount Zion and Mount Olive. Even the custom that "Mount" should precede and "Mountain" follow the proper name, came from the Biblical usage.[22]

That the early settlers showed an active interest in the Hebrew language or in Hebrew nomenclature should not be surprising. Cotton Mather, to cite only one example, was extremely preoccupied with Hebrew; it is reported that he began his study of Hebrew grammar at the age of twelve, and that he likewise taught his eldest daughter, Catherine, to read Hebrew.[23] Hebrew words and phrases are found throughout his writings. In Book I of his *Antiquities,* the introduction begins with the Hebrew words *Im yirzeh ha-Shem* ("God willing"); chapter six leads off with the words *ba'ale nefesh* ("men of spirit"); and the title of Book VI is headed by the Hebrew equivalent of *liber memorabilium.* In Volume II of his *Magnalia Christi Americana* the following datum appears: "The Jews tell us of *kilya* or a scarecrow upon the top of the temple, which kept the fowls from defiling it. . . . The same practice was used for candidates for admission to the church—only defilers of the temple were kept out." In speaking of the first ministry when they left England, Mather refers to them as *Hasidim Rishonim* ("our first good men"). As to the conduct of the magistracy, he states that it was according to Jewish wishes—*Be'ahavah Veyir'ah, cum mansuetudine ac Timore.* And William Bradford's *History of Plimouth Plantation* bears in Hebrew the motto "God succors the modest."

The Puritans may have frequently bent the Book to serve their own peculiar needs, often in an arbitrary fashion. Often they resorted to a primitivism contradictory and alien to the spirit of Deutero-Isaiah. Such failings, however, should not obscure the positive contributions of the Hebrew Scriptures to Puritan belief and practice. The legacy of Judaism was a genuine inspiration to America's early settlers, and it was this spirit that they handed on to their American posterity with intense religious devotion and sincerity.

The Early Popularity of the Hebrew Language

I devoted myself to the Hebrew language because I perceived the great value which it would have for religion and true theology. To this end I have always devoted my labors, and continue to direct them more than ever.

Johann Reuchlin

Without this language there can be no understanding of the Scriptures. . . .it is rightly said that the Hebrews drink from the fountains, the Greeks from the streams, and the Latins from the pools.

Martin Luther

A quiver full of steel arrows, a cable with strong coils, a trumpet of brass, crashing through the air with two or three sharp notes, such is Hebrew. A language of this kind is not adapted to the expression of scientific results. . . . The letters of its books are not to be many; but they are to be letters of fire. This language is not destined to say much, but what it does is beaten out upon an anvil. It is to pour out floods of anger, and utter cries of rage

*against the abuses of the world, calling the four winds of heaven
to the assault of the citadels of evil. Like the jubilee horn of the
sanctuary, it will never be put to profane use.*

Ernest Renan

While the Hebrew language has always occupied a prominent position in the intellectual history of the Western world,
its formative role in the spiritual and intellectual life of
Europe since the Protestant Reformation cannot be overem-
phasized. The significance of Hebraic learning as a wellspring
for Christian theology is incontrovertible. Equally remarkable
is the high esteem in which the Hebrew language has traditionally been held by Christian scholars. The intellectual
prestige of Hebrew only increased during the Reformation,
thus deepening the Hebraic impact on the West. The renewed study of the Hebrew tongue and of Hebraic sources
was an inevitable corollary of the reforms which the Protestants were attempting to introduce into a still medieval Chris-
tendom. The leaders of the new movement, who shared the
view that many abuses had crept into Christian faith and
practice, set out to correct what they considered the errors of
the Catholic tradition. For justification and inspiration the reformers turned to a tradition older and, in their eyes, more
venerable than that of the church, namely, the Holy Bible.
Repudiating the mainstay of the medieval Catholic interpretative tradition, the Vulgate of St. Jerome, the official Catholic
translation of the Scriptures, Protestant scholars returned to
the primary sources for both Testaments; and once Christian
theologians had renewed the study of the original Hebrew
and Greek versions in order to begin fresh translations, the
use of other Hebraic writings soon became indispensable.
Thus Hebrew exegesis and rabbinic learning entered the corpus of Western religious study. The key to this renewed
interest in Hebrew in the West lies in the very nature of the
Reformation as a pristine movement: the return to the pristine sources of Christianity had the inevitable effect of
deepening the Christian attachment to the language and cul-

ture in which these sources were steeped, and of further disseminating the Hebrew language and Hebraic culture among the nations of the West.

Puritanism, as a main branch of the Protestant movement, was profoundly affected by these processes. The Biblical tinge of Calvinism heightened the Hebraic and Biblical bent of Puritanism, and the status of the Hebrew language rose commensurately; the literalistic and fundamentalistic nature of the movement only added to the prestige of the antique tongue of the Jews. Out of this cultural ferment grew a virtual renaissance of Hebrew in Puritan society. The detailed study of the Hebrew language and literature (including the rabbinic writings) flourished in Puritan England's centers of scholarship under the impetus of such vociferous leaders as John Selden and Brian Walton. This was the age in which the great universities of Oxford and Cambridge developed their outstanding reputations in the field of Oriental languages, to which the pioneering works of such Puritan Hebraists as Edward Pococke (1604–91), Emanuel Tremellius (ca. 1579), and John Lightfoot (1602–75) contributed incalculably. This keenly intellectual environment and profoundly humanistic tradition constitute the English roots of the plant which was soon to flourish so hardily in the "New" England on the other side of the Atlantic.

Even as Hebrew nomenclature, Hebrew forms of expression, and Hebrew patterns of thought became widely disseminated throughout colonial America due to the Puritan affection for the Bible, the Hebrew language itself also enjoyed a prominent position in colonial education and in the intellectual life of the colonies in general. As might be expected, the study of Hebrew was a favorite pastime of the clergy in New England, who carried on the strong tradition of Hebrew learning among their English prototypes. Cotton Mather records in Volume II of his *Magnalia Christi Americana* that at the second session of the Synod of Elders and Messengers of the New England churches, an article was drawn up to provide for the study of the Old Testament in the original He-

brew, "the native language of the people of the God of Old."[1]
Education in colonial America was closely linked with religious studies: the main impulse behind the establishment of
most of the early institutions of higher education, and the
function they chiefly served, was the training of ministers to
meet the spiritual needs of the colonies. This course of action
was dictated by the gradual passing away of the first generation of colonial ministers and the lack of a properly trained
American-born clergy to take its place. Most of the early
American universities were thus founded in the service of a
specific denomination, and most (in New England at least)
grew up under Puritan auspices, so that Hebrew played a
significant role in their curriculum and development. Regard-
less of creed, however, the study of Hebrew was generally
considered not only "the foundation for an exact understanding of the Old Testament, but it was then as later thought to
be the mother of languages; a knowledge of it therefore was
believed to advance learning in the best sense."[2] An early
president of King's College (later Columbia University) was
only giving expression to a widely held belief when he said:
"As soon as a lad has learned to speak and read English
well, it is much the best to begin a learned education with
Hebrew. . .the mother of all Languages and Eloquence."[3]
Both Jews and Christians had long believed Hebrew to be the
proto-language of mankind from which all other languages
were merely subsequent derivations. The basis for this con-
tention was initially sought in the text of the Bible, while in
more modern times pseudo-scientific philological and popular etymological proofs have been adduced in support of the
theory. It was naturally assumed by earlier scholars that
Hebrew was the language spoken by Adam and Eve in the
Garden of Eden; and since it was demonstrably the language
of primal man, Hebrew must certainly have been created simultaneously with the world,[4] and if not indeed the very
medium through which the Lord effected the Creation. In an
intellectual climate where fanciful folk-etymology was often
confused with philosophic or scientific statement, the Biblical

account of the creation and naming of Adam and Eve:

> And the Lord God formed man [*adam*] out of the dust of the ground [*adamah*] . . . (Gen. 2:7)

> she shall be called woman [*ishah*] because she was taken out of man [*ish*] . . . (Gen. 2:23)

> And the man called his wife's name Eve [*Hawwah*] because she was the mother of all living [*hai*] . . . (Gen. 3:20)

only lent further credence to the idea. And traditional Hebrew lore not only supported but even embroidered upon the theory; in *Pirke d'Rabbi Eliezer,* for example, it is related that Abraham, whom the heads of the court of Nimrod sought to destroy, was at birth hidden in a cave, only to emerge thirteen years later speaking Hebrew! This popular conception of Hebrew as the primal language of the human race flourished and developed so, throughout the Middle Ages and the Renaissance, that by the time the Puritans settled in the New World it was a well-known "fact" that Hebrew was not only the language in which the Lord communicated with His celestial messengers, but it was the current vernacular of Heaven.

Thus, for secular as well as religious reasons, many of the leading citizens among the very early settlers in America possessed a good knowledge of Hebrew and some were excellent Hebrew scholars.

> John Cotton (1585–1652), Thomas Shepard (1605–1649), Nathaniel Ward (1578–1652), John Harvard (1607–38). Michael Wigglesworth (1631–1705), whose son and grandson (both named Edward) occupied the earliest Harvard chair (Hollis Professorship of Divinity, 1721) from 1722 to 1791, Richard Mather (1596–1669), his son Increase (1639–1723) and his grandson Cotton (1663–1728), Thomas Welde (1595–1661), Henry Dunster (1609–1659, first President of Harvard College), Charles Chauncy (1592–1672, second President of Harvard College), and other learned divines

were good Hebraists; but the knowledge of Hebrew was also current among laymen like (printer) William Bradford (1663–1732), (Pilgrim father) William Brewster (1560–1644), and (self-appointed "apostle to the Indians") John Eliot (1604–1690), whose translation of the Bible into an American Indian language was the first Bible printed in North America.[5]

Indeed, the history of Hebrew in Massachusetts is as old as the Plymouth Colony itself; its second governor, William Bradford (1590–1657), who came to America with the Pilgrims on the *Mayflower,* began in his declining years to study Hebrew, as he himself relates:

> Though I am grown aged, yet I have had a longing desire to see with my own eyes something of that most ancient language and holy tongue in which the Law and the oracles of God were writ, and in which God and angels spake to the holy patriarks of old time; and what names were given to things from the creation. And though I cannot attain much herein, yet I am refreshed to have seen some glimpse thereof as Moses saw the land of Canaan afar off. My aim and desire is to see how the words and phrases lie in the holy text, and to discern somewhat of the same for my own content.[6]

And when Increase Mather became president of Harvard (1685–1701), he brought to that office an excellent knowledge of Hebrew and a profound dedication to Hebrew scholarship. His command of the language was such that he challenged the translation of certain words in the Authorized Version; he was also familiar with certain of the rabbinic writings, making occasional reference to the Talmud and Kabbala, and to the medieval Biblical commentators, Rashi, Abarbanel, Ibn Ezra, Saadia, and Kimhi. Cotton Mather was likewise a prominent Hebrew scholar, having studied Hebrew at Harvard, like his father before him, and in 1681 delivering a commencement address on the divine origin of the Hebrew vowels. (The Hebrew system of vocalization, or *nikkud,* incidentally, seems to have been a popular thesis among Harvard graduates from the first commencement in 1642 onwards.) Among the younger Mather's prolific writings are *Magnalia Christi Americana* (1702), a sort of ecclesiastical history of New England and the source of much of our information about its cultural life, and *Biblia Americana,* a work of encyclopedic proportions preserved largely in manuscript form in the library of the Massachusetts Historical Society.

Many of the signers of the Declaration of Independence, as graduates of colonial colleges, possessed at least a basic knowledge of Hebrew. Isaac Norris, speaker of the Pennsylvania Assembly (the man responsible for the selection of the text, Leviticus 25:10, cast on the Liberty Bell), and his father-in-law, James Logan, chief justice of the Supreme Court of Pennsylvania, were both noted students of Hebrew. Roger Williams (1603–83), founder of the Rhode Island Colony, received, during a visit to England, several lessons in Hebrew from the great Puritan poet John Milton, in return for lessons in Dutch; Williams later utilized his knowledge of Hebrew in the treatise *Christening Make Not Christians* (1645), in which he gives a good exposition on Hebrew terms. Active in the field of translation was Henry Ainsworth, author of a metrical version of the Psalms; as a result of his work he was known as the "great Rabbi of his age" and a "Pilgrim Solomon." The first book published in the colonies, the *Bay Psalm Book,* was a rendering of the Psalms into English from the original Hebrew by a group of American clergymen. This joint effort was later submitted to Henry Dunster, the first president of Harvard College, who, drawing upon his own extensive knowledge of Hebrew, revised and polished the translation. Dunster was so proficient in the language that he corresponded with the great German Hebraist, Christian Ravis, correcting his European colleague's work at numerous points! But perhaps the best example of how deeply rooted the tradition of Hebrew learning became among the more erudite of the colonial families is Cotton Mather's account of how his sixteen-year-old brother, Nathaniel, "entertained the auditory with a Hebrew oration which gave good account of the academical affairs among the ancient Jews. Indeed the Hebrew language was become so familiar with him, as if. . .he had apprehended it should quickly become the only language which he should have occasion for. Rabbinical language he had likewise no small measure of."[7]

It was in this intensely intellectual climate that the first American institution of higher education was established in 1636 and endowed by John Harvard in 1639. The truly pioneering spirit of the founders is expressively memorialized by Stephan d'Irsay in his *Histoire des Universités*, commenting on "the heroic energy, of those who in the midst of material daily cares on the very outposts of civilization struggled to establish only fifteen years after the landing of the Pilgrim Fathers, on the still wild coasts of New England, Harvard University."[8]

The earliest account of Harvard College indicates the twofold aim of the new institution: "to advance *Learning* and perpetuate it to Posterity; dreading to leave an illiterate Ministry to the Churches, when our present Ministers shall lie in the Dust."[9] The early history of the college reflects the early popularity of Hebrew and Hebraic learning in New England generally; following the English tradition, the curriculum from the very beginning included Hebrew as an essential course, on a par with Latin and Greek. In this respect, the cultural contribution of England to America, especially in the academic sphere, is incalculable. At Cambridge, for example, from 1549 onwards, a knowledge of Hebrew was required in order to qualify for the master of arts degree, and a Regius Chair for Hebrew was established by King Henry VIII as early as 1540 (first occupied by the noted Hebraist and student of Johannes Reuchlin, Thomas Wakefield).[10]

As almost all of the original clerics of the Bay Colony had been educated at the great English seats of learning, and under the influence of such renowned Hebraists as Wakefield, it is not surprising to find the English pattern of collegiate study perpetuated in the first university established in the New World. Thus, generations of students at Harvard devoted a day a week for three years to the formal study of Hebrew and its cognate languages, using primarily the text of the Hebrew Bible, in addition to the grammatical and syntactical texts discussed below. Beyond these formal lessons students were, according to the earliest statutes of the college (1642–46), required to study the Scriptures twice a day in private before exhibiting their knowledge to their tutors, giving "theoretical philological observations and with spiritually practical examples." Finally, a prerequisite for graduation was a demonstration of the ability to translate the Old and New Testaments from their original languages into Latin. This rigorous program doubtless received the unconditional endorsement and continual encouragement of the college's first two presidents, Henry Dunster and Charles Chauncy, both of whom were noted Hebraists.

Since the college had been founded on the Puritan principle of Scriptural influence, Hebrew was regarded as a key to the right course of action in all affairs, practical as well as speculative; in all matters of administration, averred Cotton Mather, the leaders "were agreed in declaring the Scriptures, as the *direction* of all. . . . It is *not* the opinion of *men,* but the *Scriptures* which must decide the controversy."[11] Regarding the cultural background of this secular insistence on the study of Hebrew, Samuel Eliot Morison comments:

Authorities on the history of education have too readily assumed that colonial students were forced to study Hebrew and Greek simply in order to read the Bible. As regards Hebrew, that may well have been the real reason, though the *good* one assigned in an early commencement thesis was, that Hebrew is the mother of languages. This theory that Hebrew was the archetype of all western tongues, was common in the Renaissance; the great English Hebraist, John Selden, among others believed it. A smattering of that language was then supposed to be a classical education in England; Sir Humphry Gilbert had it on the program for his proposed academy for young gentlemen of the court and even in the late eighteenth century, President Samuel Johnson of Columbia declared that Hebrew was part of a "gentleman's education." Wilhelm Schickard, professor at the University of Tubingen, prepared especially for his pupils a Hebrew text with the attractive title (in Latin) "The Hebrew Sun-dial, or advice as to how the elements of that Holy Language may be sufficiently apprehended by College students in a space of twenty-four hours."[12]

In a similar vein, Mather writes:

The reader knows that in every town among Jews, there was a *school,* whereat children were taught in the reading of the *law;* and if there was any town destitute of a *school,* the men of place did stand excommunicate, until one were erected: besides and beyond which they had *midrashoth,* or *divinity-schools,* in which they expounded the law to their disciples. Whether the churches of *New England* have been duly careful or not about *their* other *schools,* they have not been altogether careless about their *midrashoth;* and it is well for them that they have not.[13]

While Mather's analysis of the Jewish educational system may be somewhat imprecise, it nevertheless indicates the favorable Puritan attitude toward education and the prevailing ideas regarding the suitable course of studies in their schools.

For whatever reason, then, freshmen at Harvard began with Hebrew. Their program of study was modeled after that of the great English universities and based largely on the serious Renaissance works. One such early program of Hebrew studies reads, in part, as follows:

The fifth day reads Hebrew, and the Easterne Tongues
Grammar to the first yeare houre the 8th
To the 2d. *Chaldee* at the 9th houre,
To the 3d. *Syriack* at the 10th houre,
Afternoone

The first practice in the Bible at the 2d. houre
The 2d. in *Ezra* and *Daniel* at the 3d. houre.[14]

Divinity students began their professional studies only after obtaining a preliminary college degree; undergraduate students, therefore, studied and analyzed the Bible in Hebrew. The first formal textbook in use at Harvard was Wilhelm Schickard's *Horologium ebraeum (Hebrew Sun-dial,* mentioned above; London, 1639); other technical aids employed were: Francois du Jon, *Grammatica Hebraeae Linguae* (Geneva, 1596); Johann Buxdorf (the elder), *Epitome Radicum Hebraicarum et Chaldaicarum* (Basel, 1607), *Thesaurus Grammaticus Linguae Sanctae Hebraeae* (Basel, 1609), and *Lexicon Hebraicum et Chaldaicum* (Basel, 1615; essentially a newer edition of the *Epitome Radicum);* Johann Buxdorf (the younger), *Dissertationes Philologico-Theologicae* (Basel, 1645).[15] There were only two Hebrew grammars in English available: John Udall, *The Key to the Holy Tongue* (Leyden, 1593; a translation of Petrus Martinius, *Grammaticae Hebraicae libri ii,* Paris, 1568), and Christian Ravis, *General Grammar for the ready attaining of Ebreu, Samaritan, Chalde, Syriac, Arabic, and the Ethiopic Languages* (Berlin, 1650).[16] Such works necessarily had to be brought from afar; the renowned Dutch Hebraist John Leusden, for instance, once received an order for fifty copies of the Hebrew Psalter for use by Harvard students. The college also benefited from a number of donations in the form of books; in 1638 it inherited the library of John Harvard, which included Schickard's *Horologium,* Udall's *Key,* and Buxdorf's *Thesaurus* and *Lexicon,* as well as a set of Old Testament commentaries, an Aramaic dictionary to the Talmud, and John Lightfoot's *Erubhim.*[17] The original Hebrew collection was augmented by "a good number of *Targumes,* Talmuds and rabbinical exegesis" sent by certain English Hebraists sympathetic to the principles upon which the college was founded and the goals toward which it was striving. The Hebrew books at Harvard constituted a respectable collection of more than one hundred volumes. Included in the holding of 1723 were: Isaac ben Jacob

Alfasi's Talmudic Code, *Halakot* (Venice, 1521–22); Joseph ben Ephraim Caro's code of rabbinic law, *Shulchan Aruch* (Hanau, 1627); Maimonides' *Sefer ha-Mitzvot* with the commentary to *Megillat Esther* by Isaac Leon ben Eliezer Zur Sefardi (Venice, 1619); and the Babylonian Talmud in fourteen folio volumes (Amsterdam, 1644–45). There were in addition several Latin translations of certain post-Biblical Hebrew texts, including two copies of Buxdorf's translation of the *Moreh Nevuchim* (Basle, 1629).

Interest in Hebrew at Harvard manifests itself recurrently in theses presented for the baccalaureate degree. A survey of bachelor theses from the latter part of the seventeenth century, dealing with Hebrew and related areas, illustrates how vital the subject was to educators in colonial America; and the fact that the student body of the college in 1680 numbered only about twenty, lends further significance to the already large proportion of such theses. The topics covered between the college's inception in 1642 and the year 1700 included the following: Hebrew is the mother of languages (1642); the consonants and vowels of the Hebrews are contemporary (1642); the *hateph* vowel points do not produce a real syllable (1642); the *shewa* is neither a vowel nor a consonant, nor does it constitute a syllable (1643); the *aleph,* in accordance with its vowel points, has the sound of every vowel (1646); no Hebrew vowel points, except ten, basically constitute a syllable (1646); by contracting sentences the Hebrews expand the meaning (1646); vowel points received on either side of a letter remove the *shewa* (1647); either tense in Hebrew verbs expresses both times (1647); verbs often govern Hebrew nouns of the same root (1647); a guttural letter determines both its own vowel and that of the preceding letter (1653); *benoni* (the participle) takes the place of the present, which the Hebrews do not have (1653); the four guttural letters among the Hebrews are interchangeable (mock thesis, 1663); no word can begin with two *shewas* (1687); all Hebrew letters are in a single verse, Isaiah 5:25 (1689); all languages originated from Hebrew (1691); and, the Hebrew language is the "archetype" of all languages (1693).[18] Nor was the graduate division of the college lacking in an active interest in Hebrew, judging from the titles of certain dissertations (in the form of *Quaestiones*) offered by candidates for the master of arts degree during the same period: Are the Hebrew vowel points of divine origin? Yes (1693). Is the Hebrew language the oldest of all? Yes (1693). Are the Apocrypha canonical? No (1696). Are the Americans Israelites? No (1699). Are the Hebrew text of the Old Testament and the Greek text of the New Testament exclusively authentic? Yes (1699).[19] Incidentally, an interesting custom inaugurated at Harvard in 1655, and maintained for many years thereafter, called for the translation by all students, except freshmen, of a verse from the Hebrew original of the Old Testament into Greek as part of the morning prayer service.

Harvard College employed as its first full-time instructor of Hebrew Judah Monis (1683–1764), a Portuguese Marrano Jew who came to America from Italy in 1720. Monis, although converted to Christianity through the efforts of Increase Mather, was referred to throughout his life as "Rabbi." He taught Hebrew at Harvard from 1722 to 1760, and in 1735 he published the first Hebrew Grammar printed in America, *Dickdook Leshon Gnebreet. A GRAMMAR of the Hebrew Tongue, Being An Essay to bring the Hebrew Grammar into English to Facilitate Instruction Of all those who are desirous of acquiring a clear Idea of this Primitive Tongue by their own Studies; Composed and accurately Corrected by Judah Monis, M.A.* Boston, N. E., MDCCXXXV.

Monis's successor at Harvard was Stephen Sewall (1734–1804), who taught Hebrew at the college from 1760 to 1785. In 1764 Sewall was appointed the first Hancock Professor of Hebrew and Other Oriental Languages. Equally competent in Arabic, Syriac, and Samaritan, and a good classicist as well, Professor Sewall wrote a number of learned works on Hebrew, among them the anonymous publication, *A Hebrew Grammar collected chiefly from those of Mr. Israel Lyons and the Rev. Richard Grey. . . .With a Sketch of the Hebrew Poetry as re-*

trieved by Bishop Hare (Boston, 1763).

However, student interest in Hebrew at Harvard was declining even in the second half of the seventeenth century; in 1653 some of Michael Wigglesworth's students attempted to drop Hebrew, apparently without success. In 1787 the first concessions were made in the Harvard curriculum regarding the study of Hebrew, and students were allowed to substitute French for Hebrew under special permission. Hebrew classes declined drastically, and the situation soon became so serious that the second Hancock Professor of Hebrew (1786–1807), Eliaphet Pearson, was asked to supplement his duties by teaching English grammar and rhetoric and correcting English themes and exercises. Yet despite this decline in the popularity of the subject among the student body, Hebrew was still honored at official functions and ceremonies. For over a century and a half, until 1817, the commencement exercises at the college included a Hebrew oration, which during the early years dealt solely with matters of syntax and grammar, and in later times was extended to the discussion of broader and more varied topics.

Yale University followed the same rigorous tradition with no less illustrious results, indeed ranking second only to Harvard in the advancement of Hebraic studies and in the cultivation of the intellect in colonial America. From the very beginning, the university seal depicted an open Bible displaying the Hebrew inscription *Urim Vetumim,* to which the founders, "in charity to their successors who might be less familiar with the language of scholars. . .happily added a translation in the vernacular: *Lux et Veritas.*"[20] From its inception in 1701, the university recognized Hebrew as a major academic discipline, requiring the study thereof by all its students. The language was introduced into the curriculum by the first president of the university, Thomas Clap, who had himself studied it diligently as an undergraduate at Harvard. But the individual most responsible for the advancement of Hebraic studies at Yale, and for the immense prestige which the language attained in academic circles in colonial America, was the university's seventh president, Ezra Stiles. Stiles, who surely ranks among the most learned men ever to hold such an office, was a lifelong ardent "Hebraician" (as he styled himself) and true Semitophile. Charles Seymour comments that Stiles "was a thorough master of the Hebrew language, which he wrote and spoke with a fluency unusual even for those days. . . .He regarded it [Hebrew] as an important element in a liberal education as the key to a vast storehouse of knowledge which could make possible an understanding of a highly significant aspect of human culture."

In 1755, Stiles, a recent Yale graduate and newly ordained minister, took over the pulpit of the Second Congregational Church of Newport, Rhode Island; his enduring friendship with the members of that town's Jewish congregation (established in 1762) is recorded in his *Literary Diary*—a remarkable documentary on the cultural life of that early and important community, of immense value to later historians. In 1767, in his fortieth year, and with virtually no previous knowledge of, or training in, the language, Stiles resolved to study Hebrew; he benefited greatly in this endeavor from his intimate association with the Jews of Newport, as attested by his son-in-law, who writes: "Some light, indeed, he derived from the Jews of Newport, particularly from their Hazzans, or teachers." Stiles began his studies under Newport's resident *hazzan,* Isaac Touro, reading through the Psalms and the Pentateuch, and acquiring grammatical texts and technical works in the field of Semitics; a diligent student, he soon became so proficient in the language as to be able to discourse with visiting rabbinical authorities on the Mishna, Talmud, and Kabbala. In Stiles's own words, he had "been taught personally at the mouth of the Masters of Wisdom, at the mouths of five Rabbis, Hochams of name & Eminence viz, R. Moses Malchi of Saphat in the holy Land. . . ; R. Moses Askenazi; R. Raphael Hajim Karigal of Hebron & Jerusalem. . . ;R. Tobiah Bar Jehuda. . .and. . .R. Samuel Cohen of Jerusalem."[21]

When a traveling Kabbalist, Rabbi Moses Bar David (surnamed "Askenazi" from his Polish origins), sojourned in Newport, Stiles hastened to pay his respects, discussing at length with the learned Gaon the intricacies of mysticism, and securing the loan of two volumes from the rabbi's personal collection, *Sefer Shaarey Orah* and Nathan Hanover's *Sefer Shaarey Tziyon,* upon which he comments in his *Literary Diary:* "I read it thro' immediately. It is in good Hebrew." And when our zealous "Hebraician" exhibited his own prized copy of the *Zohar,* the good rabbi "was much delighted." Similarly, for the two months in which Rabbi Karigal of Hebron stayed at Newport, he and Stiles engaged in many day-long discussions on Biblical interpretation, Jewish and Christian theology, Kabbala, etc.; and after the rabbi's departure in 1773 the dialogue continued for the next four years (until Karigal's death) in a correspondence of lengthy letters in Hebrew initiated by Stiles.[22] Since these learned rabbis probably knew little or no English, it is to be assumed that their conversations with Stiles, like the letters between Stiles and Karigal, were conducted in Hebrew—a remarkable testimonial to the achievement of a unique man. No less remarkable, and perhaps even more indicative of his profound humanity, is the report that the ordinary members of the Jewish community of Newport often came to Stiles for translation of letters in Hebrew.

In 1781, at his first public commencement at Yale, President Stiles delivered "An Oration upon the Hebrew Literature," originally written in Hebrew in 1778, the year of his election to office, but delivered three years later in English. In his oration Stiles lauded the traditional Wisdom of Israel with which he was so familiar, and proposed the inauguration of a program of Hebraic studies at Yale in particular, and in the American colleges generally.[23] Evaluating Hebrew as "a glorious language which throws more light on the Old Testament than all the Commentators," Stiles persisted in his enthusiasm for the *leshon qodesh* throughout his life; in his eyes it was essential for a properly balanced liberal education, and particularly indispensable in the preparation for a career in the ministry.

Before Stiles assumed the presidency of Yale, Hebrew had been taught only sporadically; but he was determined to have every graduate know something of the holy tongue, lest he "be entirely ignorant of the holy language when he got to Heaven." Thus, under his administration there was considerable emphasis on the Bible and other classical Jewish sources. Hebrew was taught five days a week between 1780 and 1790, with Stiles himself teaching the freshmen. By 1782 there were two classes in Hebrew, a development which was assisted by an endowment fund for a professorship of Hebrew and other Oriental studies, established by the Reverend Richard Salter. There were, in addition, prizes awarded to those who excelled in Hebrew. Yet by 1790 there seems to have been a damper on the earlier enthusiasm for Hebrew at Yale.

> From my first Accession to the presidency. . .to 1790 I have obliged all Freshmen to study Hebrew. This has proved very disagreeable to a number of the students. This year I have determined to instruct only those who offer themselves voluntarily, and that at subsecivis horis only without omitting any of the three daily classical recitations to their Tutor.[24]

Nevertheless, at least some students had learned enough during this period to have been able to deliver Hebrew orations at commencement exercises. Nor did interest in Hebrew at Yale ever really die; toward the end of the nineteenth century, the popularity of the language reached a new peak as a result of the lectures of Professor William Rainey Harper, a colorful and erudite personality as well as a brilliant Hebraist. Harper's students are reported to have filled the largest of the lecture halls at Yale. Furthermore, as one of the founders and later the first president of the University of Chicago, he turned the study of Hebrew into a national fad, establishing summer courses and correspondence courses; it is reputed that he received so much mail in connection with his instructional activities that it was necessary to raise the salary of the local postmaster!

Samuel Johnson, first president (1754–63) of King's College (later Columbia University), reflected the intellectual stance of his age when he referred to Hebrew as "being essential to a gentleman's education." Johnson was the most scholarly American of his day, and together with Jonathan Edwards, another student of Hebrew, he "takes rank as one of the two really powerful and constructive philosophers of the 18th century." An ardent devotee of Hebrew and Hebraic learning, he insisted that all tutors engaged in instruction at King's College possess at least a basic knowledge of the language. Johnson himself had studied Hebrew in his early years at the Guilford Grammar School in Connecticut, and later in life he taught his own children and grandchildren the rudiments of the language. He also wrote *An English and Hebrew Grammar, Being the First Short Rudiments of those Two Languages Being Taught Together, to Which is Added a Synopsis of all the Parts of Learning.*

Clement Clarke Moore, the son of one of Johnson's successors, graduated from King's College in 1798 at the head of his class; he was also an outstanding student of Hebrew. Moore composed a *Compendious Lexicon of the Hebrew Language* in two volumes, a work which is presumed to be the first of its kind in this country. In his middle years he taught Hebrew and Greek to students at the General Theological Seminary in New York, established under the auspices of the Protestant Episcopal Church as a result of his efforts. In 1859 the seminary established the Clement Clarke Moore Professorship of Hebrew in recognition of the latter's contribution to the field. Ironically, Moore is now known almost exclusively as the author of the ever-popular "A Visit from Saint Nicholas."

King's College and the Philadelphia Academy (later the University of Pennsylvania) were exceptions to the usual pattern among institutions of higher learning in early America. Other universities were, in effect, denominational divinity schools; the Philadelphia Academy, on the other hand, at the insistence of Benjamin Franklin, was not limited exclusively to the study of the classics, but was the first university in America to offer a true liberal arts course. And in time its curriculum was broadened to include subjects rarely offered in the other universities, such as applied mathematics, physical science, natural history, international law, and modern languages. Franklin's pragmatism is readily sensed here; yet despite this new utilitarian attitude toward higher education, one of the seven professorships at the academy in 1782 was in Hebrew and Oriental languages. In 1792 a combined professorship of Hebrew, Oriental languages, and German was established. Nearly a century later, in 1885, the noted Jewish scholar Dr. Morris Jastrow, Jr. became head of the Semitics Department; Dr. Jastrow also distinguished himself as the university librarian.

Dartmouth College, which was instituted in 1769 (just prior to the outbreak of the American Revolution) in order to train missionaries to work among the Indians, also followed in the "Hebraic" tradition of the older American colleges. Professor John Smith, for instance, who was appointed to the chair of Oriental languages while still a very young man, prepared a treatise on Hebrew grammar during his junior year (1722), and in 1803 published a grammar for the use of his students, *A Hebrew Grammar, without Points, designed to facilitate the study of the Old Testament in the original* (Boston, 1803). Hebrew is said to have been as familiar to him as his mother tongue. Likewise, Benjamin Hale, professor of medicine at Dartmouth from 1827, held "recitations in Hebrew" for two years, "not perhaps," as he himself modestly puts it, "much to the profit of my classes but because I happen to be fresher in that study than any college officer."

Many other American colleges founded in the eighteenth century, such as William and Mary in Virginia, Rutgers and Princeton in New Jersey, and Brown University in Rhode Island, were conducted in a religious or classical motif and regarded Hebrew as essential to the curriculum. The tradition was maintained, by and large, at least until the time of the Civil War, while Harvard, Yale, King's College, the Philadelphia Academy, Brown, Princeton, and Johns Hopkins have been teaching Hebrew without interruption since their inception. Thus, it is hardly surprising to find Hebrew words and phrases in the official emblems of many of these schools (see appendix A).

It has been said that in order to fully understand a poet one must dwell in his homeland, but that is actually a secondary prerequisite; primary, of course, is the poet's language, for it is through his language that one discovers the expressive spirit of his thought and creativity. And this was the attitude of the Puritans and others among the early settlers of America, perhaps epitomized in William Bradford's attempt to master Hebrew despite his advanced age; though he knew French and had mastered Greek and Latin, he finally concentrated on Hebrew because he wanted to see "with his own eyes the ancient oracles of God in their native beauty." And not only in the colleges but also in the lower schools was Hebrew studied. As Miller and Johnson point out, it was taught at the Boston Latin School in the seventeenth century; in an act dated 1695, providing for the establishment of a free school in St. Andrew's Parish, a clause was inserted which read: "Along with instruction in reading, writing, Latin, Greek. . .arithmetic. . .the scholars were to receive instruction in Hebrew." Earlier still, the Baptist town of Swansea, in New England, voted in 1673 to establish a grammar school, the plans for the curriculum of which were ambitious, to say the least, but indicate the importance which this country's earliest settlers attached to education. The proposed course of studies provided for the teaching of grammar, rhetoric, arithmetic, and three languages—Latin, Greek, and Hebrew. Similarly, John Davenport, an able Hebraist and colleague of John Cotton, "was directly instrumental in introducing the study of Hebrew in the first public school of New Haven, an action which was in part inspired by a bequest in the will of Governor Hopkins; according to the records of the colony, the instructor was appointed June 28, 1660." It was precisely this early and continuing acquaintance with the language on the part of students that enabled (and perhaps mandated) the colleges to require of their freshmen further instruction in Hebrew, in an attempt to build upon the basic knowledge acquired in the lower grades.

At any rate, such an attitude toward Hebrew did, as intimated above, inspire many first-rate scholars of the language. Increase Mather (whose very name is obviously a literal translation of the Hebrew *Yoseph)*, father of Cotton (from the Hebrew *katan,* "small," "junior"), knew the language well enough to discourse in it; his writings, furthermore, contain numerous quotations from the Talmud, Midrash, and Kabbala, and from the works of Saadia Gaon, Rashi, Ibn Ezra, Bahya Gaon, Maimonides, and many other classic Jewish commentators. The younger Mather was similarly absorbed in the language, and produced a respectable dissertation on Hebrew punctuation.

John Udall's translation of Marinius' Hebrew grammar, his own compilation of a Hebrew dictionary (*The Key to the Holy Tongue),* and Harvard President John Dunster's revision of the *Bay Psalm Book,* are but a few outstanding examples of the prevailing Puritan affection for the Hebrew language. The phenomenon is perhaps epitomized precisely in the fact of the publication of the *Bay Psalm Book;* an original translation of the Psalter from the Hebrew, it was one of the first books published in the colonies, so that copies are now among the rarest treasures of Americana, and, as such, priceless. The purpose of the publication was to replace the then popular Sternhold and Hopkins version, a rather free rendering which frequently sacrificed the original meaning for the sake of poetic effect. Such an inaccurate reading of the Hebrew text troubled the consciences of Puritans and offended their love of the language, and they sought to rectify the situation by the publication of the *Bay Psalm Book.* In a similar spirit, Cotton Mather wrote:

But of all the more than twice seven versions which I have

seen, it must be affirmed, that they *leave out* a vast heap of
those rich things, which the Holy Spirit of God speaks in
the original Hebrew; and that they *put in* as large an Heap
of poor things, which are entirely on their own. . . .I am
therefore strongly of the opinion that the *Poesie* of the Ancient Hebrews, knew no *Measure,* but that of the unknown
music, wherein it was to be accommodated. Our Psalms in
the Hebrew, are not so much *metrical* as *musical.*

The most famous of grammar school texts, *The New
England Primer,* was first published in America in 1683; better
known as *Milk for Babes,* it was based largely on Biblical
episodes, teaching the alphabet by means of verses, beginning with

A: In Adam's Fall
We Sinned All
and ending with

Z: Zacheus, he
Did climb the Tree
His Lord to see.

By 1840, *seven million* copies of the primer had been published.

At the time of the American Revolution, the interest in and
knowledge of Hebrew in the colonies was so widespread as
to allow the circulation of the story that "certain members of
Congress proposed that the use of English be formally prohibited in the United States, and Hebrew substituted for it."
Whether or not there is any basis of fact for the story, it is
plausible that in their patriotic zeal some people were eager
to replace the tongue of the British with one which they regarded as their spiritual language; but the essential thing is
that the people of that period considered the rumor likely
enough to circulate it.

The above examples illustrate the prominent place which
Hebrew occupied in the early academic life of this country,

and the high esteem in which it was held by the pioneers of American collegiate education, religious thought, and scholarship. The subsequent decline in the study of Hebrew in American institutions of higher learning may be attributed to numerous and diverse factors. Almost immediately after the Revolutionary War, following the growing tradition of the separation of the churches from the governing bodies, education in general was shifted from a religious to a national basis. This was regarded as essential to liberty and to the preservation of the state; and higher education also began to reckon with this broader aim, rather than merely with the sectarian training of ministers.

Moreover, the rapid and extensive growth of the natural sciences compelled the universities to broaden their curricula to meet the growing demand for professional, technical, and scientific training. The older colleges, now endowed by men of wealth, expanded their facilities and established schools of engineering and law, medicine and science. This new tendency reflected a utilitarian educational philosophy advocating the application of knowledge to everyday affairs, and derogating the value of the study of the classics for mental discipline, or of learning for its own sake. Education, according to this doctrine, was to provide for a useful and happy life. In this pragmatic view, Hebrew and the classics inevitably played a less significant role. The colleges, which greatly increased in number during the nineteenth century, and the state universities which began to spring up all over the country, following the new mode, made no provisions for Semitics courses. Courses in the Bible were still offered, but these were studied in the English translation, as part of English literature rather than (as previously) a sacred text.

Knowledge of Hebrew was, accordingly, not considered essential for either teacher or student in this type of course. Consequently a number of American universities during the nineteenth century transferred their early function of training for the ministry, with its attendant courses in Classics and Hebrew, to theological departments or seminaries. In most instances, universities assigned their courses in Hebrew to the Semitic or Oriental languages departments, which were associated strictly with their graduate divisions, thus restricting these studies to a more limited number of students. The secularization of the universities and colleges also resulted in a departure from the custom of appointing clergymen to university presidencies—a practice which in the past had strengthened the religious tenor of the institutions.

The archaeological movement, spurred by the deciphering of the Rosetta Stone (1830), found ardent exponents and supporters in America. In 1814 Colonel Mendes J. Cohen (1796–1879) of Baltimore traveled extensively up the Nile and brought back a collection of Egyptian relics, which was presented in 1884, several years after his death, to Johns Hopkins University. Edward Robinson, a gifted professor at the Union Theological Seminary in New York, together with a missionary, Eli Smith, traveled through Palestine in 1838, and again in 1852, and located many Biblical sites, obscured by Arabic names. When Paul Emil Botta, a Frenchman, formerly consul at Alexandria, was appointed in 1842 to a similar post in Mosul, opposite the site of ancient Nineveh, he unearthed in that region the palace of King Sargon of Assyria (722–705 B.C.E.) mentioned in Isaiah 20:1.

These archaeological breakthroughs of the nineteenth century in the Middle East prompted many American universities to establish or strengthen departments of Semitic studies in order to train scholars in the analysis of inscriptions and texts in the ancient tongues. Union Theological Seminary had already introduced the teaching of Hebrew and related ancient languages early in the century. In 1822 a Semitics program was launched at the Princeton Theological Seminary. New York University, under the name of the University of the City of New York, had also been teaching classical Hebrew and Oriental languages since its founding in 1831 by a splinter group among Columbia's trustees. Vanderbilt launched its Semitics program four decades later, in 1875, Johns Hopkins in 1876, Cincinnati in 1882, Pennsylvania in 1886, Columbia in 1887, Bryn Mawr in 1891, Chicago in 1892, Michigan in 1894, Minnesota and Syracuse in 1895. Other institutions, including Wisconsin and McGill, soon followed suit.[25]

A new approach was effected in the teaching of Hebrew as a Semitic language rather than as the sacred tongue of the Old Testament. It was now regarded as one ancient language among many, in relationship to which it could now be studied philologically and scientifically, so that the religious motivation for the study of Hebrew began to fade into the background. The stress was now on grammatical declensions, exemplified in the *katal, katalti* pattern, which helped to "kill" the fervor of students, so that its popularity also began to wane. But there were other reasons as well for its decline, chief among which was the increasing secularization of American life in general. Freethinking had undermined the belief in the divine revelation of the Scriptures and the historicity of many of the narratives of both Testaments. Biblical scholars in their turn began to offer rationalistic explanations for the authorship and compilation of the Biblical text. Aside from this, the rapid expansion of the natural sciences, and the expanding technocratic and industrial requirements of the country, provoked a need for training facilities in the scientific fields, in engineering, and in law. By this time the older colleges had accumulated sufficient funds for this purpose, so that schools now began to concentrate on these secular fields, relegating instruction in Hebrew to the newly established divinity schools.

Thus the originally religious character of these venerable institutions was lost, and the large number of new public and private colleges opening at this time were imbued from the start with the current secular and pragmatic outlook, so that they also subordinated the study of Hebrew and classical languages. Rabbi William Rosenau, an instructor in Hebrew and Semitics, described the situation thus: "Semitic studies occupy a minor place in American colleges as such. The American college, while in many localities the highest seat of learning, is only a station on the road to scholarship. The American college corresponds to the European Gymnasium. Hebrew and Arabic are the only Semitic branches taught in the college course and are optional in every case." Another contemporary had indicated that the teachers of Hebrew were poorly prepared, recalling that "the number of professors of Hebrew throughout the Country who had approximately scientific training in the Semitic languages could have been counted on the fingers of one hand. Such as had any training had acquired it perforce in Germany."

The 1880s were a turning point in this regard. In 1883 Professor Paul Haupt, a brilliant young Assyriologist, was brought from the University of Göttingen to Johns Hopkins, where he did much to improve conditions by training teachers for Semitics programs. From two schools (Harvard and Yale) in 1883, the number of fairly complete Semitics programs had by 1896 grown to no less than sixteen. Other colleges and universities throughout the country offered partial programs in Semitics, which commonly included Hebrew.

In 1917–18 the *American Jewish Year Book* published a list of the American colleges offering Hebrew, generally as part of a Semitics program. It listed fifty-five institutions providing such instruction, among them Boston University, Brown, Butler College, the University of California, the University of Chicago, Colgate, Columbia, Cornell, Dropsie University,* Johns Hopkins, Oberlin, Pennsylvania, Smith, Temple, Trinity, Tulane, Wisconsin, and Yale. These were only the major schools; seven of the remaining smaller institutions evidently taught such courses intermittently, only when there was sufficient demand. The Lucius Littauer Chair of Jewish Literature and Philosophy at Harvard, founded in 1925, was occupied from its inception (and until his retirement) by the late scholar Harry A. Wolfson, himself an alumnus of Harvard. The Nathan Miller Chair at Columbia (created

*Established in 1907 as a postgraduate institution for Hebrew and cognate learning.

several years later) had as its first incumbent the late Dr. Stephen S. Wise (1874–1949), a student of Professor Gotheil. After 1930 it was held by the noted Jewish historian Salo Baron, who retired in the fall of 1963.[26]

The first academic course in modern Hebrew was introduced by the writer in 1933, in the Division of General Education of New York University. Several years later, in 1937, this course was incorporated, with the help of the then Dean E. George Payne, into an accredited curriculum of the School of Education. The success of this course led to the introduction of additional courses, and the first chair of modern Hebrew culture and education in any American institution of higher learning was established in 1944.* In 1962, after nearly thirty years of effort in the field of Hebrew, the Institute of Hebrew Studies was founded. The Institute was designed to give cohesion to the work carried on in the undergraduate and graduate divisions of New York University.† Today, students may receive the bachelor's, master's, and doctoral degrees in the fields of Hebrew and Hebrew culture in the School of Education now headed by Dr. Nathan Winter, while at the undergraduate and graduate Schools of Arts and Sciences there is a program leading to the degrees of bachelor of arts, master of arts, and doctor of philosophy in the new Department of Near Eastern Studies, formerly Hebrew and Near Eastern Studies.

Happily, other colleges and universities soon followed this lead. A series of studies carried out by the author indicate that in recent years the study of Hebrew, modern as well as classical, has been rapidly gaining ground.[27] In 1940, 124 institutions of higher learning offered Hebrew, only ten of which treated it as a modern language. A decade later the number rose to 206 institutions teaching Hebrew in some form, and 38 institutions listed courses in modern Hebrew

*In 1957 the chair was named the Abraham I. Katsh Professorship of Hebrew Culture and Education.

†This Institute lasted until 1968, when the writer left New York University to assume the presidency of Dropsie University in Philadelphia.

and in Hebrew culture in their curricula. The survey carried out in 1958 showed that this figure had risen to 245, with 48 offering instruction in modern Hebrew, while in 1963, 252 taught Hebrew in some form, with 55 institutions offering courses in modern Hebrew.

Although the number of universities today providing instruction in Hebrew is indeed large, it is not only a matter of quantity, for the list of institutions offering such courses includes the most famous in America: Boston, Brandeis, Brown, Chicago, Columbia, Cornell, Dartmouth, Denver, Harvard, Indiana, Iowa, Johns Hopkins, Kentucky, Maryland, Miami, Michigan, Missouri, Oberlin, Pennsylvania, Princeton, Rutgers, Smith, Southern California, Temple, Texas, Vanderbilt, Washington, Wayne State, Wisconsin, Yale, Yeshiva University, and the Dropsie University, which established a chair in Hebrew and cognate studies in 1907. Their catalogues abound with an endless variety of courses, from the most basic instruction in elementary Hebrew to literary criticism of the nineteenth- and twentieth-century Hebrew essayists; and this trend is evidently increasing among students throughout the country.

Initially, the popularity of the study of Hebrew was due to the theological interest in the Bible. With the increasing secularization of American society, this original impulse weakened. However, since the creation of the State of Israel in 1948, there has been a new trend—toward the study of Hebrew as a living language within the context of a renascent culture. Just as the colleges and universities in the early days of America provided a firm foundation in the Hebrew language and tradition, so today the institutions of higher learning are striving to keep pace with the expanding horizons in Hebrew education.[28]

4

The Judaic Spirit

The priceless jewel of Hebrew religious development, a pure ethical idealism of the prophets, was not lost to the religious experience of Israel, but was rather preserved for her and for all ages and for all races, through the ritual legalism of the priests. The world's richest treasures of religious and moral truths are the gifts and fruitage of Jewish ethical idealism. [1]

The passage quoted as the epigraph to this chapter expresses the opinion of one scholar on the far-reaching effect of the spirit epitomized in the Old Testament. It was this spirit that captured the imagination of the Puritans as they sought to establish a society in accordance with the life which the "elect" of God chose to live. Relating this more specifically to American life, we find that mastery of Hebrew served to deepen the Puritans' roots in the ethical idealism which they derived as much from Judaism as from the Christian tradition of which they were a divergent branch. The knowledge of the Hebrew language enabled the Puritans to breathe more deeply of the spirit and meaning of the Old Testament. It is,

in fact, almost axiomatic that in every period of Christian reform, the effort to understand the Biblical word in its original
form leads to the overcoming of limited established orthodox
doctrines, even as the shift of emphasis from the New Testament to the Old usually results in a concomitant emphasis
on the spirit and ideals contained specifically in the Hebrew
Scriptures. Whether this emulation of the Judaic ideal was
conscious or not, the Puritans, at least, were not unaware of
where their ideals and Bible-bound spirit were leading them.
This peculiarly Hebraic type of idealism, as the Puritans
chose to interpret and apply it, not only dominated their
theology but permeated the pattern of their daily life. It
helped them to discipline their minds; it fortified their will; it
confirmed in divine terms the principles for which they
stood; and these were the factors which enabled them to
survive. Perhaps as much as any more practical factor, this
belief in their divinely inspired mission equipped the Puritans to triumph over the difficulties which had defeated previous colonists. It gave them the hardihood and tenacity of
purpose, the will and courage necessary to withstand the
rigors of life in the wilderness that was America during the
early years of the seventeenth century.

Before proceeding further, however, one point needs
clarification. The fact that the Puritan colonists were nurtured
on the Bible, grew up in its spirit, and lived according to its
precepts, does not necessarily mean that they held any deep
affection for the contemporary heirs of the Biblical tradition,
i.e., the flesh-and-blood Jews of the seventeenth century. Although they did consider the Jews of their day fit objects for
their missionary efforts, and would have been overjoyed had
these efforts borne fruit, the Puritans held no brief for obdu-
rate Jews who remained faithful to their own religion. This
was not a manifestation of anti-Semitism per se, such as the
twentieth century has witnessed in horror, but simply the
natural and inevitable result of a faith predicated on the principle of divine "election." Nor was Puritan intolerance directed solely against the Jews; for the Quakers who came to

preach in the Massachusetts Colony were met with persecution and torture. Similarly, John Endicott, the first governor of the Massachusetts Colony, petitioned the British Parliament in London in 1652 on the matter of the presence of other religious sects in the colony, demanding that "strange religious groups" be barred from the territory; among those so designated were the Arians, Mahumetans, Familists, Adamites, Raantrees, Levellers, Papists, Atheists, and Jews. It was thus not the contemporary Jew that was so appealing to the Puritan, but rather the timeless Judaic spirit and its concomitant philosophy.

Thus, according to the historian Fiske, there was in the Massachusetts Commonwealth "the same ethical impulse which animates the glowing pages of the prophets and which has given to the history and literature of Israel their commanding influence in the world." This very idea finds expression in the 1656 revision of the Pilgrim Code:

> It was the great privilege of Israel of olde and soe was acknowledged by them, Nehemiah the 9th and 10th, that God gave them right judgements and true laws. They are for the mayne so exemplary, being grounded on the principles of moral equitie as that all Christians especially ought alwaies to have an eye thereunto in the framing of their politique constitutions. We can safely say both for ourselves and for them that we have had an eye principally unto the aforesaid platforme in the framing of this small body of Lawes.

Thus the Pilgrims sought to re-create the conditions of the old Canaan in the new Canaan which they were endeavoring to establish. As A. A. Neuman contends,

> Puritanism was, in essence, the rebirth of the Hebrew Spirit in the Christian conscience. It was the Hebrew religious genius come to life to wage battle for God and soul-freedom, once more to impress upon the world the sovereignty of God and the holiness of life. . . . The most

drastic reforms which Puritanism introduced in the Church polity, when it broke away from the Anglican Episcopacy, lay in the decentralization of the Church, the abolition of the hierarchy, and the bridging of the gap between the minister and the laity. In all of these directions, Puritanism paralleled or unconsciously followed Jewish precedent. Every synagogue was an independent entity; and the rabbi, like the Puritan elder . . . laid no claim to super-naturalism in any form. Learning, piety, interpretation of God's will as revealed in the Law—a source open to all—these were the essential qualifications for spiritual author-ity as in the Puritan Churches. In both institutions, the re-ligious head was chosen by the people.[2]

The parallel is valid on every level. For example, the gov-ernment and administration of the Puritan colony was not strictly in the hands of the ministers, so that in this respect the Puritans never really achieved an "ideal" theocracy; yet there is little doubt that they hoped to establish one. It was to this end that the early Puritan settlers drew from the Old Testament numerous examples of the procedure of the He-brews in this regard. The question of precedent and sanction was always of the greatest moment, because they were more concerned with the religious ideals involved than with mere concepts of political and social democracy. As Millar Burrows observes, the Hebrew ideal "was not democracy but theo-cracy. The days when 'there was no king in Israel,' when 'ev-ery man did that which was good in his own eyes,' were re-garded in retrospect, not as a time of hateful anarchy, but as a time when God ruled his people directly."[3] Although Bur-rows's description of the situation is accurate enough, there is, in fact, considerable difficulty in applying any arbitrary label to the system of the Hebrews, and equally so to that of the Puritans. In any case, however, the parallel between the two systems remains a remarkable coincidence.

In more ways than one, the Puritans, knowingly or not, followed the Jewish ethical tradition. One of the most strik-ing examples of this is the almost complete lack of asceticism

in the Puritan outlook and practice. Nor should what is traditionally conceived of as Puritan "sternness" be confused with
asceticism; the opinion of the British historian R. H. Tawney,
that the Puritans were a folk willing to come to terms with
this world, is surely a more accurate estimation of this Puritan characteristic. Genuine asceticism, according to the
medieval outlook, is rather the belief that perfection in this
life and in this world is to be attained only by means of a
monastic retreat from life and the world; Puritanism, however, firmly maintained that one could best serve God in this
world by genuine devotion to one's chosen profession or
trade. Thus, the farmer or the village smith could lead a life
every bit as exemplary and "holy" as that of the pious monk
by fulfilling to the best of his ability the role which the circumstances of this world determined for him. If the
craftsman plied his trade and lived his life in an ethical and
charitable fashion, fulfilling his responsibilities to the best of
his ability, then his share of the hereafter was assured.

It was constantly emphasized in all the Puritan sects that
God preferred a man who served Him in the manner for
which he was best suited to one who sought to escape his
responsibilities through retreat from the world. The correspondence to the Judaic spirit and belief on this point is
worthy of note, for the Hebrews were likewise a decidedly
unascetic people in the main. Although the practice of
monasticism was not prohibited, it was discouraged. The
preference for finding spiritual fulfillment in the vigorous
pursuit of these occupations, and the affirmation of the religious value (or "holiness") of such vocations, was shared
by Puritan and Jew alike.

This attitude extended naturally enough to the realm of
love and marriage, in which the Puritans adopted a course
divergent from that held by medieval Christianity. Indeed,
the religious group to which the Puritans bore the closest resemblance in this regard was the Jews. A natural outgrowth
of the Puritan attitude toward asceticism and worldliness was
the dim view which they took of the practice of celibacy. As

they could not condone monastic retreat or mortification of the flesh, so they also regarded celibacy with distinct disfavor. The Puritan ideal in this regard is expressed with eloquent simplicity by Milton: "Hail, wedded love!"

The Biblical command to increase and multiply was understood by the Puritans, as by the Jews, quite literally; marriage was considered the natural (and ideal) state for mankind. The clergy, accordingly, married young in the New England colony, and there was no retreat within the bosom of the church for those who desired a celibate life. Although continence in all things might be considered a moral ideal of the Puritans, who, again like the Hebrews, abhorred excess, the logical conclusion of this was by no means complete abstinence. Sexual abstinence was not considered in Puritan society the mark of a morally virtuous person, but rather took on an obstructionist cast, as confounding the intent of the Creator and of His plan of Creation. Indeed, married men who came to settle in New England without their wives were ordered to send for or return to them. A corollary of the importance of marriage in the Puritan colony was that divorce was easier to obtain in the New World than in England; since wedded love was so highly valued by the Puritans, it was felt that every marriage should be a success.

In a study of Puritan love and marriage[4] it is shown that the Puritan wife occupied an enviable position in comparison not only with the wife of early Rome or of the Middle Ages, but even of contemporary England. The reason for this is that "the husband's authority was strictly limited. He could not lawfully strike her, nor could he command her to do anything contrary to the *Laws of God,* laws which were explicitly defined in the civil codes." Love in marriage was a duty imposed by God. "The Great God commands thee to love her," exclaimed Benjamin Wadsworth. Not to love one's wife was to disobey God. Wadsworth further explains, "The indisputable Authority, the plain command of the Great God, required Husbands and Wives, to have and manifest very great affection, love and kindness to one another."[5] When John

Cotton preached a sermon at a marriage ceremony in 1694, he condemned the fortitude of a couple who had had no conjugal relations, saying that they followed not the "Holy Spirit, which saith 'It is not good that man should be alone.' "[6]

On the other hand, moderation in love was also dictated by God's word. Too much love, according to John Cotton, "benumbs and dims the light of the Spirit." The reasoning behind this was that too much affection tended to cause man and wife to forget their Maker. True love demands that "such as have wives look at them not for their own ends, but to bee better fitted for God's service, and bring them nearer to God."[7]

Notwithstanding the many natural differences between Puritan and Jew in many areas, the similarities, then, are striking. The parallels between the town government of the Puritans and the community organization of the *kahal;* the synagogue and the meetinghouse; the rabbi and the elder; the beadle and the tithingman; and the respective attitudes toward education are extremely noteworthy. With these similarities the suggestion is certainly not being made that one group derived its conduct from the other. Rather, as Neuman said, "Puritanism and Judaism spoke the same spiritual language."[8] The common source from which both drew inspiration was the Bible. Therein lies the kinship between these two communities.

Even the Puritan attitude toward predestination was mitigated by the influence of the Hebraic spirit. Although the theology of the Puritan movement operated under a strong Calvinist influence, there were many factors conditioning that theology in New England. The Massachusetts Puritan was not strongly predestinarian; like the Jew, he conceived of the world and mankind as a divine enterprise, whose management was God's main interest. Both peoples felt that God was deeply concerned with the ways of the world, the paths its nations chose, and the actions of its peoples. The element of a personal God was very strong, and His interest in the individual was felt with keen conviction. But the overriding sentiment was that in the event a person was incapable of receiving God's grace, there was always hope as long as there was life. Thus Calvinist predestinarianism in the New World was moderated by a strong note of optimism.

But the similarities between the Puritan spirit and the Judaic spirit were not confined to the theoretical and esoteric realm of belief; life in general was modeled as much on the Hebraic pattern as was possible for the New England colonists under the circumstances. But before considering the more concrete examples of the impact of the Judaic spirit on the Puritans, a few words must be said about what later came to be known as "Puritan strictness." The earliest Puritans were not opposed to the lighter side of life; but the extremely low moral conditions of English society in the late sixteenth and early seventeenth centuries had an ineradicable effect on the Puritan consciousness. In addition, the Puritans in America had to struggle incessantly against the harsh physical realities of the New World, which forced them into a self-discipline at which we in the twentieth century can only marvel. These factors combined with the natural Puritan inclination toward the Biblical spirit to give the Puritans a strength of will comparable, perhaps, only to that of our Biblical prophets. Under such circumstances, the Puritans were strongly influenced by the nature and strictures of Judaic law, so that they hedged life about with "thou shalts" and "thou shalt nots" in a manner distinctly reminiscent of Judaic law. At the inception of the Puritan movement, this attitude derived from and thrived on the Hebraic spirit; only later, after the Puritan decline, did it degenerate into unnecessary legalism and strictness.

Thus, the influence of the Judaic spirit on the early colonists in the New World was sharply felt in the area of ritual and in the form taken by the celebration of holy days. The first Thanksgiving celebration in 1621 was not a joyous holiday but rather an imitation of a Jewish fast day: it was a purely religious service, with the emphasis placed rather on fasting than on feasting (as has become the custom in more recent years): "Let us, we beseech you (all you that love Zion) your prayers, and helpe in heaven and earth for the furtherance of this great and glorious worke in our hands; great works need many hands, many prayers, many tears."

Likewise, the Puritan attitude toward the observance of the Sabbath, so similar to that of the Bible, is best expressed by Cotton Mather: "It has truly and justly been observed that our whole religion fares according to our Sabbaths, that poor Sabbaths make poor Christians, and that a strictness in our Sabbaths inspires a vigor in all our other duties." It was in this spirit that the Sabbath in New England was kept, for the Puritan Sabbath developed along lines completely divergent from the tradition of the Catholic Church. Under Catholicism, the Sabbath has traditionally been a festival celebrated by an early mass, with recreation or even work afterwards not being forbidden.[9] The manner in which the Puritans observed the day of rest was completely different.

The first indication of a stricter observance can be seen in the *Treatise of the Sabbath* by Dr. Richmond Bound in 1595, wherein he maintained that "for the proper regulation of the Christian Sunday we must look to the Old Testament precepts regarding the Jewish Sabbath." Strict Sabbatarianism evolved with the increased influence of Puritanism. In Scotland, whose national church was influenced even more by Geneva, citations for breaking the Sabbath were frequent. (It even became a sin for mothers to kiss their children on the Lord's Day!) Once in America, the Puritans continued their tradition of strictly observing their Sunday Sabbath. They sought to establish the principle of the literal observance of many Hebraic laws, sometimes even including rabbinic injunctions. This was most pronounced in their Sabbath laws and customs. Like the Jews, the Puritans began their observance of the Sabbath in the early evening of the previous day, and would not, within the space of twenty-four hours, shave, perform work of any kind, or have their rooms swept, beds made, dishes washed, or cooking done. The Sabbath was intended as a day of worship and meditation. John Cotton went so far as to doubt the propriety of preparing a sermon on the Sabbath "so far as it might beweary some labour to invention or memory." Traveling on the Sabbath was forbidden in Massachusetts, even through a small village, in mockery of which John Mayhew wrote:

> Henceforth let none, in peril of their lives,
> Attempt a journey; or embrace their wives.

Another contemporary observer describes a Boston Sabbath in the early years of the town's existence: the gates were shut and the ferry was guarded to prevent anyone, man, woman or child, from leaving the town. Within the precincts of the town itself, moreover, the citizens were constantly watched, and were prohibited from walking along the waterfront or on the common, even in the heat of summer. Any gathering was regarded as an opportunity for the violation of the Sabbath, so that if a few people met by chance on the street and stopped a moment to chat, they were warned by officers to disperse. "All trade and business ceases and every shop in town is shut up, even a barber is finable for shaving after that time." The punishment for breaking the Sabbath, as set forth in the General Laws of the Massachusetts Colony of 1658, was severe: all men or women above fourteen who indulged in "playing, uncivil walking, drinking, travelling from town to town" on the Sabbath could be warned or fined; if the offender had no money for the fine, the resulting whipping should "not exceed five stripes for ten shillings fine."[10]

Again, as in the Orthodox Jewish synagogue, the sexes were segregated in the Puritan churches; beyond which, Joseph Banvard states,

> The peculiarities of some of the forms of legislation were occasioned by their imitation of ancient Jewish customs. Thus, in New Haven the members of the constituent

committee were called the "seven pillars hewn out of the house of Wisdom," and Rhode Island performed for one or two years a "Jewish masquerade." Their language was quaint because [it was] interlarded with the phraseology of Scripture.

The extent to which Hebraic concepts and ideals had permeated the Puritan mind is indicated by the report that some of Cromwell's officers suggested that his Privy Council consist of seventy members, along the lines of the Jewish Sanhedrin.[11]

The Puritans followed the spirit of the Bible even in matters of dress, disapproving of all forms of apparel that seemed to be at variance with the simplicity and purity of the Hebraic spirit. Modest clothing was prescribed for women; although they were permitted to appear in public with face and hands bared, it was considered evil to be seen wearing clothes with short sleeves, low necklines, or hemlines above the ankles. In 1656 a law was enacted in Massachusetts banning "short sleeves, whereby the nakedness of the arm may be discovered." But even if a woman's clothes did meet the standard of Puritan modesty, she could be censured for "pride of raiment" if her clothes were too ostentatious or richly decorated. Men also were subject to dress-regulations in conformity with the proper standard (that of the Bible).

In 1634 the General Court of Massachusetts, as a result of "some new and immodest fashions," forbade the wearing of any clothes "with lace on it, silver, gold or thread . . . slashed clothes, other than one slash in each sleeve and another in the back; also all cutworks, embroidered or needlework caps, bands and rails . . . all gold and silver girdles, hat-bands, belts, ruffs, beaver hats." The General Court in 1639 added to the list of prohibited clothes for males "immoderate great breeches, knots of ribbon, broad shoulder-bands and rails, silk rases, double ruffs, and cuffs," since these "superfluities" inclined "to little use or benefit, but to the nourishment of pride."[12]

The reasoning behind these regulations was voiced by the early New England preacher, Uriah Oakes:

> Hath God brought us into a wilderness and caused us to dwell alone and separated us for a peculiar people to Himself, that we should imitate the nations in these vanities? . . .When persons spend more time in trimming their bodies than their souls. . .you may say of them, as a worthy divine wittily speaks that they are like the cinnamon tree, nothing good but the bark.

The Biblical echoes in this chastisement are unmistakable!

The Puritans regulated not only ordinary apparel, but also prohibited the use of crosses and beads, surplices and prayerbooks, which they regarded as "Romish" abuses. Nor could they countenance rites and rituals which they felt to be distortions of the ancient practices recorded in the Hebrew ordinances. They also denied the superiority of religious leaders, how high soever their rank; the Puritans, like the Jews, believed in an equality among the servants of the Lord, all members of this common ministry possessing the same rights and enjoying the same privileges.

The manner in which ministers were ordained was likewise influenced by the Judaic spirit and practice. The first minister in a community was selected by the elders, and installed in his position by them in the symbolic laying-on of hands. When he resigned his ministry, he would similarly place his hands in turn on the head of his successor, thus insuring the continuity of the ministry. The custom doubtlessly originates from an identical custom among the ancient Israelites, beginning with the laying-on of hands by Moses upon Joshua.

The structure of the church hierarchy is also reminiscent of the Judaic model. The Puritans felt that the church was independent of the ministry, that every church enjoyed the right and privilege of selecting its own minister. It was a cardinal belief of Puritanism that no authority on earth outside the community, whether it be king, prince, or church hierarch, had the authority to impose on the community, in disregard of its will, a pastor. The keynote of this structure was autonomy and simplicity. All towns were responsible for the moral character of their citizens; all churches were responsible for the souls of their members. But the leaders of the Puritan churches were elected by majority vote, and were granted a great deal of authority in the affairs of their respective flocks. There is in this a decided repudiation of the top-heavy hierarchy which had come to characterize the Catholic and Anglican churches, and a resurgence of the vastly more independent spirit which marked the ancient Israelites. Though the power of the ministry remained strong in civil affairs, the people had a say in the choice of their ministers. The spirit of exhortation had returned to religion, and the voices of the prophets were heard again, calling for the correction of sins in government as well as in the church. In all this the Bible and the Judaic spirit served as very real models; hence, for example, trial by jury was rejected, since it was not a part of Mosaic law.

In fine, the state civil laws, the Sabbath, the general rules of conduct and behavior, justice and equity, both in deed and in thought, had to derive their sanction from the Old Testament, which the Puritan so revered. As James Ernst comments, "God had revealed for all time in its entirety all true religion, a revelation absolute and final." In view of this repeated and devoted use of the Bible, this highly conscious emulation of Biblical models, this infusion of the general spirit of Hebraism, one can readily agree with Simms that "the American people owe more to the ancient Hebrews than to any other people. More than to either the Greeks or the Romans, because to the Hebrews we owe our ethical and spiritual ideals."[13]

Chapter

5

Legislation and Justice

One of the most significant and far-reaching results of the Protestant Reformation was the accessibility of the Bible to all who sought it for their eternal salvation; with the new translations, the precepts of the Bible became binding upon each individual reader, who was now no longer dependent solely upon the interpretative office of the church for his understanding of the faith. Moreover, the ornate liturgical apparatus of the medieval church was supplanted by a direct and austerely simple way of religious life, the most rigorous proponents of which were undoubtedly the Puritans. Since Puritanism was essentially a return to the Hebraic concept of a "compact" with God, the covenant, it followed that the laws, regulations, and ordinances by which Puritan society was to be governed should be those contained in the Hebrew Bible, or the Puritans' Old Testament, through which document the Lord had manifested His will and revealed the laws that were pleasing in His eyes. Professor Harold Fisch gives the following explanation of the concept of covenant as understood by the Hebrews:

In the Covenant-doctrine, Man is seen to be created from nothing. He starts out merely as dust, with no claims whatever to any specially assigned place in a cosmic chain. In this sense, the Covenant preserves the sense of an enormous, indeed apparently unbridgeable distance between an omnipotent Creator and His human creation. On the other hand, impotent and without claim as he is, man is miraculously elected to be the partner of Deity in an historical enterprise. His life is invested not merely with purpose but with divine purpose; and within the categories of Covenant, he and his divine Creator enter into mutual obligations to one another. This is the audacious claim of the Hebrew Religion; to the Greeks it should have seemed an example of incredible *hubris*. [1]

Although this doctrine was early adopted by Christianity in some degree, it was not developed very fully until the time of the Reformation, and was only completely realized by the Puritans, who accepted the concept in toto as the bedrock of their society and its legal structure. The most serious implication of this concept of covenant was its exaction of righteous and moral behavior; there was a felt urgency to act, and to act along the proper ethical and moral lines as described in the Lord's own dictates. And since the boundaries between the moral behavior of the individual and that of the body politic were scarcely perceptible, the ethical laws regulating the activity of the community as a whole were often virtually indistinguishable from those pertaining to the individual.

The theoretical basis for Puritan legislation began to crystallize and to take shape as early as the closing years of the reign of James I (1625) in England, during which period the English Congregationalists (the forerunners of the New England church) began to expound vigorously the belief that each individual congregation constituted a separate church, each deriving its authority and sanction directly from God and ruled by His precepts and ordinances alone. [2] While the proponents of this school of thought continued to recognize the Church of England, their credo reduced that church, in theory at least, to a very loose confederation of congregations. The founders of this amorphous body assumed that it would maintain its unity through the vigilant support of the civil government, whose appropriately religious and zealous magistrates would faithfully maintain the tenets of the true church while endeavoring to expunge the influence of all other churches; in other words, both the religious law of the church and the civil law of the secular community were to derive alike from the precepts of the Holy Bible, since the Word of God was manifestly superior to that of man.

If the Congregationalists failed to impose this theological and legislative blueprint upon their fellow Englishmen, they did succeed in impressing the basic pattern of their utopian vision upon their brethren who were leaving the Old World to settle in the New. Thus the Puritans, upon their arrival in America, vigorously set about putting into effect the ambitious plan of their English precursors. But the New England Congregationalists proved far more literal in their interpretation of Scripture than their counterparts in England, for reasons which lie in the psychological makeup and historical background of these early settlers. Since the psychological impetus of their whole enterprise was the conviction that they had in fact entered a new Canaan, under the guidance of the Lord Himself and the leadership of His appointed spokesmen, the Puritans felt themselves bound by the express dictates of their divine mentor, and under particular obligation to conduct themselves faultlessly in every area of human conduct. Consequently, as might have been expected, the resultant Puritan legislation was dominated by this strict construction of the Biblical moral imperatives; their conception of ethics, of integrity, honesty, industry, being wholly determined by their severe and unequivocal reading of the Scriptural text. At times they even exceeded the letter of Biblical law, legislating, solely on the basis of their understanding, particular problems in a Biblical spirit, where textual justification or precedent was lacking.

As mentioned previously the Hebraic influence on the

Mayflower Compact, the first major legislative document in the New World, which in turn served as a precedent for later colonists in their attempts to formulate legislation appropriate to the new circumstances. The covenant drawn up by the Salem colonists, for instance, reflects the same spirit of the Hebrew Bible from which the Mayflower Compact derived: "We covenant with the Lord and with one another, and doe bynd our selves in the presence of God to walk together in all his waies, according as he is pleased to reveale himself unto us in his Blessed word of truth." This document likewise constitutes an explicit acceptance of a contractual relationship of a religious and social nature. Implicit in this relationship is the acceptance of certain obligations, the criterion for which ("his Blessed word of truth") leaves little doubt as to the form which the Salem colonists intended to give to the legislative basis of their society.

A similar spirit prevailed among the New Haven colonists when, in 1639 (as yet independent of Connecticut), they assembled at a general meeting in order to determine the structure their proposed civil government would take, the outcome of which was the unanimous decision to establish an administrative structure based on a legislative framework in accordance with the wishes and uses of God. In a sense, this meeting marks the inception of the unique type of legislation adopted and spread by the English colonists in America. Although the manner in which the various colonies evolved the general form of their respective codes was largely determined by their different circumstances and backgrounds, they all scrupulously followed the example of Hebraic law in their legislative models. Cotton Mather's profusely Scriptural interpretation of this process illustrates the point quite explicitly:

When the great God of Heaven had carried His *peculiar* people into a *wilderness* the theocracy wherein He became. . .the Lord of Hosts, unto them and the four squadrons of the army, was most eminently displayed in His enacting of their *laws,* His directing of their *wars,* and His electing and inspiring of their *judges.* In some resemblance hereunto, when *four* colonies of Christians had marched like so many *hosts* . . . unto an American *wilderness,* there were several instances wherein that *army* of confessors was under a theocracy; for their laws were still enacted, and their *wars* were still directed by the voice of God, as far as they understood it, speaking from the *oracle* of the *scriptures.*[3]

The Biblical impulse of the English settlers in America is self-evident. It is precisely in their legislative system that this impulse coalesces with the legal portions of the Old Testament to form a Biblical superstructure for the newly founded society. The image of the "hosts" marching into the "American wilderness" under the direct guidance of God, so reminiscent of the ethical forces that motivated the ancient Israelites with such vigor, only strengthens this impression.

The colonial leaders were highly respected and honored by all the colonists, and their influence penetrated every aspect of life in the colonies. These remarkable men left their impress on business, politics, theology, and morals throughout the colonies proper, and, in the case of Roger Williams, it even extended to new and unsettled areas. In a pioneering age these leaders were in the forefront of every new effort and broke the ground for every new enterprise. It is not surprising, therefore, that those matters which were of concern to men like Roger Williams, William Bradford, and John Davenport, were of vital concern and focal interest to the vast majority of colonists as well. In almost all of their undertakings these men resorted to the Bible for inspiration, justification, and guidance. John Davenport, the Puritan clergyman who helped found New Haven, had come to New England resolved to follow the precepts and pattern of the Scriptures; when faced with the dangers which the New World presented, Davenport customarily drew a parallel from the Biblical narrative. In a letter to Alexander Leighton, for example, he writes:

How much better would it beseme us to combine together
in an holy league against the common Adversary, according to Joab's agreement with Abishai, if the Aramites be
stronger than I, thou shalt helpe me, and if the children of
Amon be too strong for thee Ile come and succor thee,
than thus to resemble those servants of Saul and David,
under the command of Abner and Joab, each of which
caught his fellow by the head, and thrust his sword into
his fellowes side so they fell downe together?

Similarly, Roger Williams, whose speeches and manner are
so reminiscent of the prophets of the Hebrew Bible, remarks: "Yea, one Scripture in the mouth of a mechanic before any decree of the whole council. . .[is] a far greater light
than yet showes." This confidence in the ability of the common man to find spiritual righteousness led Williams eventually to formulate his doctrine of the separation of church and
state. Williams believed that it was incumbent upon the state
to abstain from interference in religious affairs, not because
religion was trivial or unrelated to the needs of society, but
rather because its unique and supremely important truths
and verities could be revealed and spread among men only
in an atmosphere of liberty and freedom of conscience. Williams anticipated that this could not but result in a certain
degree of error, but was confident that " 'tis Light alone,
even Light from the bright and shining Sunne of Righteousness, which is able, in the soules and consciences of men to
dispell and scatter such fogges and darknesse."[4]
Again, when, at the time of the Restoration of 1660, Major
Generals Goffe and Whalley and Colonel Dixwell fled to the
colonies and were pursued from New York, they found ref-
uge in the Massachusetts and Connecticut colonies. To secure the safety of the refugees and to prevent their possible
betrayal, Davenport undertook to preach publicly from a text
appropriate to his sentiments in the matter: "Take counsel,
execute judgement; make thy shadow as the night in the
midst of the noon day; hide the outcasts, betray not him that
wandereth. Let mine outcasts dwell with thee, Moab; be

thou a covert to them from the face of the spoiler" (Isa. 16:3–4). The sermon had the desired effect and the refugee officers were assured of a safe haven in the colonies.

Davenport's influence on the legislation enacted by the New Haven Colony was paramount, and it was in the New Haven settlement that the Biblical influence on legislation is most marked. At the first assembly of the New Haven colonists, held in June 1639, Davenport asked the settlers whether they believed that the "Scriptures do hold forth a perfect rule for the direction and government of all men in all duties which they are to perform to God and men as well in the government of families and commonwealth as in matters of the church." No one debated the point with Davenport; in view of the attitudes and beliefs of the settlers, the thesis he posited was irrefutable. Upon further questions of a similar nature, it was agreed upon by all present "that the Word of God," as revealed in the Bible, "shall be the only rule to be attended unto in organizing the affairs of government in this plantation." The supremacy of the Bible as a guide in the enactment of legislation was not subject to dispute. The fundamental thesis of New Haven's legislative principle was that "the judicial laws of God, as they were delivered by Moses, and as they are a fence to the moral law, being neither topical nor ceremonial, nor had any reference to Canaan, shall be accounted of moral equity, and generally bind all offenders, till they be branched out into particulars hereafter."

This spirit is clearly evident in all the legislation of 1639 and in the subsequent enactments in 1642 and again in 1644. In the New Haven Code of 1655, forty-nine of the seventy-nine topical statutes derive their authority from the Bible, and of these, thirty-eight are from the Hebrew Bible. The New Haven settlers were concerned not only with imparting a Biblical nature to their legislation, but also gave much consideration to the efficacy with which their laws were executed, and to the appointment of officials qualified to impose the laws in the spirit in which they were conceived. Thus, before selecting any official, Biblical verses (taken from Exodus, Deuteronomy, and I Corinthians) dealing with the appointment of the council of elders by Moses were read. This form of selection seems to have been widespread in the colonies, and not restricted to the selection of civil officials. As previously mentioned, this form of election was customary in Massachusetts. In Salem, in July 1629, for instance, the election of John Endicott as minister was preceded by a "solemn day of humiliation" and meditation upon the gravity of the action which the congregation was about to undertake. Even Endicott's ordination closely parallels the installation of a civil official—a solemn ceremony, consisting of prayer, appropriate citation from the Bible, preaching, and the laying-on of hands by neighboring ministers of the congregation. The high standard of justice and equity, the care with which Moses chose his leaders (without forcing them upon the people of Israel), were carefully studied by the leaders of New Haven so that these hallowed examples might serve as a pattern for their own actions. In matters of crime and the administration of justice, a prisoner was always reminded that "he that hideth his sins shall not prosper, but he that confesseth and forsaketh his sins shall find mercy" (Prov. 28:13).

The neighboring colony of Connecticut also enacted legislation along the lines indicated by the statutes and regulations of the Bible. The man most responsible for the nature of the laws instituted here was Thomas Hooker (a close friend of the Reverend John Cotton of Massachusetts), whose role in the process is described by Ralph Barton Perry as follows:

> The Fundamental Orders of Connecticut, drafted in response to a sermon delivered by Thomas Hooker before the General Court of Hartford on May 31, 1638, has been referred to as the "first written constitution of modern democracy." The Biblical injunction, "Take ye wise men, and understanding, and known among your tribes, and I will make them rulers over you," was cited by Hooker

with the emphasis on the "taking" rather than the "making"; and was interpreted as meaning "that the choice of public magistrates belongs unto the people by God's own allowance." "They who have power to appoint officials and magistrates," he went on to say, "it is in their power, also, to set the bounds and limitations of the power and place unto which they call them"; because, in short, "the foundation of authority is laid, firstly, in the free consent of the People."[5]

Several years later, the Connecticut Code of 1650, also based on the Hebrew Bible model of government, derived many of its laws from the legislative codes of the "Bible State," Massachusetts.

The Massachusetts settlers, under the leadership of John Cotton, likewise based their administration on Scriptural precedent, claiming that

the government might be considered as a theocracy, wherein the Lord was the judge, law-giver and king; that the laws of Israel might be adopted so far as they were considered God's people in a covenant with him; that none but persons of approved piety and eminent abilities should be chosen rulers; that the clergy should be consulted in all matters of religion; and that the magistrates should have a superintending and coercive power over the churches.[6]

Thus the doctrine in Massachusetts diverged widely from that propounded by Roger Williams; there was no clear distinction in the Massachusetts Bay Colony between the authorities responsible for the civil administration and those charged with the responsibility for religious affairs. This coalescence of state and church in Massachusetts was a direct outgrowth of the Congregationalist philosophy as it had evolved in England, with a heavy emphasis on localism. Because of this doctrine, the Congregationalist churches of England throughout most of their history failed to exert a very great influence, since they did not enjoy the support of the local civil authorities, vital to the successful implementation of a religious localism, and the very nature of that doctrine made the absence of such support doubly hazardous for the Congregationalist churches. This was one of the main reasons for the migration of the Congregationalists to America in the first place. Thus it was not surprising that the colonists sought to fuse religious and secular authority in an attempt to forestall a recurrence of the problems which had plagued them in the Old World.

As a result of the implementation of this doctrine in New England, the church itself enjoyed a new political, social, and religious centrality in society. And as a corollary to this, church-membership assumed a determinative role in regard to social status. Since legislation and political decisions in the Massachusetts Bay Colony were closely connected with the church, political and civil influence was exercised only by those citizens belonging to the proper religious establishment. This meant, also, that the Biblical spirit (the motivating force of this establishment) had a direct and vital influence on the machinery of state and its expression in the form of legislation. Accordingly, in 1631 the General Court of Massachusetts decreed that "the body of the commons may be preserved of honest and good men" only if "no man shall be admitted to the freedom of this body politic but such as are members of some of the Churches." Membership in this secular community of Massachusetts thus depended upon religious qualifications; and membership in the church itself was likewise not easily obtained, but was restricted solely to those considered "saints." The restrictive manner in which this category was defined further indicates the pervasiveness of Scriptural morality in the Bay Colony: "By saints we understand such as have not only attained the knowledge of the principles of religion and are free from gross and open scandals, but also do, together with the profession of their faith and repentance, walk in blameless obedience to the Word, so that in charitable discretion they may be accounted saints by calling."[7]

The criteria for service in a magisterial capacity, where the individual chosen to execute the colony's ordinances would have a preponderant voice in the manner in which the laws would be executed, were no less rigorous. It was felt that it was by "a divine ordinance that none should be appointed and chosen by the people of God magistrates over them but men fearing God (Exodus, XVII:15). . . . for the liberties of this commonwealth are such as require men of faithful integrity to God and the State, to preserve the same."[8] In Massachusetts, as in New Haven, English common law was largely neglected and textual rulings from the Hebrew Bible substituted. The resentment which the Puritans felt toward English law was in part a consequence of their harsh experience of it before their departure for the New World. But the main reason for the Puritan preference of Biblical statute over the accepted common law was the overriding concept of their covenant with God. For more than ten years, the administration of justice in Massachusetts, during the Confederacy of the Four Colonies (viz., Massachusetts, New Haven, Connecticut, and Plymouth, Rhode Island having been excluded because of its radical and separatist views), "was without the security of either a system of statutes, or of any recognition of the authority of the Common Law. The law dispensed by the Magistrates was no other than equity, as its principles and rules existed in their own reason and conscience, instructed by Scriptures."[9] Moreover, a great many of the laws framed by all the New England colonies reveal a similar dependence on the Bible. The choice of magistrates, legislation, and the rights of inheritance were typically decided according to the example of Scripture. Following the bold and shocking work of such seventeenth-century religious thinkers as Robert Browne, the Puritans had declared the sanction of the Mosaic legislation for their own regulatory laws. Their authoritative statute-book was the Pentateuch, directly from which was drawn the first formal code of laws, framed at the request of the General Court of Massachusetts.

More specifically, the capital laws enforced in the New England colonies reveal a particularly close dependence on Biblical jurisprudence, which may be precisely the reason for the enormous influence they exerted on the direction taken by similar legislation enacted throughout the rest of the northern colonies. These fifteen Capital Laws, instituted in 1641–42 by the General Court of Massachusetts, dealt with the three chief areas of the colony's concern, viz., religion, the civil order, and the social order. The manner in which this body of legislation regulated these vital areas is remarkably similar to its Biblical precedent; in fact, the fifteen Capital Laws of New England were originally published with marginal notations citing the Old Testament passages from which they originated and which justified their present resuscitation.

The first three Capital Laws dealt with the religious basis of society. The first law stated that

> If any man after legall conviction, shall have or worship any other God but the Lord God, he shall be put to death. (Deut. 13:6. Exodus 22:20.)

Thus the Puritans established the keystone of their social order and assured divine sanction for their act by citing the Old Testament sources. The second and third laws dealt in a similar manner with those who threatened the established religious beliefs.

> If any man or woman be a Witch, that is, hath or consulteth with a familiar spirit, they shall be put to death. (Exodus 22:18. Lev. 20:27. Deut. 18:10, 11.)

> If any person shall blaspheme the Name of God the Father, Sonne, or Holy Ghost, with direct, express, presumptuous, or high-handed blasphemy, or shall curse God in the like manner, he shall be put to death. (Lev. 24:15, 16.)

Such issues as blasphemy and witches were not merely rhetorical. These laws were considered vital to the obstruction of the forces of evil, which, the colonists believed, constantly threatened their puny community. This constant fear became all too palpable in the historic witch-hunts of 1691–92. In this seemingly senseless outburst of hysteria, the American colonists were merely in step with the prevailing intellectual atmosphere, in which not only the common folk but even such giants of the age as Shakespeare, Bacon, Selden, Sir Walter Raleigh, and Sir Thomas Browne firmly believed in the existence and influence of such supernatural phenomena.

The second major area dealt with in the Capital Laws was the internal civic order, and these measures also derived their authority from the precepts of the Hebrew Bible. These laws determined the penalties for crimes against the community itself, such as murder, kidnapping, false witness, and insurrection. The various degrees of murder were outlined in detail in the fourth through the sixth Capital Laws.

If any person shall commit any wilfull murder, which is manslaughter, committed upon premeditated malice, hatred, or cruelty, not in a man's necessary and just defence, nor by mere casualty, against his will, he shall be put to death. (Exod. 21:12, 13, 14. Num. 35:30, 31.)

If any person slayeth another suddenly in his anger, or cruelty of passion, he shall be put to death. (Num. 35:20, 1. Lev. 24:17.)

If any person shall slay another through guile, either by poysonings, or other such devilish practice; he shall be put to death. (Exod. 21:14).

Protection of the individual against kidnapping was provided by the thirteenth law, wherein it is stipulated that

If any man stealeth a man, or man-kinde, he shall surely be put to death. (Exod. 21:16.)

The Biblical injunction against false witness was incorporated in the fourteenth law.

> If any man rise up by false witness wittingly, and of purpose to take away any man's life, he shall be put to death. (Deut. 19:16, 18, 19.)

Finally, the political threat of insurrection and subversion was accounted for in the last of the Capital Laws.

> If any man shall conspire, or attempt any invasion, insurrection, or publick rebellion against our Common-wealth, or shall endeavor to surprize any Towne or Townes, Fort or Fortes therein; or shall treacherously, or perfidiously attempt the alteration and subversion of our frame of pollity, or government fundamentally, he shall be put to death. (Num. 16:2. Sam. 3 & 18. & 20.)

The third area regulated in this manner was the social order and crimes against it. Since the foundation of social order in the Puritan community was the home, these laws dealt primarily with sexual offenses, in an attempt to secure the integrity of the family unit and, in turn, that of the community. Thus, such unnatural sexual acts as sodomy and homosexuality were sternly prohibited in the seventh and eighth Capital Laws.

> If a man or woman shall lye with any beast, or bruit creatyres, by carnall copulation, they shall surely be put to death; and the beasts shall be slaine, and buried. (Lev. 20:15, 16.)

> If a man lyeth with man-kinde, as he lyeth with a woman, both of them have committed abomination, they both shall surely be put to death. (Lev. 20:13.)

Adultery, a dreaded sin in the pious and well-ordered Puritan world, was regarded as a dire threat to the family structure; hence the ninth Capital Law:

If any person committeth adultery with a married, or es-
poused wife, the Adulterer, and the Adulteresse, shall
surely be put to death. (Lev. 20:10. and 18:20. Deut. 22:23,
24.)

The rape of a married woman was considered an equally
grave crime, but in this case only the rapist was to be executed.

If any man shall forcibly, and without consent, ravish any
maid or woman that is lawfully married or contracted, he
shall be put to death. (Deut. 22:25.)

It is interesting to note that only the tenth and the twelfth
Capital Laws do not cite Biblical precedents:

If any man shall unlawfully have carnall copulation with
any woman-childe under ten years old, either with, or
without her consent, he shall be put to death.

If any man shall ravish any maid or single woman (committing carnall copulation with her by force, against her
will) that is above the age of ten years, he shall be either
punished by death, or with some other grevious punishment, according to circumstances, at the discretion of the
Judges: and this law to continue till the Court take further
order.

In these cases, since a Biblical precedent was lacking for
these offenses, the Puritans went beyond the letter of Biblical
law, legislating in what they considered to be the spirit of
Biblical jurisprudence.

Five years later, in 1646, the General Court issued an additional law, the Law of the Incorrigible Child, which also had
a precedent in the Pentateuch and was in keeping with the
other Capital Laws. It stipulated that if the parents were un-
able to deal with an incorrigible child, he could be sum-
moned before the court by any magistrate in order to answer
for his behavior. If the child was found guilty, the magis-

trate, adhering to the 1646 Order of the General Court, was empowered to "sentence him to endure . . . corporal punishment by whipping . . . not exceeding ten stripes for one offense." In the event the child continued in his unlawful ways, the parents were instructed to produce him before the magistrate again, by force if need be, in which case (if proved against him), the child could be sentenced to death by hanging.

These were the most serious offenses, which the Puritans felt should be punished as severely as possible. Their legal concern, however, extended to all facets of their society, for which again precedent was sought in the pages of the Holy Bible. For instance, the Sabbath Laws, still in existence to this day in many areas of New England, testify to an entire realm of Puritan legislation directly inspired by Biblical injunction. In October 1692, all the inhabitants of the Massachusetts Bay Colony were instructed to "apply themselves to duties of religion and piety, publicly and privately" on the Sabbath, and participation in "any game, sport, play or recreation" was strictly forbidden by law. The manufacture of coffins and the digging of graves on the day of rest was prohibited in May 1701; even if all the preparation was made by sunset of Saturday, the burial itself must still be postponed until the following Monday morning.

The period between 1716 and 1727 saw numerous new laws of this sort enacted. An interesting notice appeared in the Boston *Newsletter* in 1746, stating that the city was to be patrolled by justices in order to apprehend people "walking, standing in the streets or other ways breaking the laws made for the observation of the Lord's Day." Similarly, as was the case with two of the above-mentioned Capital Laws, a number of minor prohibitions were enacted in the Massachusetts Commonwealth without specific Biblical justification, but in what was considered the spirit of Biblical morality. Cards and dice, for example, were prohibited because lots were used in the Scriptures to discover God's will in important matters, and it was thus felt that their profane use in gambling would be sacrilegious. An even more curious example of such laws is the ban on the drinking of toasts, on the grounds (which Cotton Mather cites) that

> It is too notorious to be denied that it was originally a heathen custom to drink those which were called the cups of health. That which very much adds to the obligation lying upon Christians to abandon this relic of paganism is the idolatrous and diabolical intentions that gave the first rise unto it. We are aware from all the monuments of antiquity that the healths drunk by the pagans were first of all drink offerings to the demons.[10]

A law forbidding this "abominable practice" gives additional justification for its proscription; it led to "drunkenness, quarreling, bloodshed, uncleanness." These forebodings, however, appear to have had little effect since many citizens of Massachusetts continued to drink the health of their neighbors.

In 1641 a Body of Liberties was framed in Massachusetts. (This came about as a result of numerous requests by the General Court for the codification of the laws of the colony.) The Reverend John Cotton, therefore, "requested by the General Court, with some other Ministers, to assist some of the magistrates in compiling a body of fundamental laws, did this Court present a copy of *Moses, His Judicials,* compiled in an exact method." Cotton's proposed draft of laws was based almost in toto on the Mosaic Code—with appropriate adaptations to the circumstances of Massachusetts. Cotton claimed it was "all the judicial laws from God by Moses, so far as they are moral, that is, of universal equity."[11] Although in the end Cotton's draft was not accepted, his proposals for laws dealing with magistrates, burgesses, and free inhabitants, defense of the country, inheritance, commerce, trespassing, and other minor crimes influenced subsequent legislation. The code that was accepted by the General Court, drafted by Nathaniel Ward, nonetheless bore a striking resemblance to Cotton's draft—which is not surprising in light of the fact that both men used the Pentateuch as a source for their proposed laws. In 1648 a new code, based on the previous one, was adopted and published. This code, though never formally enacted in a legal sense, was considered the general standard.

The General Court itself fully recognized its role in a society based on the "Judicials of Moses":

> When, in 1646, the General Court found it necessary to convoke a public assembly of the elders they did so protesting, however, that "their lawful power *by the word of God* to assemble the churches or their messengers upon occasion of counsel" is not to be questioned, and therefore the said assembly of elders, after having "discussed, disputed, and cleared up *by the word of God* such questions of church government and discipline . . . as they shall think needful and meet," is to report to the General Court, "to the end that the same being found *agreeable to the word of God*," it may receive from the said General Court such approbation as is meet. . . . Not only the church synod is to judge what is "agreeable to the holy Scriptures" but the civil government takes it as its own duty to make sure that the resolutions of the synod are really in accordance with the Scriptures and only then to give their approbation.[12]

Even individual litigations were frequently decided on the basis of Scriptural precedent. One notable case is cited by James Truslow Adams wherein the court was divided on a complicated dispute concerning the ownership of a cow. The question of precedent was raised: was it possible for a small number of judges to hamper lawfully the decision of a large number of deputies? Winthrop forthwith prepared a treatise on the subject, declaring that "were the magistrates forbidden to veto the action of the deputies, the colony would not be a democracy, and *there was no such government in Israel.*"

The Cambridge Synod was drafted as a broadened covenant to accommodate the ever-increasing numbers of immigrants to the Massachusetts Bay Colony. The commonwealth's government was called a democracy insofar as it was a brotherhood, and an aristocracy insofar as power was so constituted. The synod speaks of the form of government adopted: "This Form is the *Visible Covenant,* agreement, or consent whereby they [the members] give up themselves unto the Lord, to the observing of the ordinances of Christ together in the same society, which is otherwise how members can have Church-power over one another mutually." The marginal references ("Exod. 29:8; Deut. 19:19; Zech. 1:3") are all taken from the Old Testament.

The Plymouth Colony likewise returned to the Old Testament for the basis of the judicial system it established. The fact that the Pentateuch was used as the source for Pilgrim legislation was a crucial factor in the development of the colony's institutions. Like their Massachusetts neighbors, the Pilgrims believed that the "judicials of Moses are immutable and perpetual," as evinced by the legal codes established in the Plymouth Colony. In November 1636, before any general code of law had been instituted, the Court of Associates of Plymouth declared that the English laws "present or to come" were not valid in Plymouth Colony. Just as later in the Massachusetts Commonwealth, the Scriptures served the Plymouth community as the basis for legislation. The code drafted and adopted in 1636, and the revisions thereto in 1656, clearly show the predominance of this influence. And later still, in 1685, when the colony's law of inheritance was revised, the revision was only for the purpose of bringing the law into line with Biblical usage, as was the procedure in much of the legislation throughout the colony's history.

In summary, then, throughout the period of colonization in New England, the Mosaic rulings and Biblical laws were considered the supreme authority in any question requiring the citation of a precedent. These Biblical injunctions were willingly and reverently accepted as the Word of God, so that there can be no question here of the imposition of a foreign code of laws; rather, the practice only reflects the fervent desire of the colonists to abide by these Biblical precepts. For therein, the colonists felt, was to be found the model of society as they envisioned it. From these initial efforts Hebraic laws and principles extended and prevailed throughout the colonies, to eventually occupy a central place in the more unified laws of the separate colonies, and, still later, in the national system of American constitutional law.

Biblical
Background of
American
Legislation

*I hope the time will come when the laws and literature of the
ancient Hebrews will be studied in all of our schools as now are
studied the laws and literature of the ancient Greeks and Romans, and when it will be universally recognized that no man
who is ignorant of the laws and literature of the ancient Hebrew
is a well-educated man.*

Lyman Abbott

The development of the American polity—that is to say,
the evolution of the political system of America, its fundamental principles of government, its Constitution, and the
spirit behind the formal framework of its society—is one of
the more interesting chapters in the annals of the country's
history; for it is precisely in this area that the full impact of
the Hebrew Bible, the Judaic spirit, and the ancient ideal of

the Israelite commonwealth on American life is manifest in all its ramifications from colonial times to the present. The commonwealth of ancient Israel, from the days of the Exodus from Egypt until the anointing of Saul as first king of Israel, was a unique social and political system; that the Puritan settlers of the New World so regarded it, and that the new society which they established in America (as well as the political order of the new republic a century and a half later) was profoundly influenced by this ancient Israelite model, is undeniable. There were, of course, several reasons for this conscious emulation of a socio-political system thousands of years old.

Primarily, the Biblical impulse of Puritanism provided the Puritan settlers with a strong theological or religious motive. The effort to reconstruct the Israelite system in the wilds of the New World naturally received its inspiration and basic justification from the divine sanction of the Scriptures, which were the lifeline of these pious Pilgrims. But such an ambitious enterprise was not supported by religious considerations alone; certain significant psychological and practical exigencies were also at work. Initially, the circumstances surrounding the arrival of the early English colonists in America—the persecutions which drove them from their homeland, and the primeval conditions with which they were faced in the new land—forced upon them a conscious identification with the lot of the ancient Israelites. Under these circumstances, there were certain features of the Israelite commonwealth which made its imitation particularly appropriate. The Puritans had, after all, left England in repudiation of the archaic and oppressive political and religious structures, and their aim in coming to America was to establish a new society, based on an equality of "saints" and administered on the basis of their character and achievements. Rule was to be vested in the members of the community (in this case, members of the church) and was to be no longer the hereditary prerogative of an entrenched hierarchy. Thus, the principles upon which the ancient Israelite commonwealth

had been established seemed, in retrospect, particularly fit-
ting for the framework of the new society which the Puritan
settlers intended to create, for the Israelites had similarly left
the Land of Goshen with the aim of establishing a new society in a strange new land. And even though their efforts
were to a great extent divorced from their contemporary environment (for their commonwealth was not founded on the
remains of a shattered monarchy, but was a fresh creation),
the political structure which Israel developed was likewise
not an aristocracy ruled by members of an elite class, but derived its power from the members of the community itself,
from the people. When the ancient Israelites fled across the
wilderness of Sinai, they took with them no titled class, no
royal institutions—only themselves, and their abiding faith in
an abiding Lord. And this, then, was the theoretical basis of
society that so appealed to the Puritans, and these the ideals
which they hoped to incorporate in their new society. In this
light, the historical analogy between the Pharaoh of Egypt
and the King of England, and between the Israelites and the
Pilgrims, seems a natural outgrowth of the Puritans'
practical-minded devotion to the Holy Scriptures.

This Hebraic influence gradually deepened as the institutions of the diverse colonies evolved and eventually merged
into the underlying framework of the American Republic.
The natural channels of this influence were from the first the
spiritual leaders of the communities, who drew their very
livelihood from these Scriptural sources. Due to the religious
nature of the new society, it was the ministers and preachers
who in effect molded the forms of polity through their influence and nurtured its spirit by their personal examples and
exhortations. This process had early antecedents in America.
From 1633 on, the governors and their assistants in the New
England colonies appointed the most outstanding and
eloquent ministers to preach on the day of election. The subjects "chosen by these ministers in their 'election sermons'
were invariably political and were often printed as pamphlets, meeting with great success."[1] It is not surprising

that the invariable source of these sermons was the Holy
Scriptures, and the popularity they enjoyed is an indication
of how receptive the colonists were to Biblical concepts and
ideals of polity. In these "election sermons," which were of a
political-religious nature, the ancient Israelite commonwealth
was held up as a model for American democracy. Jonathan
Mayhew, in one such sermon, developed in detail the idea
that the Hebrew commonwealth was a God-given government, and that a king was given to Israel only because the
nation had not been virtuous.[2]

In the same vein, an important development in the principles of society in New England, which stemmed directly
from the precepts of the Bible, was the almost instinctive
abhorrence which the men of the colonies felt for the
"slavish" doctrine of "unlimited submission and nonresistance." The ideal of the Hebrew commonwealth became a
major weapon in the arsenal of colonial resistance to raw absolutism disguised as the "divine right of kings." This trend
was to grow to overwhelming proportions in the years immediately preceding the War of Independence and during
the establishment of the Republic itself. In this regard, the
Biblical verses to which the Puritans resorted would surely
have struck a responsive chord in the ears of the ancient Israelites; taken from Samuel's warning of the evils of kingship, they were to the American colonists wholly consonant
with the circumstances of their own age:

> And the Lord said unto Samuel, "Hearken unto the voice
> of the people in all that they say unto thee; for they have
> not rejected thee, but they have rejected me, that I should
> not rule over them." (I Sam. 8:7)

> "Now therefore hearken unto their voice: howbeit yet pro-
> test solemnly unto them, and show them the manner of
> the king that shall reign over them." (I Sam. 8:9)

These verses served the colonists as the theological and political underpinnings of their revolt against English absolutism, both in the colonial period and during the Revolutionary War.

Even the fundamental sentiments of patriotism and love of country, the keynotes of the revolutionary period, were given a Biblical cast by the colonists. In his editorials denouncing the Tea Act, Benjamin Rush declared patriotism to be "as much a virtue as justice," pointing to the example of the spirit of "the holy men of old": "What did not Moses forsake and suffer for his countrymen! What shining examples of Patriotism do we behold in Joshua, Samuel, Maccabeus and all the illustrious princes, captains and prophets among the Jews." The need for Scriptural justification for so basic a sentiment as national spirit provides a further indication of the deep influence of the Bible as a major and constant strain in early American history.

The impact of the Hebraic influence on early America is further seen in statistical data compiled from the various legal codes of the New England colonies. An example of this is the Code of 1655, which was drawn up in New Haven: the code contained seventy-nine statutes of government, of which fifty percent contained Biblical references, forty-seven percent of which references were to the Old Testament and the remaining three percent from the New. A body of legislation derives essentially from the underlying body of polity which motivates it; formal law in general is the direct outgrowth and expression of polity. And particularly in the case of the United States, there is an outstanding parallel between the basic concepts of the Old Testament and the law of the land as exemplified in the Constitution. The Declaration of Independence, endorsed by the Constitution, states that governments are accountable to a higher power. It affirms that the duty of the government is to uphold the rights of man as ordained by divine law, and that the duty of the citizen is to defend the same against any encroachment— even by his own government. In short, the politics of Puritanism developed from its theology. And the main political idea of the day—resistance to absolutism—could find no direct and specific support in the Christian Scriptures. George E. Ellis, a leading authority on the Puritan age, maintains that "if the colonies of Massachusetts had been Episcopalian there might have been no American Revolution."[3] Similarly, the argument against monarchy in Thomas Paine's fiery pamphlet, *Common Sense,* is drawn entirely from the example of the Hebrew commonwealth; after citing Samuel's warning to Israel, Paine concludes his exhortation thus: "These portions of the Scriptures. . .admit of no equivocal construction. That the Almighty hath here entered his protest against monarchical government is true, or the Scriptures are false."[4]

As we have seen, the "Divine Law" or "Higher Law," which was of such deep concern to the framers of the Constitution and the Declaration of Independence, was in effect the restoration of the authority of the God of the ancient Hebrews and of the principles upon which the ancient Israelite commonwealth had been established. The phrase "laws of nature and of nature's God," of course, reflects superficially the preoccupation of the Age of Reason (late sixteenth–early seventeenth century) with the philosophical concepts of God, Nature, and Reason. But it is also apparent that there runs through these two prime instruments of American government the deeper meaning and higher purpose of a constant regard for principles and religious ideas, based on a profound sympathy with the Scriptures and an intimate acquaintance with the Hebrew Bible. Though the precise words of the Scriptural text are avoided, the same spirit is present to a remarkable degree. Henry W. Field, the distinguished Christian clergyman, remarks that it does not occur to readers of the Hebrew Bible that there is a great similarity between the Hebrew Commonwealth and the American Republic; that the one basic principle which separates a republic from a monarchy—viz., the natural equality of men—is fundamental both to the Mosaic law and to the Declaration of Independence. The fact that under the Mosaic Code even the poorest member of society was not to be deprived of tenure of land, establishes the ancient Israelite commonwealth as a pure democracy.

As indicated above, the government of the New England colonies constituted as near an approach to a theocracy or a monocracy as the world had witnessed since the ancient Jewish state, although diversity of opinion has prevailed in the attempt to determine the true nature of the government in Massachusetts as it existed both in theory and in practice. Thomas Jefferson Wertenbaker sums up the matter as follows:

> When the historian seeks a name for the Massachusetts type of State he encounters difficulties. The use of the word "theocracy" has been criticized. In a theocracy, it is argued, the clergy are rulers, whereas in Massachusetts the ministers, even though they had a deciding vote in picking the electorate, did not themselves hold civil office. The word "commonwealth" is also open to objection, since it is defined as "a state especially viewed as a body in which the people have a voice" or "a government chosen directly by the people," and none of these definitions fits the society established in Massachusetts.[5]

In any case, Massachusetts was technically, like the other New England settlements, a charter colony. Consequently, their governments, unlike those of the royal colonies in the South, were almost wholly autonomous entities. The result of this was a situation wherein the New England settlers were virtually unimpeded in establishing a society based on the principles most consistent with their beliefs.

That the governments of New England were based to a remarkable extent on the principles, customs, and spirit of the Scriptures cannot be gainsaid, even if there may be some room for debate as to whether these governments fulfilled all the requisite conditions of a true theocracy. On this point, John Higginson the Puritan minister of Salem, comments: "It is never to be forgotten. . .that our New England is originally a plantation of religion and not a plantation of trade. If any man among us makes religion as twelve and the world as thirteen, let such a man know that he hath neither the spirit of a true New England man nor yet of a sincere Christian."[6] This was the underlying spirit of the New England governments.

This religious basis and Biblical precedent, however, was not confined solely to the internal mechanism of the governments of New England; even the relations between the different colonies were often patterned after Old Testament relationships and structures. An outstanding example of this is the above-mentioned confederacy of the four New England colonies, which existed from 1643 to 1684, modeled on the structure of the confederacy of the twelve tribes of Israel during the Hebrew commonwealth. The ramifications of this development were such that "this confederacy of the four New England Colonies served as the basis of the great confederacy afterwards between the thirteen States of America."[7]

With respect to internal structure, the similarities between the fundamental institutions and social attitudes, which served as the bedrock of both the New England colonies and the ancient Israelite commonwealth, are striking indeed. In certain respects there are even distinct similarities to the attitudes and institutions of the later Jewish *kahal* ("community") during the exilic period. While it is doubtful that the Puritan had any direct knowledge of the details of the Jewish *kahal*, the fact of such a remarkably parallel development suggests, at least, that similar motivating forces were at work in both circumstances. The main institution of the community in New England was the meetinghouse; this was the focus of the autonomous township and served a variety of purposes. Even the terminology used in this instance is strikingly similar to that of the *kahal*, since the term for "synagogue" in the original Hebrew is *Beth-HaKnesset* or "the house of meeting." That the Puritans chose the term "meetinghouse" for the central structure of their community, which served their social, political, and religious needs, while avoiding the use of the term "church," was not due to chance; Cotton Mather writes that there could be "found no just ground in Scripture to apply such a trope as church to a house of public assembly."[8] It was incumbent upon all Puritan communities to build such a "house of public assembly." Like most synagogues, this meetinghouse was constructed on the top of a central hill overlooking the settlement. The parallel also applies to the interior of the edifice, and the complete lack of ornamentation and absence of musical instruments furthers the impression; the physical austerity found in the New England meetinghouse would not have been alien to the *Beth-HaKnesset*.

Likewise, many of the positions established in the Puritan communities of New England also had their counterparts in the ancient Hebrew commonwealth. One of the most important of these positions was that of the elder. The functions of the elder were both religious and civil; he performed many tasks of a religious nature within the community and acted as the religious advisor to the magistrate. He was also consulted by the magistrate on political matters.[9] The actual authority of the individual elder was in direct proportion to his character, ability, and knowledge. His comments and advice were always based on the Scriptures, as was the precedent for the office itself; the origin of the office can be traced to Moses' delegation of authority to the elders of Israel upon the advice of his father-in-law, Jethro:

> "The thing that thou doest is not good. This is too heavy for thee; thou art not able to perform it thyself. Moreover, thou shalt provide out of all the people able men, such as fear God, men of truth, hating covetousness, and place such over them to be rulers of thousands and rulers of hundreds, rulers of fifties, and rulers of tens." So Moses hearkened to the voice of his father-in-law, and did all that he had said. (Exod. 18:13–24; cf. Deut. 1:13–15)

If the Puritan elders at times fell short of this Mosaic ideal, the example of the Hebrew prophets was still the ideal of the

New England men. The rudimentary democracy found in the above passage may have reached fruition only in later years, but the nucleus existed from the start of the Puritan enterprise. The injunction "take you wise men" bore the implication of election, while the instruction that these leaders were to be taken from "out of all the people" definitely ran counter to the prevailing custom of class distinction. Finally, the stipulation that these elders be "wise men, and understanding" established merit, not birth, as the criterion of leadership.

The attitude of a society toward education is another clear reflection of that society's fundamental polity, and here too the Puritans were strongly influenced by the Bible and by Hebraic principles. The Puritan attitude toward the role of education in the larger framework of society itself was roughly parallel to that of the Hebrews, and was conditioned by the Puritans' intention to impart the enduring values of the Scriptures to succeeding generations.

The importance attached to education in New England is evidenced by the provisions made for education in the Puritan colonies. In 1670 the British commissioners of foreign plantations made a survey of the general conditions prevailing in the American colonies. It was reported of the Connecticut Plantation that one fourth of that colony's annual revenue was set aside for the maintenance of free schools for the settlers' children—a striking parallel to the use of public revenue for education which was one of the primary functions of the Jewish *kahal* throughout the ages. The attitude toward education in Massachusetts is indicated in the Preamble to the Act of the General Court in 1642, where "forasmuch as the good education of children is of singular behoof and benefit to any commonwealth, and whereas many parents and masters are too indulgent and negligent of their duty in this kind," it was the decision of the court to make legal provision for such education. The educational system of Massachusetts was extended in the statute of 1671, which outlined the basic tenets of the colony on this matter and also the practical steps to be taken:

> It being one chief project of Satan to keep men from the knowledge of the Scriptures, as in former times keeping them in unknown tongues, so in these latter times, by persuading from the use of tongues, so that at least the true sense and meaning of the original might be clouded and corrupted with false glosses of deceivers; to the end that learning might not be buried in the graves of our forefathers, in church and commonwealth, the Lord assisting our endeavours; it is therefore ordered by this court and authority thereof, that every township within the jurisdiction, after the Lord hath increased them to the number of fifty householders, shall then forthwith appoint one within their towns to teach all such children as shall resort to him to write and read, whose wages shall be paid either by the parents or the masters of such children, or by the inhabitants in general, by way of supply, as the major part of those that order the prudentials of the two shall appoint: Provided that those which send their children be not oppressed by paying much more than they can have them taught for in other towns.
>
> And it is further ordered that where any town shall increase to the number of one hundred families or householders, they shall set up a grammar school, the master thereof being able to instruct youth so far as they may be fitted for the university; and if any town neglect the performance hereof above one year, then every town shall pay five pounds per annum to the next such school till they perform this order.

As to the extent to which this attitude toward education was an indigenous development, and the extent to which it resulted from the influence of the Judaic spirit, we may cite Cotton Mather's account of what he thought constituted the educational system of the Jewish *kahal:* "The reader knows that in every town among Jews, there was a *school,* whereat children were taught the reading of the *Law;* and if there was any town destitute of a *school,* the men of place did stand excommunicate until one were erected."[10]

Thus the Puritan settlers contributed to the polity of New England the spirit of the Bible and their practical devotion to its principles. The structure of their society was modeled upon the one they saw therein, so that every facet of their society was touched by the Bible in one way or another. In 1635, for instance, John Cotton drew up for the use of the General Court a law code based on "Moses, his judicials" and this became the basis of legislation in the Bay Colony for many years. The Biblical influence on this code is readily apparent in the numerous laws concerning land, the detailed laws regarding slavery, the heinousness of the crime of blasphemy, and the constant legislation of the Sabbath laws. Later, the Continental Congress leaned heavily on the sanctions of the Bible, which became its main strength since its legislative authority was weak. Biblical precepts became political maxims. Congressional proclamations are filled with Biblical phrases.[11] But the role of religion in New England society is perhaps best understood when one considers the fact that, to the early English settlers in the northern reaches of the North American continent, matters such as worship were not mere impulse but almost a final objective in themselves. One of the cornerstones of the original conception of the Puritans' Bible state was the attempt to introduce into the theocracy of New England the minute control and punctiliousness of the laws which had so successfully governed the ancient Hebrew theocracy in its wanderings in the wilderness; for to the Puritans their period of uncertainty, of trial, of violent conflict with the elements and with the savage inhabitants of the new land, was in every way comparable to the trials of the Israelites in the desert. This spirit of religious idealism and sensitivity to the religious need for worship are eloquently expressed in a letter from the General Court of Massachusetts to Charles II. Sent in December 1660, it was written in defense of religious liberty in the Bay Colony:

We could not live without the publicke worship of God.

Wee were not permitted the use of publicke worship without such a yoake of subscription and conformity as wee could not consent unto without sinne. That wee might therefore enjoy divine worship without the humane mixtures, without offense wither to God, man, or our owne conscience, wee, with leave, but not without teares, departed from our country, kindred, and fathers' houses unto this Pathmos. Ourselves, who came away in our strength, are, by reason of very long absence, many of us become grey-headed, and some of us stooping, for age.

The eloquence of the Puritans, in recounting their profound motives for leaving their homeland and establishing a new society in the wilderness, is compelling, and their thirst for religious liberty inspiring indeed. Yet while the Puritans were incensed by the tyranny and religious persecution which they had endured in England, they themselves did not hesitate to impose their own beliefs on others through the agency of their near-theocratic political structure. Freedom of belief was in most New England colonies assured to the "chosen" alone. There was bitter truth in the old gibe, "the world belongs to the saints and we are the saints." In the words of the late Chief Justice Charles Evans Hughes, in his address at the laying of the cornerstone of the National Baptist Memorial Church in Washington, D.C., in April 1922: "The New World, despite its freer atmosphere, was affected by the traditions of the Old. Freedom to worship God was one thing. Freedom for someone else to worship God was quite another." Yet the depth of the Biblical influence on New England polity is indicated by the fact that even in such a chauvinistic exercise of their liberty, the Puritans acted in the name of the Lord and sought Biblical sanction. The issue here extends beyond the question of religious freedom to the matter of popular democracy. There is no doubt that freedom of the individual and popular democracy as understood today were frowned upon in colonial New England. Winthrop "expostulated about the unwarrantableness and unsafeness of referring matters of counsel or judicature to the body of the people, *quia* the best part is always the least and of that best part the wiser part is always the lesser." Or, in John Cotton's words: "Democracy, I do not conceive that ever God did ordeyne as a fitt government for church or commonwealth. If the people be governors, who shall be governed?"

At the same time that the forms and structures of polity were acquiring a distinct cast in the Puritan colonies of New England, a second element became operative in America, the consequences of which were to be no less far-reaching than those in New England. This other major trend was that of civil liberties, and it began its inexorable course when Roger Williams was banished from the Massachusetts Commonwealth in 1636 for his subversive doctrines. Williams was the prophet of a new era. Although he may well have been as narrow as his Puritan contemporaries on points of church dogma (and this is to be doubted), his basic belief, nevertheless, was that "all men may walk as their consciences persuade them, everyone in the name of his God."[12] This radical vision led Williams to a more radical belief, that of tolerance and even goodwill between different faiths:

> I humbly conceive it to be the duty of the civil magistrates to break down that superstitious wall of separation (as to civil things) between the Gentiles and the Jews, and freely without their asking to make way for their free and peaceable habitation among us. . . . For who knows but that many of the Jewish religion may be clear and free from scandalous offenses in their life, and also from disobedience to the civil laws of the State.[13]

Williams's biographer carries this idea forward: "Actuated by the lofty idealism of Williams and the significant Jewish interest in things Biblical of the first settlers, Rhode Island paved the way for the recognition of the rights of the Jewish people in all American colonies."[14] Williams's humanistic acceptance of others whose beliefs differed from his own can best be understood in light of his credo that "the armies of

Truth like the armies of the Apocalypse, must have no sword, helmet, breastplate, shield or horse, but what is spiritual and of a heavenly nature." Essentially, the difference between the Massachusetts Commonwealth and Williams's vision was that between a religious state and a system which provided for the separation of the powers of church and state; nevertheless they derived their sanction from Scriptural word and example.

Williams's struggle for religious freedom began while he was still a minister to the Puritans of Salem. His first overt rebellion against the more intolerant aspects of Massachusetts polity was regarding what was known as the "Two Tables of Law." The basis of the Bay Colony's legislation was the Bible, specifically the Hebrew Bible, and the cornerstone of this system was the Decalogue, which in turn divided into "Two Tables": the "first table" (i.e., the first four commandments) dealing with man's duties toward God (viz., worship, oaths, and Sabbath observance), and the "second table" (consisting of the last six commandments), which concerns man's duties toward his fellowman. The root of the conflict between Williams and the Massachusetts government was the former's refusal to accept the authority of civil magistrates to impose punishments for infractions of the "first table," or the laws of religion. This debate, dangerous and heretical in the eyes of the more orthodox Puritan leaders, eventually led to Williams's banishment from the Bay Colony in 1636 and his proscription as an outlaw.

Williams outlined his beliefs in a public exchange of letters in 1643 with Cotton Mather on the charges brought against him during his trial in Massachusetts. In answer to the charge that he had disturbed the civil peace with his pernicious doctrines, Williams declared:

Acknowledging the ordinance of Magistracie to be properly and adequately fitted by God, to preserve the civill state in peace and order; as he hath also appointed a spiritual government and Governours in matters pertaining to his worship and the consciences of men, both which

> Government, Laws, Offenses, Punishments are essentially
> distinct, and the confounding of them brings all the world
> into combustion.

Thus Williams in one breath disavows the authority of the
civil government to interfere in matters of religion, while at
the same time admitting that the "Magistracie" was "fitted
by God." This dichotomy is present throughout the society
which Williams created at Providence in 1636, and confirms
the common origin of two divergent concepts of polity.

The new colony was established by Roger Williams and
five friends in June 1636, in remembrance of "God's merciful
providence to him in his distress" and was so named Providence. The actual government in the new settlement was at
first a pure democracy; the legislative, judicial, and executive
functions of the community were all performed by the general assembly of citizens in a monthly town meeting. As the
colony grew, however, this procedure proved ineffective,
and a new form of government was soon instituted, based
on the model of the Hebrew commonwealth. As one historian relates, "in imitation of the form of government which
existed for a time among the Jews, the inhabitants chose Mr.
Coddington to be their magistrate, with the title of Judge;
and a few months afterward they elected three elders to assist him."[15]

The theoretical basis of government for Providence was
given in the town's compact, written in 1638, and in the Providence Code of Laws in 1647. The compact of 1638 embodied the principles of polity on behalf of which Williams
suffered exile, and constitutes the most radical document of
America's early colonial period:

> We whose names are hereunder written, being desirous to
> inhabit the town of Providence, do promise to submit our-
> selves, in active or passive obedience, to all such orders or
> agreements as shall be made for the public good of the
> body, in an orderly way, by the major consent of the pres-

ent inhabitants, masters of families, incorporated together into a township, and such others whom they shall admit unto the same, *only in civil things.* [16]

Here again the dichotomy appears; on the one hand the colony patterned its government after that of the Hebrew commonwealth, and on the other it vigorously endorsed the principle of the separation of church and state.

The main principles governing Providence were reiterated when a general assembly of the inhabitants of the plantation adopted a code of laws in May 1647, the concluding phrases of which express the basic tenet of religious freedom in language that seems to derive directly from the Old Testament:

These are the laws that concern all men, and these are the penalties for the transgression thereof, which by common consent, are ratified and established throughout the whole colony. And otherwise than thus, what is herein forbidden, all men may walk as their conscience persuade them, everyone in the name of his God. And let the Saints of the Most High walk in this colony without molestation, in the name of Jehovah their God, forever and ever.

In light of the conflict between the opposing concepts of polity present in America's early colonial period, some historians have misinterpreted William Lecky's famous statement with regard to the Biblical sanction invoked:

It is, at least, an historical fact, that in the great majority of instances the early Protestant defenders of civil liberty derived their political principles chiefly from the Old Testament, and the defenders of despotism from the New. The rebellions that were so frequent in Jewish history formed the favorite topic of the one, the unreserved submission inculcated by St. Paul, of the others. When, therefore, all the principles of right and wrong were derived from theology, and when by the rejection of traditions and ecclesiastical authority, Scripture became the sole arbiter of theological difficulties, it was a matter of manifest importance in ascertaining the political tendencies of any sect, to discover which Testament was most congenial to the tone and complexion of its theology.[17]

Although Lecky's interpretation is basically sound in relation to the colonial struggle against absolutism, it should not be invoked in a discussion of *religious* liberty in the colonies. For in the struggle against absolutism, both the Puritans and the followers of Roger Williams moved in the same direction, setting the stage for the eventual break with England in 1776 and the War of Independence. The colonial struggle against English absolutism was a large step in the direction of America's eventual separation from the mother country, and left a lasting impression on the ethos of the Republic. The origins of this struggle were a mixture of religious, social, and political forces, and had an enormous effect on the subsequent direction of American polity.

As Lecky points out, the Bible and Scriptural citations were employed by both sides in the conflict over absolutism. Initially, the conflict was between those in support of and those in opposition to the concept of the "divine right of kings." This concept was perpetuated by members of the ecclesiastical establishment in England, who had also abetted its inception. In time, the king who ruled by virtue of "divine right" came to be "King by the Grace of God." Although the distinction was a subtle one, its implications were enormous, as it led to the inordinate expansion of the authority and power of the royal person. A divinely awarded prerogative required divine sanction. This the proponents of absolutism found in the New Testament. The doctrine of "unlimited submission and nonresistance to Higher Powers" was justified by means of such passages as I Peter 2:13–14: "Be subject for the Lord's sake to every human institution, whether it be to the Emperor as supreme, or to governors as sent by him to punish those who do wrong and to praise those who do right"; and Romans 13:1–3: "Let every person be subject to the governing authorities. For there is no authority except from God, and those that exist have been instituted by God. Therefore he who resists the authorities resists what God has appointed, and those who resist will incur judgement." These verses, or their distortion, provided divine sanction for the absolute authority of temporal institutions, and were used to establish the "divine right" of Britain's rule over the American colonies, just as it had been used by James I in an earlier period to sanction the "divine right" of his rule over the British Isles.

Opposition to this dogma in the northern colonies of America was as fierce as the efforts to implement it were persistent. What the Puritans objected to essentially was the worship of the person of the king. The authority which they chose for their opposition must be just as valid and just as sacred as the text used in support of the absolutist doctrine. Selections from the Old Testament, therefore, were chosen as counterweight to those from the New. The prior Puritan identification with the ancient Israelites only bolstered their instinctive reaction to the idea of temporal kingship, which they had abhorred from the very beginning of their settlement in the New World. The concept ran counter to their creed, even as it had been considered an evil by the earliest leaders of the Hebrew commonwealth (the ideal toward which the Puritan society strove). The institution of kingship thus became to them the embodiment of the forces of Satan working to undermine the new Canaan, a theme early taken up by the clergy and constantly reiterated. To discredit the very idea of monarchy, preachers like Boston's bold and clever Jonathan Mayhew repeated the warnings of the prophet Samuel against the establishment of a king in Israel. Samuel Langdon, president of Harvard, considered the Jewish government to have been a "perfect republic," while Yale's Ezra Stiles saw in the new American government the fulfillment of Biblical prophecy. The nineteenth-century historian William Edward Lecky considered that the Hebrew mortar provided the cement for the foundations of American democracy. And Oscar S. Straus, in his *Origin of Republican*

Form of Government, concluded that "in the spirit and essence of our Constitution, the influence of the Hebrew Commonwealth was paramount."

Throughout the seventeenth century, in the struggles between Massachusetts and the throne over the all-important charter for the colony, the religious and political leaders of the colony fought side by side against the doctrine of absolutism. As mentioned above, of the three forms of settlement in the British possessions on the American continent, royal, proprietary, and charter colonies, the New England colonies were all chartered, thus enjoying the rights of local self-government. The structure that this form of government usually evolved was that of governor, council, and assembly (chosen by the people). The autonomy which these colonies enjoyed gave them the opportunity to implement their concepts of polity derived from the Bible and from the example of the Hebrew commonwealth. When the crown asserted what it considered to be its right to alter or abrogate these charters (over the colonists' vigorous protests), the political and religious considerations mitigating against absolutism coalesced. Massachusetts, as well as the other New England colonies, felt that its rights had been guaranteed by charter, and resented the royal encroachment on these rights. The fact that Moses had been reluctant to allow any monarchic considerations to enter into the government of Israel served the latter-day "Israel" as a guide in their struggles. Samuel had shown nothing but ill will when called upon by the elders of Israel to establish a monarchy; the prophets of New England could do naught but follow his lead. Indeed, long after the clergy had lost its effectual power, after devastating inroads had been made into the colonial government by the royalist elite, the Congregationalist ministers kept up the battle; *there was no king but God!* They had so thoroughly assimilated the Hebrew Bible idea and spirit that, though virtually ineffectual and seemingly out of touch with the realities of the eighteenth century, they still opposed valiantly an institution which they felt violated both the letter and the spirit of the Scriptures. The long-range effect of their courageous resistance, however, is indicated by the following comment of James Madison on the eve of the Revolution: "If the Church of England had been the established and general religion in all the northern colonies, as it had been among us here [in Virginia], it is clear to me that slavery and subjection would have been gradually insinuated among us."

Though the Biblical concepts of polity and the opposition to absolutism originated from the pulpit, the masses of New Englanders readily turned to the Hebrew Bible for their ideas and principles of government, and found there what was for them full justification for their antagonism to any idea of absolute rule or divine right. Samuel's distaste for monarchy and Gideon's refusal of the kingship were frequent starting points for the clergy's exhortation of the citizenry. The clergy continued their active resistance up to and including the time of the Revolution; although they no longer enjoyed their previous political influence, they maintained their grip on the people through their sermons. Jonathan Mayhew, for example, a leading minister and often referred to as the father of true civil and religious liberty in America, in his "Discourse Concerning Unlimited Submission and Non-Resistance to the Higher Powers," flayed the concept of absolutism. In this sermon, delivered on January 20, 1750 (the anniversary of the death of Charles I), Mayhew declared that opposition to absolute rulers was the will of God:

> We may very safely assert these two things in general, without undermining government: One is, that no civil rulers are to be obeyed when they enjoin things that are inconsistent with the commands of God. All such disobedience is lawful and glorious. . . . Another thing that may be asserted with equal truth and safety is, that no government is to be submitted to at the expense of that which is the sole end of all government—the common good and safety of society.

"To say that subjects in general," wrote J. W. Thornton, "are not proper judges when their governors oppress them and play the tyrant, and when they defend their rights, administer justice impartially, and promote the public welfare, is as great treason as ever man uttered. 'T is treason, not against one *single* man, but the State—against the whole body politic; 't is treason against common sense, 't is treason against God.''[18]

'' 'T is treason against God.'' This became the rallying cry of Mayhew and his sympathizers during those eventful years. Yet the question may well be asked as to what Mayhew proposed in place of the absolutist form of government which he so vigorously opposed; to which Mayhew himself responded in the same discourse: ''Why then should not these parts of the Scripture which relate to civil government be examined and explained . . . ?'' In this, the ''morning gun of the revolution,'' Mayhew cited the Scriptural example of the call of the Hebrew prophets to resist illegal taxation and royal infringements on the rights of the people. The effect of Mayhew's exhortation was the absolution of the last vestige of divine authority which the king may have enjoyed in the eyes of the American people, and the firm entrenchment of the model of the Hebrew commonwealth in the emerging pattern of American polity.

In his famous sermon, ''The Snare Broken, a Thanksgiving Discourse,'' delivered on May 23, 1766, Mayhew gives further expression to the growing desire for freedom. This sermon, celebrating the repeal of the notorious Stamp Act, reveals the great impact of the Bible on the leaders of this period:

> Having . . . learnt from the Holy Scriptures that wise, brave and virtuous men were always friends to liberty; that God gave the Israelites a king in his anger, because they had not sense and virtue enough to like a free commonwealth, and to have himself for their king . . . and that ''where the Spirit of the Lord is, there is liberty''; this made me conclude, that freedom was a great blessing.

Clearly, Moses' foreboding and Samuel's admonition against

monarchy played a considerable role in actuating the polity of colonial America at the crossroads of its life in the crucial third quarter of the eighteenth century. Hebraic idealism had inspired many of the practical considerations which spurred the patriots to challenge monarchy in a decisive manner, and to lay down their lives in the Revolution. Monarchy was termed "un-Biblical" and "un-Hebraic" by Mayhew, and so it was to the clergy; to the masses it had more and more come to be "un-American." The illustration par excellence of this attitude is the draft for the seal of the newly established United States drawn up by Benjamin Franklin and Thomas Jefferson; it portrayed Pharaoh, crowned, sword in hand, passing in an open chariot and with all his host through the divided waters of the Red Sea in pursuit of the fleeing Israelites, while Moses, beams of heavenly light radiating from his head, stands on the farther shore with hand outstretched over the sea, causing it to overwhelm Pharaoh and his host. Beneath this representation is inscribed the motto, "Resistance to Tyrants is Obedience to God."[19]

The Continental Congress continued to maintain and uphold this Hebraic ideal in its work of providing a concrete shape and substance to the new Union. Probably because its legislative powers were extremely weak under the Articles of Confederation, the Congress leaned heavily on the sanctions of the Bible. Accordingly, one of the first acts of the Continental Congress was to propose the publication of an American Bible. On October 26, 1780, the following resolution was passed:

That it be recommended to such of the states who may think it convenient for them that they take proper measures to procure one or more new and correct editions of the Old and New Testament to be printed and such states regulate their printers by law so as to secure effectively the said books from being misprinted.

Soon, however, the new Republic turned its energies to the arduous task of creating the political base and mechanism for the new government, so that the interests of the day now became the nature of this proposed government, its principles and precedents, especially previous historical models of government after which to pattern the superstructure of the new body politic. Benjamin Franklin attests to the difficulties of this search:

> We have gone back to ancient history for models of government and examined the different forms of those republics which, having been originally formed with the seeds of their own dissolution, now no longer exist; and we have viewed modern states all round Europe, but find none of their constitutions suitable to our own circumstances.

It is thus apparent that the founders of the Republic set out not to establish a completely new political entity but sought examples from past and present alike. Thomas Jefferson, in a letter to Henry Lee of May 8, 1825, recalls their endeavor:

> not to find out new principles or new arguments never before thought of, not merely to say things which had never been said before, but to place before mankind the common sense of the subject, in terms so plain and firm as to command their assent and to justify ourselves in the independent stand we are compelled to take.

This, then, was the basis for Jefferson's immortal declaration: "We hold these truths to be self-evident."

The origins of the concepts embodied in the Declaration of Independence and the Constitution, then, lie as much in the secular political thought of the day as in the pious impulses of the early American settlers. Yet both these streams derived much from the Biblical ideal state, the Hebrew commonwealth. In the light of Jefferson's comment (in the letter to Lee cited above) that "all its [the Declaration of Independence] authority rests on the harmonizing sentiments of the day," there can be little doubt that current European political thought exercised considerable influence on American statesmen. The most influential work in this area in the eighteenth century was perhaps Algernon Sidney's *Discourses Concerning Government*, which was read throughout the colonies and was familiar to all the leading men of letters and politics. Even the liberal minister Jonathan Mayhew states (in his famous sermon, "The Snare Broken") that one of the chief sources through which he had "been initiated, in youth, in the doctrines of civil liberty" was Sidney's work. Sidney's book became the guide of the Founding Fathers, and was to be found in the libraries of Franklin, Adams, Jefferson, and others. Sidney's description of the Hebrew commonwealth is particularly pertinent to the present discussion:

> Having seen what government God did not ordain, it may be reasonable to examine the nature of government he did ordain and we shall find it consisted of those parts, besides the magistrates of the several tribes and cities: They had a Chief Magistrate, who was called Judge or Captain, as Joshua, Gideon, and others: a Council of seventy chosen men, and the General Assembly of the people. The first was merely occasional, like to the Dictators of Rome. . . . The second is known by the name of the Great Sanhedrin, which, being instituted by Moses, according to the command of God, continued till they were all, save one, slain by Herod. And the third, which is the Assembly of the people, was so common that none be ignorant of it, but such as never looked in the Scripture.

The correspondences between the above synopsis of the government of the Hebrew commonwealth and the political system evolved by the Founding Fathers of the American Republic is so close as to bear further investigation. In the first place, as we have seen previously, the model of the Hebrew commonwealth provided a clear precedent for the two formative principles of the new Republic, viz., the denial of absolutism, whether in the form of hereditary aristocracy, oligarchy, or monarchy; and the affirmation of democracy as the most desirable and viable structure for society. Beyond

this basic philosophical and theoretical correspondence, however, the ancient Israelite system itself actually served the
Founding Fathers of the United States as a concrete and
practical governmental model for the new state which they
were laboring to bring forth. For example, Moses' successor,
Joshua, was succeeded by a line of popularly elected
"judges" (*shoftim*) from Othniel to Samuel, whose administration of the ancient Israelite commonwealth bears a striking
resemblance to our own federal system, in that each tribe
constituted an autonomous political unit with jurisdiction
over its own internal affairs, even while ultimately accountable to a central authority presided over by the "judge." In
fact, the official function of the judge closely resembles that
of our President: in wartime he was the commander-in-chief
of Israel's citizen army, and in peacetime he served as the
chief magistrate (which was actually not a magistracy in the
ordinary sense of the term, for, although the judge did possess supreme judicial authority, he was, in effect, what we
understand as the "chief executive" of the nation; and, interestingly enough, a further function of the judge was the
convening of the general assembly). The parallel further extends to the system of internal governmental checks and bal-
ances: the "chief executive" of the Hebrew commonwealth
never enjoyed absolute power, since he was accountable to
the council of the seventy elders established by Moses (the
"Sanhedrin" of later Judaism), which many seventeenth-
century writers (such as Sidney, Grotius, and Selden)
likened to a permanent national senate, undoubtedly to the
edification of contemporary American statesmen. And in addition to this "senate" there was a popular assembly, which,
in theory, consisted of "all Israel" or "the congregation of Israel." Although this association may have honorarily included every male member of the B'nei-Israel, in actuality the
body consisted of the representatives of the various tribes.
(There can be little doubt that in the injunction "Let all Israel
stone him," the hapless offender was not meant to be stoned
by every member of the nation.) The representatives were

the embodiment of "all Israel" by virtue of the fact that they expressed the will of their constituents; in Numbers 1:16, for instance, these representatives to the assembly of Israel are termed *Qeruay HaAyda,* i.e., "those called from the people."

That these ancient political structures and precedents exercised a powerful influence on both secular and religious thought in colonial America is evident from an election sermon delivered by Samuel Langdon, president of Harvard, before the "Honorable Congress of Massachusetts Bay" on May 31, 1775, which clearly reflects American political thinking on the eve of the Revolution:

> The Jewish government, according to the original constitution which was divinely established, if considered merely in a civil view, was a perfect republic. And let them who cry up the divine right of kings consider, that the form of government which had a proper claim to divine establishment was so far from including the idea of a king, that it was a high crime for Israel to ask to be in this respect like other nations, and when they were thus gratified, it was rather as a just punishment for their folly. Every nation, when able and agreed, has a right to set up over itself any form of government which to it may appear most conducive to its common welfare. The civil polity of Israel is doubtless an excellent general model.

Once the Republic had been established and the democratic ideal had gained practicing adherents, it was natural enough that the laws governing the democracy derive from the familiar and revered Scriptural sources. But the government which the Founding Fathers eventually evolved was also based on practical experience, as observed by Lawrence Henry Gipson:

> [the new government was not only] the conscious creation of far-seeing statesmanship but of adventurous, hard working, home-loving men and women of the middle and lower classes of society of the British Isles and of Europe

who were endowed with extraordinary initiative, tenacity of purpose, and resourcefulness in meeting as individuals the problems of frontier life.[20]

And yet it is undeniable that the Bible had become an integral part of that frontier life; its letter and spirit had penetrated ineradicably into the minds and hearts of America's pioneers; its influence was, as we have seen, present in every level of society; it was, in short, an essential part of the American ethos.

Democracy as a political *modus vivendi* presupposes a moral basis and background; it is moral before it is political. For a people to rule, there must prevail among them a hunger for justice and righteousness and a thirst for liberty, both for oneself and one's brother; without these fundamental virtues, a people, even if living under a form of democracy, will find itself in fact living under tyrannous masters.[21] This truth was paramount in the minds of the earliest settlers in New England as well as the later pioneers of the interior regions, who, by their dauntless emigration and unshakable resolution to build their New World, demonstrated a genuine love of liberty which is the primary condition for a true democracy; they were, like Israel in its oppression, free within slavery. Moreover, while the Puritans, upon their arrival in America, were (like Israel under Joshua at the River Jordan) fully prepared for an ideal theocracy, it is to the everlasting credit of the American people that, as they gradually came to realize that the exacting principles of a theocracy were not feasible in their increasingly practical world, they were able to supplant the rigid code of the one with the more liberal laws of the other, while always following the moral imperatives which had motivated their initial step. This they were able to do because the ultimate source of both polities was the same—the Hebrew Bible.

The Influence of the Hebrew Bible on the Literature of England and America

On both sides of the Atlantic, in England as in America, the Bible has long been known as the best-selling book of the ages. Its popularity is an accepted fact. Perhaps more so than any other book—and for a variety of reasons—the Bible has been and is still being constantly read and re-read. Some people, as a result of their frequently repeated readings of the Bible and because of their intense attachment to it, have committed numerous verses, entire chapters, and even books to memory in the precise phraseology.

Until well into the nineteenth century, before mass production made books more readily available, the Bible was often the only book a family possessed. It was much thumbed, finger-stained and dog-eared from frequent use. The Bible came to be the repository of all major events in the history of a family over the generations. In it were recorded births and deaths, marriages and divorces. It was passed from father to son, as much a part of the material patrimony as of the spiritual.

This reverence for the Book was by no means confined to one class or restricted to any particular segment of the population. All men knew its contents, all men were exposed to its spirit, and most of them tried—outwardly at least—to live by its injunctions. Familiarity with the legend, lore, and language of the Bible grew, not only through the more formal efforts of the clergy, but through immediate personal contact with it. It came to be a source of history as well as parable, and a guide to literary excellence. It was in this manner that the English language, and through it English literature, acquired so many phrases and idioms grounded in, or directly quoted from, the Bible.

In his book *Mithridates*, published in 1555, Conrad Gesner noted that when Hebrew joined Greek and Latin as an Oriental language, scholars and linguists began to study it with particular interest. Among the students of the time it was an irrefutable hypothesis that since the Old Testament was written in Hebrew, that tongue must have been the earliest language spoken by man; that by philological analysis Hebrew was the mother language from which all other languages sprang, "a theory which has found adherents down to Gesenius in recent times."[1]

This theory, although discarded as totally groundless today, was accepted unquestioningly by scholars until a comparatively late date, adding to the intellectual influence of the Bible and of Hebrew, the language in which it was written. W. L. Roy, for example, in the introduction to his Hebrew dictionary, writes: "Hebrew is the original language, neither improved nor diminished by foreign idioms. . . .It was the language of Eber, from whom it derived its name; and was, we presume, the only language spoken before the deluge. Hence 'the whole earth was one language and one dialect' (Genesis 9,1)."[2] According to Roy, the names of men, beasts, birds, and other creatures, as well as the names of many ancient cities, towns, and peoples, were, generally speaking, of purely Hebrew origin. The fact that many of the modern-day languages, wholly different in most respects, have numerous words of apparent and easily traced derivation was seen as further proof of the antiquity of Hebrew. These were thought to be relics of the mother of all tongues—Hebrew—and were evidence of the origin of the language. Arabic, Syriac, Chaldean, and Ethiopian, as well, were felt to have been dialects of Hebrew. That these languages were sometimes resorted to in order to uncover the root of a Hebrew word was explained as resulting from the scarcity of surviving Hebrew documents, and thus these languages were classed as cognate dialects.

Roy adds that Hebrew has been studied because it is the most comprehensive of all languages. He cites numerous authorities who share this opinion with him. After a lengthy treatment he concludes that the Bible "can never be understood, unless through the medium of the language in which it was originally written, and the spirit by which it was dictated."[3]

Modern philological research has forced the abandonment of these ideas and retired them to antique obscurity, and they remain important only to the extent that they reflect the value placed on Hebrew and the Bible by early scholars. Today a more general and inclusive picture is accepted. There is no doubt, however, that Hebrew is an extremely ancient language, one of the very oldest in the Semitic group, and that it continuously maintained an active position.

The influence of Hebrew on the languages spoken in neighboring areas began at an extremely early stage in its initial development. As far back as the second millennium B.C.E., several Hebrew words are found in the letters of Tel el-Amarna in Egypt. The exact position of Hebrew, as to centrality and antiquity, in the development of the Semitic language group has never been satisfactorily established. Until recently many scholars have accepted Hebrew as the most

ancient in this language group. In the past few years, however, it has been suggested that Arabic preceded Hebrew.
Others have given precedence to either Aramaic or Assyrian.
One things appears to be fairly well agreed upon, however,
and that is that the present Semitic languages are all variant
dialects of one common ancient language—designated as
Proto-Semitic.

But these finer points are of no great concern to the social
historian. In any event, for the purposes of this discussion, it
may be stated that Hebrew is the oldest of the ancient Semitic languages to exert a continuing influence on modern languages. This is equally true of the Bible and Hebrew literature. This projected long-range influence has reached our
present English and American literature primarily through
the agency of the Scriptures. Biblical precepts, injunctions,
nobility of thought, and unmatched eloquence are the source
of much that is great in English and American literature.

If one wishes to study English literature from its beginnings, there is little doubt that an intimate acquaintance with
the Bible is an indispensable preparation. The very origins of
English literary efforts are intertwined with the influence of
the Bible and Biblical lore.

Caedmon, the seventh-century poet, who is often referred
to as the father of English poetry, won early fame for his
paraphrases of Biblical tales. Biblical stories served as the
basis of such Anglo-Saxon poems as *Genesis, Exodus,* and
Daniel which were attributed to Caedmon. Poems of this nature were common, and are symptomatic of the fact that during most of the Anglo-Saxon period of English literature, the
spheres of religion and scholarship were not particularly distinct. For the most part, secular literature did not have an
apparent and independent existence. Much of what was written, therefore, was religious in nature. These works were essentially written for the instruction and edification of the
small number of people who were able to read, as opposed
to the intent of later English poets, such as the seventeenth-
century "metaphysical" poets, who wrote for large audi-
ences.

If we turn from the early poetry of Caedmon, who is known primarily through the works of the Bede, to Anglo-Saxon poetry such as *Beowulf,* the influence of the Bible as a source book is still readily apparent. Many have felt that the Scriptural references found in this ancient epic were entered by latter-day monks when transcribing the poem. *Beowulf* is essentially a narrative poem of the genre that was recited in the manor houses by the *skops,* or poetry reciters. Yet even in this poem—pagan in so many respects—there is arresting evidence that many of the references from the Scriptures, as well as the attitudes evinced, are central to the world-outlook of the poem rather than superimposed in later centuries. The references to the monsters as the offspring of Cain are of major importance in this work and in this age, and not of peripheral interest as was supposed.

Beowulf, written between the seventh and ninth centuries, came at a time when the Anglo-Saxon world was exchanging its ancient pagan concepts for the monotheistic ones of the Scriptures. In the combination of pagan monsters as the offspring of the biblical Cain, the world-view of the past and that of the future are blended in a significant synthesis— perhaps marking the true start of the influence of the Bible in English literature.[4]

Thus, in an effort to portray the ancient pagan days in *Beowulf,* the unknown poet drew on his knowledge of the Scriptural tradition of his time. In describing the nobility of several of the poem's characters, the poet turns to the shepherd leaders and kings of the Hebrews for examples. *Beowulf* in many respects is an example of how a Christian poet utilized Christian concepts based on Biblical lore while writing a historical epic of the pagan past.

The influence of the Scriptures manifested itself in another area as well during the Anglo-Saxon period. The *Anglo-Saxon Chronicle* of King Alfred the Great, who ruled Wessex in the latter part of the ninth century, was modeled on the Hebrew Chronicles, and was prefaced with a copy of the Decalogue and other verses from the Mosaic law. Alfred's codes quoted extensively from the Five Books of Moses, and when one considers the fact that religious, political, and literary efforts were all subsumed under one category during this period, the traces of Biblical influence and the areas of impact become all the more important.

Moving to the Middle English period, from approximately the thirteenth until the middle of the fifteenth century, English literature developed in a great many respects, and with it the nature and extent of Scriptural influence. It was during this period that a burgeoning secular literature evolved. It is for this reason that the role of the Bible in literature is so interesting. The stories from the Bible were obviously found throughout the corpus of religious literature; but now, for the first time, they were used for the purpose of illustration and exemplification in the rapidly developing body of non-religious works. The possibility of such forms was due to a variety of factors. At the same time that a secular literary tradition was evolving, literature of a religious nature was taking on a secular cast. This resulted in the increased knowledge of Biblical lore by a greater number of people. This knowledge, attained through literary and non-literary vehicles alike, enabled the writers of this period to use Scriptural stories and thereby be assured that their audience would be a large one whether the works were read or recited.

Dramatic and colorful events were the ones most frequently taken from the Bible and used in literature. It was at this time that the Hebrew Bible came to be widely accepted as actual history. The narratives of the Bible were, therefore, incorporated as the starting point for most historical works written, influencing literature in another indirect manner.

However, when discussing the impact of the Bible on literature during the Middle English period, it must be remembered that the Scriptures themselves had not as yet been translated into the English language. The absence of a translation stemmed from the attitude of the church to the Bible. It was felt that the common people should know the Word of God as authorized by the Latin Vulgate and not the Bible itself. The masses were not thought to be capable of assimilating the Bible in translation. This is evident in the reply given by Pope Gregory VII in 1179 to the king of Bohemia, when the latter requested permission for the use of Slavonic: "It was not without reason that the Almighty God decided that Holy Scripture should be secret in certain parts, lest, if it were clearly apparent to all men, it might perhaps be little esteemed and be treated disrespectfully."[5] The idea that the simple folk should presume to know the Bible in its awesome holiness was inconceivable in that day and age.

The effect of this approach was that while the Bible served throughout the Middle English period as a source for stories, history, and attitudes, it never served as a literary model after which works could be patterned. This took place only after efforts to translate the Bible into English became widespread. The influence of the Bible, therefore, was expressed primarily in the use of Scriptural figures for illustration, historical content, and morality. The element of morality, as seen for instance in the *Pardoner's Tale* by Chaucer and in *Piers the Plowman,* was very reminiscent of the concepts of justice and retribution held by the Hebrew prophets. This is also seen in poems like *Cleanness* and *Patience,* which paraphrased the stories of the Bible almost in toto.

Finally, it was during these centuries that the foundations of the theater were laid with the miracle plays. These began as antiphonal chants in the church service. The chants then developed into church dramas and later became plays, albeit primitive ones. These crude plays comprised both religious and secular elements based on Scriptural incidents. In essence they were dramatizations of the Bible stories with a morally instructive purpose, often extremely robust and humorous, straying from the spirit of the original. The incidents chosen were the most striking and dramatically effective, such as *Noah and the Flood* and *Abraham and Isaac.* The events, aside from the Nativity or the Passion, were most often taken from the Old Testament. Eventually these developed into what came to be known as the "sacred plays":

Two Sins of King David (1561); *Goodly Queen Hester* (1561); *Jacob and Esau* (1568); *Abraham's Sacrifice* (1577); *Suzanne* (1578); *David and Bathsheba* (1599); and *The Tragedy of Mariam (and Herod)* (1613).[6] Invariably the sources for the "sacred plays" were the Old Testament or the works of Josephus. It was from these origins that the great English dramatic tradition sprang.

It was during the latter part of the sixteenth century that the Bible began to serve as a literary model as well as a source of material and events. As was mentioned above, the Hebrew Bible had previously served as a store of tales and history, whereas from this period on it became a model of style as well. This came about as a result of the efforts to translate the Bible into English, which culminated in 1611 in one of the greatest masterpieces of the English language: the Authorized Version, or King James Bible. The excellence of this translation was soon unequivocally acclaimed as one of the great works of the language, and since it became the most widely read, its language and style were rapidly adopted as a model. In European literatures the Bible served as the basis for many works, yet it never fulfilled the function of a guide to eloquence because of the absence of a translation that could match the King James edition.

This translation, however, was preceded by a number of other notable efforts which prepared the ground for its rapid and critical recognition. In fact, by 1604, when work on the King James edition began, the style in which the translation was done had already become considerably archaic and antiquated. The style, later so often emulated, began with Tyndale's attempts in 1525. Over the next century, Tyndale's limited efforts were followed by Coverdale's Bible, Mathew's Bible, the Great Bible, as well as by a number of others. The King James version was undoubtedly a better translation than its predecessors, but the style was one that had already been accepted as appropriate. This perhaps explains the reason for the rapid critical acceptance.

The fact, however, that this was a translation of the Word of God, important as it may be, is not the only reason for its enormous impact on the literature of the period. It must not be forgotten that this work was carried out when the modern English literary forms and traditions were taking shape— contemporary with Shakespeare's works. This period was one of transition and great flux, and the influence of the Bible was assured by its magnificent translation at a time of change. The Bible, therefore, was important for two reasons: it was the Word of God, and thus compelling from a religious point of view; and it was the fruition of one of England's greatest literary periods.

The English text of the Scriptures became known to all and was soon used in daily conversation. Quotation of passages in the course of ordinary social intercourse became commonplace, and this familiarity was easily adopted into the literature of the day. The importance of the English translation was such that by "the seventeenth century it is often impossible to distinguish the rhetorical from the ideological influence of the Bible, for familiarity with the diction of the Authorized Version came to be regarded by many as implying an acceptance of certain religious doctrines."[7]

The influence of the Scriptures in this period, however, was not solely confined to the words of the King James Bible, but was part of the spirit of the age. The body of literature that developed during the Renaissance and Reformation displayed a comprehensive wisdom. The poets, dramatists, painters, and musicians drew on the Bible for vividness of imagery and strength of spirit. Biblical grandeur pervaded their works, whether consciously or not. These artists and writers accepted the core-beliefs of the Hebrew prophets; as one English author, James Bell, felt, they were "a daily recognition of the strenuous moral forces of history," and "an insight into the Divine conditions and the spiritual tendencies of life."[8] Like the prophets, they combined the concept of righteousness with an acceptance of the agency of divine will in human history, constantly reaffirming that

> There's a divinity that shapes our ends,
> Rough-hew them how we will. (*Hamlet* I,ii)

Shakespeare's plays—a unique treasure to fall so early in the history of a national literature—are replete with references to Biblical characters and direct quotations from the Bible. (There are, for instance, eight different occasions on which Shakespeare uses the story of Cain and Abel.) Shakespeare's England, despite the fact that Jews had been expelled from the country many years earlier, was in many ways, as we have seen, influenced by Hebraic thought. Although Shakespeare did not write any Hebrew chronicles similar to his historical plays dealing with England and Rome, his numerous Scriptural references suggest that the Hebraic influence was ever present in his work. The very manner in which these references were made indicates the extent to which the Bible had become familiar. But Shakespeare's use of the spirit of the Hebrew Bible is even more striking than his citation of its words. The prophetic moral vision found in his works is not Greek nor is it Roman. It is without doubt of Hebrew origin. History and the divine will acting on it are idealized by both Shakespeare and the Hebrew prophets: the historical facts are present but perhaps not in a rigorously exacting form; and history has an instructive use—a story is not merely told but a lesson of righteousness is taught. This simlilarity is found throughout the Hebrew Bible and Shakespeare.[9]

The idealized view of history is revealed in the stories of Saul and Macbeth. There is a tragic element and a basic moral aim in both. Evil storm clouds and foreboding hover over both. The elements of the tragedy soon dominate both scenes and mold the future of the protagonists, without their knowledge. If Macbeth and Saul are to learn the moral of their imminent tragedies, they must have been basically good rather than evil at the start. Their tragedies were essentially the degeneration of an innate nobility—generally characterized by the dimensions and grandeur of their actions. Initially, Saul is described as "a choice young man, and a goodly: and there was not among the children of Israel a goodlier person than he . . . " (I Sam. 9:2). When Saul was victorious over the Ammonites, Israel's traditional enemies, he secured his position as king. Those who had opposed him previously, the sons of Belial, were then in danger of losing their lives. Saul, however, revealed his nobility by refusing to have his enemies killed: "There shall not a man be put to death this day: for today the Lord hath wrought salvation in Israel" (I Sam. 11:13).

The similarity between Macbeth and Saul is indeed remarkable. Macbeth's victory wins for him the praise of the king, and his position in the realm is but a few places below that of the sovereign himself. The wounded sergeant says of "brave Macbeth":

Well he deserves that name,
Disdaining fortune, with his brandish'd steel,
Which smoked with bloody execution,
Like valour's minion carved out his passage
Till he faced the slave.

Macbeth's noble character is evident when he first recoils from the prophecy of the witches—those "horrible imaginings." Both Saul and Macbeth are portrayed as men of great worth, with even greater promise.

Ambition, however, stands between the potential greatness of these two heroes and their promising futures. The lust for absolute power diverts the course of their lives and proves their undoing. The first indication of this in Saul is when, after his triumph over the Amalekites, he fails to await Samuel's arrival before offering a sacrifice to the Lord. Saul here usurps the prerogatives of the religious leaders, in contravention of his role as a limited monarch and military leader. Saul is denounced for his action by Samuel: "Hath the Lord as great delight in burnt offerings and sacrifices, as in obeying the voice of the Lord? . . . For rebellion is as the sin of witchcraft, and stubbornness is as iniquity and idolatry" (I Sam. 15). Saul's ambition is tied to his rejection of the Lord's word and is called "the sin of witchcraft." Can this overweening pride and ambition not be compared to the sins commited by Macbeth? Macbeth's cardinal sin is his transgression against the divine right of kings, and by so doing he fulfills the prophecy of the three witches—indeed, the "sin of witchcraft."

The effects of ambition are also similar. Saul succumbs to his jealousy of David and attempts a number of times to kill him. Macbeth finds Banquo a scourge to his conscience, a living rebuke of his unnatural ambition. But Macbeth is successful where Saul is not, and Banquo is killed. The ghost of Banquo, however, returns to haunt Macbeth. This return of a spirit to make the sinner fear the outcome of his deed is comparable to Saul's visit to the witch of Endor. Saul turns to the spirit of Samuel, recalled by the witch, for aid, since he fears that God has turned from him. But where Shakespeare's witches speak to Macbeth in incomprehensible riddles, Samuel openly tells Saul that his kingdom will be given to the House of David.

Saul's tragedy is revealed: where he once banished witches from Israel, he now consults one to hear his doom; where once he had visions, God has deserted him; his moral vision has been destroyed by his lack of control, his jealousy, and then his surrender to an evil spirit. His fall from grace is described in these words: "Then Saul fell straightway all along on the earth, and was sore afraid, because of the words of Samuel . . . " (I Sam. 28:20). The resemblance to the fall of Macbeth is striking:

> I have lived long enough; my way of life
> is fallen into the sear, the yellow leaf,
> And that which should accompany old age,
> As honour, love, obedience, troops of friends,
> I must not look to have.

Thus, despite the apparent differences in place, time, and events, both Saul in the Hebrew Bible and Macbeth in Shakespeare's tragedy are the personifications of intense tragedy, which illustrates the continuous and insurmountable action of moral law.

Even in the area of specific influence, the Bible struck deep roots. The Talmud and Midrashic literature, as well, had seeped deeply enough into the general culture to provide writers like Shakespeare with inspiration on many occasions. The Midrashic saying "Habit becomes nature" is found in *Hamlet* (III,iv,168) as "For use almost can change the stamp of nature." In the play *Coriolanus,* Cominius praises the hero for refusing recompense for his deeds. Coriolanus replies that he "rewards his deeds with doing them" (II,ii,132–33). This same sentiment is expressed in *Henry the Eighth* (III,ii,182–83) as "the honour of it does pay the act of it." This should be compared with the sayings in *Pirke Aboth:* "Do not be as slaves who serve the master in order to be rewarded" (1:3), and, "Rabbi Azai says . . . that the reward of a good deed is the deed" (4:2). It is difficult to know whether these references are indications that these were part of the general culture, or whether Shakespeare was familiar with the Latin translations of such works. The fact remains, however, that Shakespeare, the giant of English literature, was one with the Bible and the Hebraic spirit.[10]

Moving on to some of the poets of the period, we find their works marked by the Scriptures throughout. One of the most important early English poets was Edmund Spenser, who encompassed many of the elements of the poetry of his day within his own works. One of these elements was the synthesis of his joyous, often almost lush view of life with the more somber strains of the Hebrew Bible. For example, Spenser wrote the following sonnet based on the biblical phrase "And God said, Let us make man in our image, after our likeness":

> Therefore of clay, base, vile and next to nought,
> Yet formed by wondrous skill, and by His might,
> According to an heavenly patterne wrought,
> Which He had fashioned in His wise forsight,
> He man did make, and breathed a living spright
> Into his face, most beautifull and fayre,
> Endowed with wisedome's riches, heavenly, rare.

Such He him made, that he resemble might
Himself, as mortall thing immortall could;
Him to be lord of every wight
He made by love out of his owne like mould,
In whom He might His mightie self behould:
For love, doth love the thing beloved to see,
That like itselfe in lovely shape may bee.

The poet thus blends the spirit of the age of courtly love with the tones and echoes of Biblical creation that to a great extent marked the manner in which some of the poetry of the period utilized so naturally the background of the Scriptures.

In the seventeenth century the Bible left its mark primarily on the religious poetry and tracts that were written, while the prose of the period largely followed the patterns of the Greek and Latin classics. The influence of the Hebrew Bible was both as a religious document and as a literary model. The early part of this century was dominated by the metaphysical devotional poets, who, by definition, resorted to the Bible and its spirit. Poets like Francis Quarles often took direct quotations from the Scriptures for the titles and themes of their poems: "Wherefore hidest thou thy face, and holdest me for thy enemie?" (Job 13:24); or, "My beloved is mine, and I am his; He feedeth among the lilies" (Song of Songs 2:16). George Herbert's devotional poetry, grave yet lyrical, was in the style employed in the King James translation of the Bible. To an extent this was also seen in the works of Vaughan and Marvell. Dryden, in works like his *Absalom and Achitophel,* used Bible tales and figures with natural ease.

Milton, the great poet of the Puritan revolution, drew on the Scriptures for literary inspiration as well as for moral instruction. Speaking of Milton's three great narratives, Whiting says: "Milton was much more successful with the Old Testament story than with the New. *Paradise Lost* is an infinitely greater work than *Paradise Regained* and *Samson Agonistes* is so great because blind, captive Samson is, in one sense, none other than blind John Milton who had been so great, and had fallen so low."[11] The Bible was, in a sense, the basis for most of the major works of Milton. He studied Hebrew at an early age (probably while still in grammar school) and made it part of himself. He was able to paraphrase in a highly poetic manner many of the Psalms. He referred to the "great taskmaster," "Babylonian woe," "cherubim and seraphim," "the sons of morning and fountain of light." There is hardly a place in his writing where a Biblical spirit and Biblical diction do not shine through. In the Scriptures, the English writer could find history, short story, lyric, epic, ode, elegy, tragedy, as well as comedy.

This period was also the focal point for both religious and literary battles. In England this battle was a veritable "paper war," fought with pamphlets such as Hooker's *Laws of Ecclesiastical Polity* and Bunyan's *Pilgrim's Progress*. Bunyan's style was perhaps the start of the simplification of English prose.

Biblical influence is not lacking in the later period as well. William Blake's political poetry was soon forgotten after the turn of the nineteenth century and became intensely religious and mystical. The imagery of works such as *The Four Zoas* is Biblical. The two prophetic poems *Milton* and *Jerusalem*, written after 1804, established Blake's mystical and highly personalized religious style. His use of material from the Old Testament is evident in the short poem *Mock on, Mock on, Voltaire, Rousseau*. In this work, Blake rails against the skeptics who would set science above God:

> The Atoms of Democritus
> And Newton's Particles of Light
> Are sands upon the Red Sea shore
> Where Israel's tents do shine so bright.

Although the poetry of Shelley and Keats is also marked by the Scriptures, as is that of Tennyson, it is perhaps Robert Browning who best epitomizes late Hebraic learning to any considerable extent. Browning's "intellectual subtlety, the meta-physical minuteness of his argument, his fondness for parentheses, the way in which he pursued the absolute while he loaded it into a host of relatives and conceived the universal through a multitude of particulars, the love he had for remote and unexpected analogies, the craft with which his intellect persuaded him that he could insert into his poems thoughts illustrating legends and twisted knots of reasoning which a fine artistic sense would have omitted were all Jewish as the Talmud."[12] Browning's acknowledgement of his Hebraism is found in his own words. Speaking of his use of Hebrew phrases in the body of poems like *Jochanan Hakkadosh,* he said: "The Hebrew quotations are put in for a purpose: as a direct acknowledgement that certain doctrines may be found in the Old Book which the concocters of Novel Schemes of Morals put forth as discoveries of their own. I have put those into English characters with the proper pronunciation that you may see they go properly into English verse."[13] Browning, in *Jochanan Hakkadosh,* makes extensive use of phrases and words such as "Mishna," "Targums tell," "Olive-branched Tsaddik," "Ye call it *Dob* (bear)," "Three daughters weeping at *Banoth,*" and "the Ruach (Thus do we denote imparted Spirit)." There is little doubt as to Browning's keen knowledge of the language and lore of the Hebrews.

In the field of prose, Thomas Hardy might serve as an example. His plots are motivated by the Bible; his characters bear Biblical names. There is a conscious emulation of the beautifully idiomatic prose of the Bible. *In Far from the Madding Crowd,* the characters plainly speak the speech of the Scriptures. In *Jude the Obscure,* Bath Sheba speaks the ironic words of Hebrew vengeance, "burning for burning," "wound for wound," "strife for strife." In *The Mayor of Casterbridge,* the characters are strikingly reminiscent of Biblical narrative.

"All our English literature," wrote Henry Kendall Booth,

is saturated with the Bible's imagery; reference and echo

are everywhere. It underlies the pomp of Milton, the vigor of Johnson, the limpid flow of Wordsworth, the rhythms of Ruskin, the eloquence of Macaulay, the severe, swift ease of Arnold, the roll of Hooker and Browne, the perfect periods of Dryden, the rugged fire of Carlyle, the companionability of Emerson, the clarity and repose of De Quincey, the chastity of Whittier, the music of Tennyson, the conviction of Browning, Bacon, Jeremy Taylor, Charles Wesley, Southey, Newman, Webster, Froude; and so many, many more answer the trenchant mastery, the polychromatic vividness, the purged and the exalted, the liquid and pellucid style of the book that bred them.[14]

When we turn to American literature the same picture is repeated. In the earliest native efforts Scriptural influence is obvious. The one truly creative center of the early colonies was New England. Here the austerity of Puritan belief channeled self-expression toward largely religious spheres. Painting and music were regarded as either frivolous or actually the work of the devil, restricting creative efforts in the Puritan colonies to the realm of literature.

In addition to the natural direction toward which the religion of the Puritans led them, literature in the early colonial days was guided by the personal inclination of the colonies' elite. When discussing the intellectual leaders of the New England colonies, it must be remembered that of the many university alumni who had reached the shores of the New World by 1645, a good number were trained for and actively practiced a religious vocation. John Cotton, Thomas Hooker, John Davenport, Roger Williams, Nathaniel Ward, John Wilson, and many others were all well known for their deeply religious world-outlook. These men served as the intellectual and cultural focus of New England and established, to a great extent, the style of its cultural life in the early years of the colonies.

Since the intellectual bent of these leaders was basically theological, one of the major genres of early New England literature was the sermon and pulpit literature. The sermons, rarely less than an hour in duration, were a major aspect of colonial life, and if the minister was well known, were often published. The purpose of these sermons was exegetical as well as practical. Generally a verse or a passage was cited from the Bible and the sermon was built around it. The minister used the occasion of the sermon to exhibit his theological knowledge and apply it to practical examples taken from everyday life. A by-product of pulpit literature was the production of religious pamphlets and tracts. This comprised a major portion of the early colonial literary output and served as a vehicle for debating many of the burning issues of the day. Thomas Hooker's *Survey of the Summe of Church Discipline* and the pamphlets that were published when Roger Williams was banished from Massachusetts are examples of this form of literature.

Another popular genre of literature in seventeenth-century New England prose was that of historical and biographical works. This dealt with historical and political matters which are of seemingly secular nature. But this secular aspect is more imagined than real, since with the growth of the first native-born into productive maturity, the all-consuming subject was religion. Even in their diaries, everything was related to their faith. Samuel Sewall's *Diary* is replete with Biblical references. Some of the titles of the works written in this period amply illustrate the religious nature of most literary endeavors. The subtitle of a historical work by Edward Johnson, for instance, is *Wonder-Working Providence of Sion's Saviour in New England,* while Thomas Morton's history is titled *New English Canaan.*[15] We have seen in the excerpts from Governor William Bradford's *History of Plimouth Plantation* numerous Biblical references that mark the style of this leading early historical work. The conscious and intense identification with the history and lot of the ancient Israelites by the Puritans is pervasive throughout all these works.

Cotton Mather's monumental *Magnalia Christi Americana* was one of the major literary works of the period. In it Mather attempted to make use of history in order to show that God had been beneficent to New England and its inhabitants. The influence of the Bible and Mather's "Old Testamentarianism" is evident on almost every page. The *Magnalia*, however, is far more than the history of the early years of the New England settlement. It is a potpourri of biography, personal narrative, history, and political propaganda, and often comments on the personal failings of some of the Puritan citizenry. It is precisely because this work deals with so many aspects of New England life that it is so valuable for determining the extent to which the influence of the Bible had penetrated the Puritan world of America.

Another prose work of considerable interest was Sewall's *The Selling of Joseph*. By using and extending the story of Joseph and his brothers, Samuel Sewall wrote what "was probably the first published attack on slavery in America."[16] Most of the polemical literature written in America made use of this literary convention, adopting a story from the Bible upon which an argument dealing with a contemporary issue could be built.

One thing was constant throughout all the literary forms in the early colonial days—simplicity of style. The Puritans in America retained a plain and unadorned style that was fully consonant with their way of life. While their English counterparts were writing intricate metaphysical poetry that came to be identified with the school of the devotional poets, the writers of New England, with perhaps the exception of Uriah Oakes and Cotton Mather, were consistent in their use of the simple cadences of the Bible.

Poetry in the seventeenth century was the realm of all literate people. All who were able to read, read poetry, and most tried their hand at verse. Although early American poetry could not, by any stretch of the imagination, be compared with the works of the English poets, such as Donne and Dryden, it nonetheless laid the foundation for much of the future efforts.

For the most part, and with the notable exception of Anne Bradstreet's love poems, native poetry was religious in intent and imagery, and this limited the extent of poetic expression. There are basically four general types under which colonial poetry can be subsumed: the rhymed translations of the Bible, sung as hymns; morally instructive poetry; religious lyrics expressing the emotional fervor of the Puritans; and, finally, polemical poetry used in sectarian disputes. Although these divisions are somewhat arbitrary, most of the early verse written in the colonies falls into one of these four categories.

One of the first verse forms to become popular in New England was hymnal translation. We have already noted the efforts to produce an adequate translation of the Psalms for use in church services. This consumed much of the literary efforts of the colonists and finally culminated in the *Bay Psalm Book*. But this soon gave way to more original work, eventually resulting in a robust literary tradition. Michael Wigglesworth was an early contributor to the tradition. In his poem *God's Controversy with New England,* written in 1662, Wigglesworth portrays God as sternly rebuking the inhabitants of New England:

> What Should I do with such a stiff-nekt race?
> How shall I ease me of such foes as they?
> What shall befall despisers of my Grace?
> I'll surely bear their candle-stick away,
> And lamps put out, their glorious noon-day light
> I'll quickly turn into a dark Egyptian night.

Though this poetry was a far cry from the sophisticated verse produced in England, it nevertheless served as the start of native American poetry.

With the passage of time, the poetry produced in this country became less rough-hewn. The poems of Peter Folger, Benjamin Franklin's maternal grandfather, are an example of the more highly sophisticated versification in America. Yet despite the change in style, the Bible continued to exert a great influence. Folger's poem *Looking Glass of the Times,* written in 1676, is a good example of this:

New England they are like the *Jews,*
  as like, as they can be;
They made large promises to God,
  at home and at the sea;
They did proclaim free Liberty,
  they cut the calf in twain,
They passed between the part thereof:
  O this was all in vain!

Though the style of this poem is more polished, and the theme—liberty—is one not generally found in early Puritan poetry, the Scriptural imagery employed by the Puritans remains constant.

This tradition continued down to the days of the American Revolution and was consciously accepted as part of the general culture of the American colonies. This is most clearly evident in the following incident. When, in June of 1774, dissatisfaction with the rule of the British Parliament had spread through the colonies and Virginia was in turmoil, it was decided to declare a day of fasting and prayer to protest the closing of the Boston harbor. The leadership of New England in such matters was acknowledged when Thomas Jefferson was sent "rummaging for precedents and Puritan forms."[17] These he found, and promptly carried them out with a fury suggesting Jeremiah. The purpose of the fast day, he explained, "was devoutly to implore the divine interposition in behalf of an injured and oppressed people."[18]

It must be pointed out in reference to Jefferson that when Benjamin Franklin first told him of the slogan "Resistance to tyrants is obedience to God," it was then ascribed to one of the regicides of Charles I. It is, of course, a quotation from the Book of Maccabees. Jefferson at once adopted it as his own motto, and later in 1776 urged that it be used on the Great Seal of the newly proclaimed United States.

As time passed and the stresses of the Revolution relaxed, literature—as well as all aspects of life—took a more secular turn. But for many the Bible still pointed the way. Leon Spitz, with justifiable pride, if slight exaggeration, calls

Bryant the "first of America's great poets," and goes on to say that he "has shown the way to the Bible."[19]

William Cullen Bryant, born in 1794, was descended from the Pilgrim Fathers, and he took much from their spirit. His ideas were basic, simple, the common knowledge of all. In a deeper sense, however, he reverted to the past. "His metaphysics was predominantly that of the Old Testament: God is the Creator and His works and His purposes are good."[20] The Psalter had an enormous influence on this pioneer of American poetry, and traces can be found in almost all of his works. Its spirit, style, and language were part of the atmosphere of the New England in which Bryant was raised. Many of Bryant's hymns were based on Biblical phrases or language: *The Earth Is Full of Thy Riches; His Tender Mercies Are Over All His Works; How Amiable Are Thy Tabernacles;* and *Proclaim Liberty Throughout the Land.*

In his *Hymn to Death,* Bryant calls for tribute to death, otherwise "idolatry would still be rampant" and "he who bears false witness," as well as "he who spreads abroad polluted hands in mockery of prayer," could continue to live. The influence of the Psalms is, perhaps, best seen in *Thanatopsis,* the poem memorized by generations of school children:

> Thou shalt lie down
> With patriarchs of the infant world, with kings
> The powerful of the Earth, the wise, the good
> Fair forms and hoary seers of ages past
> All in one mighty sepulchre.
> All that breathe will share thy destiny.

The language is Biblical, and the phrases resound with the roll of the Hebrew Bible. In fact, this is almost a paraphrase of the 104th Psalm.

But Bryant's Biblical imagery was taken not only from Psalms. He ranged far and wide throughout the entire Bible and peopled the world of his poetic vision with the Scriptural figures of antiquity. Bryant's poem *A Lifetime* describes the following scene:

> And there the child is standing
> By a stately lady's knee
> And reading of ancient peoples
> And realms beyond the sea.
>
> Of the cruel king of Egypt
> Who made God's people slaves
> And perished with all his army
> Drowned in the Red Sea waves
>
> Of Deborah who mustered
> Her brothers long oppressed
> And routed the heathen army
> And gave her people rest.

Indeed Bryant was the true heir to his Puritan heritage, living and writing of "ancient peoples and realms beyond the sea."

Henry Wadsworth Longfellow continued the tradition of Bryant and of his predecessors. In Longfellow's poetry, the Hebraic ideals and Biblical imagery often coalesced to form an almost perfect blend of content and style. This is seen with particular vividness in the poignant poem, *The Slave Singing at Midnight:*

> Loud he sang the Psalm of David,
> He, a Negro and enslaved
> Sang of Israel's victory,
> Sang of Zion bright and free

Longfellow's great narrative poem, *The Courtship of Miles Standish,* gives further evidence of the influence of the Bible on his poetry. In it we see Captain Standish consult Caesar or the Scriptures to learn the strategy of "wars of the Hebrew." When Standish tells John Alden of his wish to marry, he says " 'Tis not good for man to be alone, say the Scriptures." And so it is with much of the rest of Longfellow's verse.

In the conflict over slavery that rent the Union for so long, the Bible was used by both sides to bolster their arguments. One of the foremost anti-slavery writers of the times was Harriet Beecher Stowe, whose interest in religious problems and social reforms was evident in all her works.[21] Theodore Weld, in 1837, published *The Bible Against Slavery,* in which he used Biblical texts to prove the evil of the South's "peculiar institution." This was answered by a host of articles and pamphlets written by slave-owners proving the validity of slavery with Scriptural texts. The climax to this battle was probably *Domestic Slavery Considered as a Scriptural Institution,* published in 1845, an exchange between Richard Fuller, a prominent clergyman from South Carolina, and Francis Wayland, then president of Brown University. Both men predicated their arguments on the Word of God as they felt it had been revealed in the Bible.

One of the most literate converts to the cause of abolition was John Greenleaf Whittier. Through all of Whittier's impassioned anti-slavery poetry burns the fierce light of Biblical inspiration. In the poem *Texas* he compares the Negro to Issachar, the son of Jacob, who bore the burdens of his brothers:

> What though Issachar be strong
> Ye may load his back with wrong
> Overmuch and overlong.

Whittier, however, did not confine his use of the Bible only to the burning issues of the age. The spirit of the Scriptures pervaded his works, and Leon Spitz maintains that "Whittier may justly be crowned the American Bible Poet."[22] His Puritan ancestry is clearly marked in much that he wrote, and though he abandoned the faith of his fathers for Quakerism, he took with him the stern New England regard for the word of the Bible. Whittier also had a strong and intense feeling for the Land of Israel. In the *Holy Land*, the poet bewails the fact that he had never seen that land, in the following words:

> Nor have I from thy hallowed tide,
> O Jordan, heard the low lament
> Like the sad veil along thy side,
> Which Israel's mournful prophet sent.
> Nor trilled within that grotto lone,
> Where deep in night the Bard of Kings,
> Felt Hands of Fire direct his own,
> And sweeps for God the conscious string.

The influence of the Bible was not restricted to poetry, but went far beyond its borders. Take away from Lincoln's Gettysburg Address the Biblically flavored words and phrases, and most of the solemn cadences and prophetic fervor would die out from what has come to be considered the "Battle Hymn of Consecration to the Republic." Numerous Biblical phrases and words from the Hebrew language have become an integral part of our daily speech and vernacular, so much so that often we are not fully cognizant of their origin when we use them.

"We simply cannot estimate the effect of the Biblical influence on English—in style, imagery, and narrative techniques, in moral and even political concepts," wrote Margaret Schlauch in "General Values of the Study of Hebrew." She went on to say:

> What, for instance, would have given so persuasive expression to the egalitarian ideas of Cromwell's followers if they had not been able to present them in a guise of a reversion to the simple, healthy ideals of the ancient agricultural commonwealth in Palestine? Even the idiom of characteristic Hebrew expressions, shining through the King James translation, has repeatedly affected English stylists. A recent example is Pearl Buck, who perhaps uncon-

sciously has recourse to Biblical style in trying to convey alien culture of quite a different kind, namely, the Chinese. Many speakers, pamphleteers, orators and allegorists have made use of the technique of balanced metaphor, so characteristic of the Hebrew poetic books like the Psalms, without being aware of its origin.[23]

This detailed enumeration of works and authors could easily be brought step by step down to the present. In sum, in the development of English and American literatures, the Bible in general, and its Hebraic elements in particular, have been a constant and potent force. In all stages of our development, in periods of peace and in times of strife, authors and poets have turned to the Scriptures for guidance and inspiration. Many of our ideas of government and morality, numerous phrases in our speech, and many of our daily customs and habits originated in the Bible. It was a book that loomed large in the life of the early New England settlers. It is still an active force today. There can be little doubt that it will continue to have a hand in shaping our civilization in the years yet to come.[24]

APPENDIX A

HEBREW WORDS AND PHRASES IN ENGLISH

Hebrew and the Scriptures have had an enormous impact on our everyday language and speech patterns, although we may not be fully aware of this. Since the Bible has found a distinct place in the corpus of English and American literature, this process was inevitable. A close examination of our speech finds numerous phrases of Biblical origin. The following examples amply illustrate this: "As a drop in the bucket" (Isa. 40:15); "a land flowing with milk and honey" (Exod. 3:8); "a still, small voice" (I Kings 19:12); "the way of all the earth" (Josh. 23:14); "the peoples arose as one man" (Judg. 20:8); "there is nothing new under the sun" (Eccles. 1:9); "a tale that is told" (Ps. 90:9); "darkness which may be felt" (Exod. 4:21); "vanity of vanities" (Eccles. 1:2); "the apple of his eye" (Deut. 32:10); "a man after his own heart" (I Sam. 13:14); "how are the mighty fallen" (II Sam. 1:25).

Whenever we use phrases such as "make a covenant with death" (Isa. 1:8) or "in the sweat of thy face" (Gen. 3:19), we are unconsciously voicing the thoughts of the ancient Hebrews in their very phraseology. When we speak of the "way of a man with a maid" (Prov. 30:18) or "weak as water" (Ezra 7:17), or in despair wonder whether indeed there is "balm in Gilead" (Jer. 8:22), we are deeply indebted to the Scriptures. Much of our popular wisdom comes from the same source, as for example: "put not your trust in princes" (Ps. 146:3); "Go to the ant, thou sluggard" (Prov. 6:6); "a living dog is better than a dead lion" (Eccles. 9:4); "can the Ethiopian change his skin or the leopard his spots?" (Jer. 13:23); "his hand will be against every man and every man's hand against him" (Gen. 26:12); "God will provide" (Gen. 22:8); "Let there be light" (Gen. 1:3); "flesh of my flesh" (Gen. 2:23); "Love thy neighbor as thyself" (Lev. 19:18); "man does not live by bread alone" (Deut. 8:3); "thou art the man" (II Sam. 12:7); "wine maketh glad the heart of man" (Ps. 104:15); "Wisdom is better than riches" (Jer. 8:11); "I have escaped with the skin of my teeth" (Job 19:20); "a man of knowledge increases strength" (Prov. 24:5); "am I my brother's keeper?" (Gen. 4:19).

About half of the verses in the Book of Psalms have virtually become English idioms. Almost all the phrases of the Books of Proverbs, Job, Song of Songs, Ecclesiastes, and others have been adapted for profaner use in daily life. For example: "a voice cries out in the wilderness"; "the four corners of the earth"; "armor of light"; "go forth in might"; "cultivate your vineyard"; "longer than the earth and broader than the sea"; "keep the fortress"; "make thy loins strong"; "chosen for an inheritance"; "ordained of God"; "gird thy loins"; "as one having authority"; "light rises in the darkness"; "as the stars of heaven"; "stand in awe"; "harbor of love"; "white with harvest"; "the angels are the reapers"; "the day is at hand"; "the day is far spent"; "heavy with sleep"; "slept with his fathers"; "mindful of the covenant"; "watch the way"; "moved with compassion"; "the stranger within thy gates"; "betray not the fugitive"; "great is the truth and mighty above all things"; "a word spoken in due season"; "the way of the wind"; "resting place"; "a righteous token"; "restore the pledge"; "convenient season"; "unprofitable servant"; "thorn in the flesh"; "the ransom of a man's life"; "the way of a fool"; "vain glory"; "wise in your own counsels"; "arrogance of the proud"; "tale-bearer"; "feigned lips"; "profane babblings"; "boast not of tomorrow"; "deal treacherously"; "as an oak whose leaf fadeth"; "a stubborn and rebellious generation"; "barren night"; "long suffering"; "as a dream of night"; "a certain Samaritan"; "the lost sheep"; "the tree of life"; "the treasure of immortality"; "clean hands"; "deep waters."

Finally, although almost every simile and metaphor uttered by the prophets found its way into the speech of most of America's great orators and writers, the speech of the common man was also affected. English has, of necessity, acquired many words from the original Hebrew, as it did from Greek, Latin, French, and other languages. The following is a list of Hebrew words that became a part of the English language, either directly from the Hebrew or indirectly through other tongues:

Abnet; abaddon; amen; agadah; asphalt; ass; ashkenazim; assidean; abbot; aloes; Aaron; Abel; Abiathar; Abigail; Abner; Abraham (Abe, Abie, Abram); Ada (Ade, Adaline); Adam; Adonis; Amos; Anna; Asaph; Asherah; Ashtoreth; Ayisch.

Baal; Baali; Babel; balsam; bath; bedelium; bedlam; beer; barracan; behemoth; bekah; belial; Ben-oni; Bethel; Bethlehem; Benjamin (Ben, Benny, Benjy); Beulah.

Cabal (Cabalah); Cab; camel; cane (canon, canyon, cannon); carmine (crimson); cask; cassia; chiton; chivun; cherub (cherubim); chutzpah; cider; cinnamon; cummin; corban; Cohen; cornet; cost; cotton; Caleb; Carmel; Canaan.

Davet; delta; date; dob; damask; Dan; Daniel; David (Dave, Davy); Deborah (Debby, Deb).

Earnest; ebony; elephant; embalm; emerald; ephod; Eli; Eliash; Elihu; El; Eliezer; Elijah; Eliphalet; Elisha; Eliza; Eden; Elizabeth (Liza, Lizzy, Bessy, Beth); Emanuel; Enoch; Esther; Eva (Eve, Eveline); Ezekiel; Ezra; Ethan; Europe.

Gauze; gerah; gonef; gun; Gehenna; Gemorah; Gideon; gopher; Gabriel; Gamliel; Gail.

Hasid; harass; hazani; hin; horn; hyssop; Halakhah; Hallelujah; Hanukkah; Hassidism; Hannah; Haman; Hephzibah; Hittite; Hesther; Hezekiah; Hosanna; Hosea; Huldah.

Ichabod; Ira; Isaac (Ike, Ikey); Isaiah; Ish; Israel.

Jew-fish; jockey; jot; jubilee; jug; Jabez; Jairus; Jehu; Jehovah; Jacob; Jack (Jacky); James (Jem, Jemmy, Jim, Jimmy); Jerusalem; Japheth; Jared; Jasper; Jemina; Jeremiah (Jeremy); Jeremiad; Jesse; Jezebel; Joab; Job; Joel; John (Joan, Joanna, Johnny, Johanna); Jonathan; Jordan;Joseph; Josephine; Johnny, Johanna); Jonathan; Jordan; Joseph; Josephine;

Kaddish; Kadosh; Kehillah; kosher; Katherine (Kathryn, Catherine, Kate, Kit, Kitty); Kezia (cassia).

Laudanum; leviathan; lot; Laban; Lo-ami; Lazarus; Leah; Leila; Lemuel; Lena; Levi; Libby; Lisa; Lilith.

Malta; manna; marionette; maudlin; megillah; metal; meribah; mezuzah; Mishna; Mishpaha; Mitzvah; moloch; myrrh; Magdaline; Malachi; Marsh; Manuel; Mary; Maud; Maun; May; Micah; Michael (Mike, Mickey); Mina; Miriam.

Naaman; nabi; nard; navy; nitre; Nabley; Nazarite; Nahum; Nancy (Nace); Naomi; Nathan; Nathaniel; Noah.

Omer; ophanim; opium; Obadiah.

Pilpul; pisgah; psaltery; psalmody; Psalm; Pharisee; paschal; Passover; Phineas.

Rabbi; race; racket; ruach; Reuel; Rachel; Rebecca (Becky); Reba; Reuben; Ruth.

Sack; sacket; satchel; sapphire; sash; scallion; salem; selah; Seder; shekel; shibboleth; shiggaieon; Shiloah; shittah; sheriff; shlemihl; simony; shadrach; sodomy; sow; sugar; sycamore; saba; sheva; Sheba; sabbatical; steer; Salome; Satan; Sephardim; Seraph (Seraphim); Seth; Shekhinah; Sheol; Samson; Samuel; Sarah; Saul; Simeon; Solomon; Sion; Sopha; Susannah; shamash.

Teraphius; terelahj; tiqua; Torah; tunic; turtur; tympanum (Tumbrel); Teraphim; Thummin; Thomas; Tobiah (Tobias, Toby); Tsaddik.

Uriah; Uriel; Urim; Uz.

Vermillion.

Wine.

Zachariah; Zach; Zachary; Zebine; Zion; Zane.

APPENDIX B

PLACE NAMES OF BIBLICAL OR HEBREW ORIGIN

Following is a list of cities, towns, and landmarks in the United States bearing Biblical or Hebrew names, and a map showing their approximate locations.

Alabama: Arab, Boaz, Dothan, Dora, Eden, Eva, Goshen, Hissop, Joppa, Jordan, Mt. Hebron, Mt. Olive, Pisgah, Rehoboth, Salem, Samson, Shiloh, Silas, Uriah.

Alaska: Bethel, Elim, Esther, Ophir.

Arizona: Asher, Ben Hur, Canaan, Damascus, Danville, Eden Isle, Elizabeth, Gamaliel, Goshen, Heth, Jericho, Jerusalem, Jordan, Mt. Judea, Mt. Levi, Mt.·Olive, Mt. Tabor, Nimrod, Palestine, Ruth, Salem, Sidon, Siloam Springs, Zion.

California: Antioch, Bethel Island, Carmel, Danville, Goshen, Havilah, Heber, Holy City, Isaiah, Joshua Tree, Mt. Eden, Mt. Hebron, Mt. Hermon, Olive, Ophir, Ruth, Susanville, Temple City.

Colorado: Bethune, Beulah, Elizabeth, Ophir, Ramah, Timnath.

Connecticut: Bethel, Bethlehem, Canaan, Gilead, Goshen, Hebron, Lebanon, Mt. Carmel, Sharon.

Delaware: Bethany Beach, Bethel, Rehoboth Beach.

Florida: El Jobean, Ebro, Mt. Carmel, Mt. Dora, Salem, Shiloh.

Georgia: Abba, Bethlehem, Damascus, Danville, Hephzibah, Hiram, Lebanon, Mt. Zion, Pisgah, Rebecca, Sharon, Shiloh.

Idaho: Eden, Joseph, Samaria, Samuels.

169

Illinois: Bethany, Carmi, Eden, Elizabeth, Hebron, Hermon, Herod, Jacob, Joppa, Lebanon, Mt. Carmel, Mt. Olive, Mt. Zion, Nebo, Olivet, Palestine, Salem, Zion.

Indiana: Bethlehem, Cana, Canaan, Carmel, Elizabeth, Goshen, Hanna, Hebron, Lebanon, Mariah Hill, Mt. Carmel, New Goshen, New Lebanon, New Palestine, New Salem, Nineveh, Salem, Samaria, South Bethany, Zionsville.

Iowa: Danbury, Danville, Ely, Estherville, Jericho, Jordan, Lebanon, Mt. Carmel, Mt. Zion, New Sharon, Pisgah, Salem.

Kansas: Asherville, Bethel, Beulah, Danville, Edna, Isabel, Lebanon, Olivet, Sabatha, Satana, Sharon, Sharon Springs, Solomon.

Kentucky: Aaron, Anna, Asa, Asher, Bethanna, Bethany, Bethel, Bethelridge, Bethlehem, Beulah Heights, Boaz, Danville, David, Eden, Edna, Elias, Elihu, Elizabethtown, Eve, Gamaliel, Goshen, Hanna, Hebron, Jacobs, Jephtha, Jeremiah, Jericho, Job, Lebanon, Lebanon Junction, Maribah, Mt. Carmel, Mt. Eden, Mt. Hermon, Mt. Olive, Mt. Pisgah, Mt. Salem, Naomi, Nazareth, Nebo, New Zion, Ruth, Salem, Sarah, Saul, Sharon Grove, Sinai, Zachariah, Zebulon.

Louisiana: Arabi, Bethany, Elizabeth, Esther, Gilead, Hanna, Mt. Hermon, Mt. Lebanon, Zachary, Zion City.

Maine: Bethel, Canaan, Carmel, East Lebanon, Gilead, Hebron, Hermon, Hiram, New Sharon, Sabbatus.

Maryland: Bethesda, Bethlehem, Damascus, Hebron, Joppa, Pisgah, Rehoboth, Salem.

Massachusetts: Goshen, Hebronville, Mt. Hermon, Padanaram Village, Rehoboth, Salem, Sharon.

Michigan: Beulah, East Jordan, Eben Junction, Eden, Nazareth, Olivet, Omer, Ruth, Salem, Samaria.

Minnesota: Bethel, Eden Prairie, Eden Valley, Edina, Elizabeth, Ely, Jordan, Mizpah, Nimrod.

Mississippi: Beulah, Canaan, Ebeneezer, Eden, Elizabeth, Goshen Springs, Mt. Olive, New Hebron, Olive Branch, Ruth, Sarah, Sharon, Sidon.

Missouri: Antioch, Arab, Asherville, Bethany, Bethel, Beulah, Canaan, Dora, Elijah, Esther, Gideon, Hannah, Hiram, Ishmael, Jericho Springs, Jordan, Lebanon, Mt. Moriah, Mt. Salem, Mt. Zion, Nebo, Olive, Salem, Zion.

Montana: Eden, Ismay, Jordan, Judith Gap, Mizpah, Nimrod.

Nebraska: Danbury, David City, Eli, Gilead, Hebron, Lebanon, Memphis, Salem, Tobias.

Nevada: Ely, Ruth.

New Hampshire: Bethlehem, Canaan, Danville, Goshen, Hebron, Salem.

New Jersey: Deborah, Elizabeth, Goshen, Jacobstown, Jericho, Jobstown,

Lebanon, Mizpah, Mt. Bethel, Mt. Ephraim, Nazareth, Salem, Shiloh, Tabor, Zarephath, Zion.

New Mexico: Dora, Jordan, Moses, Mt. Dora, Rehoboth, Salem.

New York: Babylon, Bethel, Canaan, Gabriels, Goshen, Ira, Jericho, Jordan, Lebanon Springs, Moriah, Mt. Carmel, Mt. Sinai, New Lebanon, Sabbath Day Point, Samsonville, Salem, Sharon, Sharon Springs.

North Carolina: Abner, Ararat, Bethabara, Bethania, Bethel, Bethesda, Bethlehem, Beulahville, Eden, Eleazar, Mt. Gilead, Mt. Olive, Mt. Tabor, Mt. Zion, Nazareth, Nebo, Pisgah Forest, Ruth, Salem, Salemburg, Samaria, Sharon, Shiloh, Siloam, Zebulon, Zionville.

North Dakota: Beulah, Hannah, Hebron, Jud, Mt. Carmel, New Salem, Sharon.

Ohio: Ada, Anna, Antioch, Bethany, Bethel, Bethesda, Damascus, Gahanna, Gomer, Goshen, Hebron, Hiram, Jerusalem, Kidron, Lebanon, Mt. Carmel, Mt. Ephraim, Mt. Gilead, Mt. Orab, Palestine, Pisgah, Salem, Sarahsville, Sharon, Shiloh, Zoar.

Oklahoma: Antioch, Asher, Bethany, Bethel, Eva, Harmon, Hanna, Lebanon, Pharoah.

Oregon: Beulah, Goshen, Jordan Valley, Joseph, Lebanon, Ophir, Salem.

Pennsylvania: Adah, Aleppo, Ararat, Bethel, Bethlehem, Beulah, Danboro, Danielsville, Danville, Ebensburg, Ebervale, Ephrata, Galilee, Goshen, Jacobs Creek, Jacobus, Jordan, Nazareth, New Salem, Nineveh, Sharon, Sharon Hill, South Canaan, Zion Grove, Zionhill, Zionsville.

Rhode Island: Galilee, Pt. Judith.

South Carolina: Arial, Bethera, Bethune, Hannah, Jericho, Mt. Carmel, New Zion, Salem, Sharon.

South Dakota: Agar, Bethlehem, Eden, Lebanon, Olivet, Salem, Sinai, Tabor.

Tennessee: Antioch, Beersheba Springs, Bethel, Bethpage, Eva, Lebanon, Memphis, Mt. Carmel, Sharon, Shiloh.

Texas: Abram, Anna, Asherton, Eden, Edna, Goliad, Hebronville, Jericho, Jonah, Joshua, Nazareth, Palestine, Zephyr.

Utah: Abraham, Eden, Enoch, Ephraim, Goshen, Hanna, Jordan, Joseph, Moab, Mt. Carmel, Orem, Salem, Zion National Park.

Vermont: Bethel, Canaan, Danville, Eden, Ely, Jericho, Sharon.

Virginia: Ammon, Ararat, Ark, Beulahville, Ben Hur, Cana, Damascus, Danville, David, Edom, Goshen, Hebron, Lebanon, Meadows of Dan, Mt. Hermon, Mt. Olive, Nimrod Hall, Rehoboth, Salem, Susan.

Washington: Ariel, Ephrata, Moses Lake, Sara, Selah, Zillah.

West Virginia: Abraham, Amma, Annamoriah, Bethany, Bethlehem, Big Isaac, Canaan, Danville, Daniels, David, Dothan, Elizabeth, Harman, Hebron, Hepzibah, Job, Jordan, Mathias, Mt. Nebo, Mt. Zion, Naoma, Nebo, Palestine, Pisgah, Rachel, Salem, Saulsville, Seth, Sharon.

Wisconsin: Boaz, Eden, Ephraim, Lake Beulah, Lake Galilee, Lebanon, Mt. Horeb, Salem, Sharon.

Wyoming: Beulah, Daniel, Eden, Hanna.

APPENDIX C

Illustrations

חמשה חומשי תורה

אשר נדפסו על ידי רוברטוס סטפינוס יע בשנת תקצ ועשרים למלך הקדיר
אדנינו המלך מדנקישקמא ילח קית צנת צב לפק מח טאריש
תעיר תנדולה וקאס בערשת

Quinque libri legis.

Genefis. Exodus. Leuiticus. Numeri.
Deuteronomium.

P A R I S I I S.
Ex officina Roberti Stephani, typographi Regii.
M. D. XLIII.

עָשׂוּ   עִמּוֹ

Title page of an early Hebrew Bible, printed in France, in 1593,
which was brought to this country and studied by many of the
first colonists.

THE FUNDAMENTAL AGREEMENT, OR ORIGINAL CONSTITUTION OF THE COLONY OF NEW-HAVEN, JUNE 4th, 1639.

The 4th day of the 4th month, called June, 1639, all the free planters affembled together in a general meeting, to confult about fettling civil government, according to God, and the nomination of perfons that might be found, by confent of all, fitteft in all refpects for the foundation work of a church, which was intended to be gathered in Quinipiack. After folemn invocation of the name of God, in prayer for the prefence and help of his fpirit and grace, in thofe weighty bufineffes, they were reminded of the bufinefs whereabout they met, (viz.) for the eftablifhment of fuch civil order as might be moft pleafing unto God, and for the choofing the fitteft men for the foundation work of a church to be gathered. For the better enabling them to difcern the mind of God, and to agree accordingly concerning the eftablifhment of civil order, Mr. John Davenport propounded divers queries to them publicly, praying them to confider ferioufly in the prefence and fear of God, the weight of the bufinefs they met about, and not to be rafh or flight in giving their votes to things they underftood not; but to digeft fully and thoroughly what fhould be propounded to them, and without refpect to men, as they fhould be fatisfied and perfuaded in their own minds, to give their anfwers in fuch fort as they would be willing fhould ftand upon record for pofterity.

This being earneftly preffed by Mr. Davenport, Mr. Robert Newman was intreated to write, in characters, and to read diftinctly and audibly in the hearing of all the people, what was propounded and accorded on, that it might appear, that all confented to matters propounded, according to words written by him.

The "Fundamental Orders of Connecticut," adopted under the leadership of John Davenport, whose six queries form the basis of the above document, was the first known written constitution in history. It was ratified by the inhabitants of the colony, as indicated, on June 4, 1639. (From *Old South Leaflets*, vol. I, no. 8.)

Query I. WHETHER the fcriptures do hold forth a perfect rule for the direction and government of all men in all duties which they are to perform to GOD and men, as well in families and commonwealth, as in matters of the church? This was affented unto by all, no man diffenting, as was expreffed by holding up of hands. Afterwards it was read over to them, that they might fee in what words their vote was expreffed. They again expreffed their confent by holding up their hands, no man diffenting.

Query II. WHEREAS there was a covenant folemnly made by the whole affembly of free planters of this plantation, the firft day of extraordinary humiliation, which we had after we came together, that as in matters that concern the gathering and ordering of a church, fo likewife in all public officers which concern civil order, as choice of magiftrates and officers, making and repealing laws, dividing allotments of inheritance, and all things of like nature, we would all of us be ordered by thofe rules which the fcripture holds forth to us ; this covenant was called a plantation covenant, to diftinguifh it from a church covenant, which could not at that time be made, a church not being then gathered, but was deferred till a church might be gathered, according to GOD : It was demanded whether all the free planters do hold themfelves bound by that covenant, in all bufineffes of that nature which are expreffed in the covenant, to fubmit themfelves to be ordered by the rules held forth in the fcripture ?

THIS alfo was affented unto by all, and no man gainfayed it ; and they did teftify the fame by holding up their hands, both when it was firft propounded, and confirmed the fame by holding up their hands when it was read unto them in public. John Clark being abfent, when the covenant was made, doth now manifeft his confent to it. Alfo Richard Beach, Andrew Law, Goodman Banifter, Arthur Halbridge, John Potter, Robert Hill, John Brocket, and John Johnfon, thefe perfons, being not admitted planters when the covenant was made, do now exprefs their confent to it.

Query III. THOSE who have defired to be received as free planters, and are fettled in the plantation, with a purpofe, refolution and defire, that they may be admitted into church fellowfhip, according to CHRIST, as foon as GOD fhall fit them

These early colonists were concerned with establishing a civil government and choosing a church leadership. They sought a permanent limitation on government power, and were thus the first to embody the democratic idea. In their deliberations, they looked to the Hebrew Scriptures for their guidance.

thereunto, were defired to exprefs it by holding up hands. According all did exprefs this to be their defire and purpofe by holding up their hands twice (viz.) at the propofal of it, and after when thefe written words were read unto them.

Query IV. ALL the free planters were called upon to exprefs, whether they held themfelves bound to eftablifh fuch civil order as might beft conduce to the fecuring of the purity and peace of the ordinance to themfelves and their pofterity according to GOD ? In anfwer hereunto they expreffed by holding up their hands twice as before, that they held them-felves bound to eftablifh fuch civil order as might beft conduce to the ends aforefaid.

THEN Mr. Davenport declared unto them, by the fcripture, what kind of perfons might beft be trufted with matters of government; and by fundry arguments from fcripture proved that fuch men as were defcribed in Exod. xviii. 2, Deut. 1. 13, with Deut. xvii. 15, and 1 Cor. vi. 1, 6, 7, ought to be intrufted by them, feeing they were free to caft themfelves into that mould and form of commonwealth which appeared beft for them in reference to the fecuring the peace and peaceable improvement of all CHRIST his ordinances in the church accord-ing to GOD, whereunto they have bound themfelves, as hath been acknowledged.

HAVING thus faid he fat down praying the company freely to confider, whether they would have it voted at this time or not. After fome fpace of filence, Mr. Theophilus Eaton anfwered, it might be voted, and fome others alfo fpake to the fame purpofe, none at all oppofing it. Then it was propounded to vote.

Query V. WHETHER free burgeffes fhall be chofen out of the church members, they that are in the foundation work of the church being actually free burgeffes, and to choofe to themfelves out of the like eftate of church fellowfhip, and the power of choofing magiftrates and officers from among them-felves, and the power of making and repealing laws, according to the word, and the dividing of inheritances, and deciding of differences that may arife, and all the bufineffes of like nature are to be tranfacted by thofe free burgeffes ? This was put to vote and agreed unto by lifting up of hands twice, as in the former it was done. Then one man ftood up and expreffed his diffenting from the reft in part; yet granting, 1. That magif-trates fhould be men fearing GOD. 2. That the church is the company where, ordinarily, fuch men may be expected. 3. That they that choofe them ought to be men fearing GOD ; only

---

In Query IV, Davenport turns to the Hebrew Bible to guide them in determining the type of leaders that shall be chosen.

at this he ftuck, that free planters ought not to give this power out of their hands. Another ftood up and anfwered, that nothing was done, but with their confent. The former anfwered, that all the free planters ought to refume this power into their own hands again, if things were not orderly carried. Mr. Theophilus Eaton anfwered, that in all places they choofe committees in like manner. The companies in London choofe the liveries by whom the public magiftrates are chofen. In this the reft are not wronged, becaufe they expect, in time, to be of the livery themfelves, and to have the fame power. Some others intreated the former to give his arguments and reafons whereupon he diffented. He refufed to do it, and faid, they might not rationally demand it, feeing he let the vote pafs on freely and did not fpeak till after it was paft, becaufe he would not hinder what they agreed upon. Then Mr. Davenport, after a fhort relation of fome former paffages between them two about this queftion, prayed the company that nothing might be concluded by them on this weighty queftion, but what themfelves were perfuaded to be agreeing with the mind of GOD, and they had heard what had been faid fince the voting; he intreated them again to confider of it, and put it again to vote as before. Again all of them, by holding up their hands, did fhow their confent as before. And fome of them confeffed that, whereas they did waver before they came to the affembly, they were now fully convinced, that it is the mind of GOD. One of them faid that in the morning before he came reading Deut. xvii. 15, he was convinced at home. Another faid, that he came doubting to the affembly, but he bleffed GOD, by what had been faid, he was now fully fatisfied, that the choice of burgeffes out of church members, and to intruft thofe with the power before fpoken of is according to the mind of GOD revealed in the fcriptures. All having fpoken their apprehenfions it was agreed upon, and Mr. Robert Newman was defired to write it as an order whereunto every one, that hereafter fhould be admitted here as planters, fhould fubmit, and teftify the fame by fubfcribing their names to the order: Namely, that church members only fhall be free burgeffes, and that they

In this debate concerning the indirect or direct election of government officials, in Query V, these founders turned quite frequently to the Bible. The Deuteronomy 17:15 referred to is the famous, "You shall be free to set a king over yourself, one chosen by the Lord your God. Be sure to set as king over yourself one of your own people; you must not set a foreigner over you, one who is not your kinsman."

only fhall choofe magiftrates and officers among themfelves, to have power of tranfacting all the public civil affairs of this plantation ; of making and repealing laws, dividing of inheritances, deciding of differences that may arife, and doing all things and bufineffes of like nature.

This being thus fettled, as a fundamental agreement concerning civil government, Mr. Davenport proceeded to propound fomething to confideration about the gathering of a church, and to prevent the blemifhing of the firft beginnings of the church work, Mr. Davenport advifed, that the names of fuch as were to be admitted might be publicly propounded, to the end that they who were moft approved might be chofen ; for the town being caft into feveral private meetings, wherein they that lived neareft together gave their accounts one to another of God's gracious work upon them, and prayed together and conferred to their mutual edification, fundry of them had knowledge one of another ; and in every meeting fome one was more approved of all than any other ; for this reafon and to prevent fcandals, the whole company was intreated to confider whom they found fitteft to nominate for this work.

Query VI. WHETHER are you all willing and do agree in this, that twelve men be chofen, that their fitnefs for the foundation work may be tried ; however there may be more named yet it may be in their power who are chofen to reduce them to twelve, and that it be in the power of thofe twelve to choofe out of themfelves feven, that fhall be moft approved of by the major part, to begin the church?

THIS was agreed upon by confent of all, as was expreffed by holding up of hands, and that fo many as fhould be thought fit for the foundation work of the church, fhall be propounded by the plantation, and written down and pafs without exception, unlefs they had given public fcandal or offence. Yet fo as in cafe of public fcandal or offence, every one fhould have liberty to propound their exception, at that time, publicly againft any man, that fhould be nominated, when all their names fhould be writ down. But if the offence were private, that mens names might be tendered, fo many as were offended were intreated to deal with the offender privately, and if he gave not fatisfaction to bring the matter to the twelve, that they might confider of it impartially and in the fear of God.

BY THE COVRT,

In the Years 1.641. 1642.

Capitall Lawes, Eſtabliſhed within the Iuriſdiction of *Maſſachuſets*.

1. IF any man after legall conviction, ſhall have or worſhip any other God, but
the Lord God, he ſhall be put to death. *Deut.* 13. 6, &c. and 17. 2. &c.
Exodus 22. 20.

2. IF any man or woman be a Witch, that is, hath or conſulteth with a familiar ſpi-
rit, they ſhall be put to death. *Exod.* 22. 18. *Lev.* 20. 27. *Deut.* 18. 10, 11.

3. IF any perſon ſhall blaſpheme the Name of God the Father, Sonne, or Holy
Ghoſt, with direct, expreſſe, preſumptuous, or high-handed blaſphemy, or ſhall
curſe God in the like manner, he ſhall be put to death. *Lev.* 24. 15, 16.

4. IF any perſon ſhall commit any wilfull murther, which is manſlaughter, committed upon premeditate malice, hatred, or cruelty, not in a mans neceſſary and juſt
defence, nor by meer caſualtie, againſt his will ; he ſhall be put to death. *Exod.* 21.
12, 13, 14. *Num.* 35. 30, 31.

5. IF any perſon ſlayeth another ſuddenly in his anger, or cruelty of paſſion, he ſhall
be put to death. *Num.* 35. 20, 21. *Lev.* 24. 17.

6. IF any perſon ſhall ſlay another through guile, either by poyſonings, or other
ſuch diviliſh practice ; he ſhall be put to death. *Exod.* 21. 14.

7. IF a man or woman ſhall lye with any beaſt, or bruit creature, by carnall copulation, they ſhall ſurely be put to death ; and the beaſt ſhall be ſlaine, and buried.
Lev. 20. 15, 16.

8. IF a man lyeth with mankinde, as he lyeth with a woman, both of them have
committed abomination, they both ſhall ſurely be put to death. *Lev.* 20. 13.

9. IF any perſon committeth adultery with a married, or eſpouſed wife, the Adulterer, and the Adultereſſe, ſhall ſurely be put to death. *Lev.* 20. 10. and 18.
20. *Deut.* 22. 23, 24.

10. IF any man ſhall unlawfully have carnall copulation with any woman-childe
under ten yeares old, either with, or without her conſent, he ſhall be put to
death.

11. IF any man ſhall forcibly, and without conſent, raviſh any maid or woman that is
lawfully married or contracted, he ſhall be put to death. *Deut.* 22. 25. &c.

12. IF any man ſhall raviſh any maid or ſingle woman (committing carnall copulation with her by force, againſt her will) that is above the age of ten yeares ;
he ſhall be either puniſhed with death, or with ſome other grievous puniſhment, according to circumſtances, at the diſcretion of the Judges : and this Law to continue
till the Court take further order.

13. IF any man ſtealeth a man, or man-kinde, he ſhall ſurely be put to death.
Exod. 21. 16.

14. IF any man riſe up by falſe witneſſe wittingly, and of purpoſe to take away any
mans life, he ſhall be put to death. *Deut.* 19. 16. 18, 19.

15. IF any man ſhall conſpire, or attempt any invaſion, inſurrection, or publick rebellion againſt our Common-wealth, or ſhall indeavour to ſurprize any Towne
or Townes, Fort or Forts therein : or ſhall treacherouſly, or perfidiouſly attempt
the alteration and ſubverſion of our frame of pollity, or government fundamentally,
he ſhall be put to death: *Num.* 16. 2 *Sam.* 3. & 18. & 20.

Per exemplar Increaſe, Nowel, Secret.

Printed firſt in *New-England*, and re-printed in *London*
for *Ben. Allen* in *Popes-head Allen.* 1 6 4 3-

An early sample of colonial legislation, the
capital laws of Massachusetts, listing fifteen
capital offenses, thirteen of which are followed
by biblical citations. The colony of Connecticut
passed similar capital legislation.

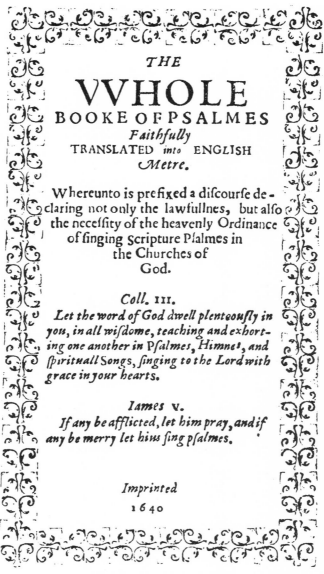

THE

VVHOLE

BOOKE OF PSALMES
Faithfully
TRANSLATED *into* ENGLISH
Metre.

Whereunto is prefixed a difcourfe de -
claring not only the lawfullnes, but alfo
the neceffity of the heavenly Ordinance
of finging Scripture Pfalmes in
the Churches of
God.

Coll. III.
*Let the word of God dwell plenteoufly in
you, in all wifdome, teaching and exhort-
ing one another in Pfalmes, Himnes, and
fpirituall Songs, finging to the Lord with
grace in your hearts.*

Iames V.
*If any be afflicted, let him pray, and if
any be merry let him fing pfalmes.*

Imprinted
1 6 40

The very first book published in the American Colonies was an English translation of the Hebrew Psalms, the famous *Bay Psalm Book*, printed by Stephen Daye in the Massachusetts Bay Colony, which contained a number of Hebrew words and letters.

members, but the whole Church is commaund-
ed to teach one another in all the severall sorts
of Davids psalmes, some being called by himselfe
מִזְמוֹרִים : psalms, some תְּהִלִּים : Hymns
some שִׁירִים : spirituall songs. soe that if the
singing Davids psalmes be a morall duty & ther-
fore perpetuall; then wee under the new Testamēt
are bound to sing them as well as they under the
old: and if wee are expresly commanded to sing
Psalmes, Hymnes, and spirituall songs, then either
wee must sing Davids psalmes, or else may affirm
they are not spirituall songs: which being penned
by an extraordiary gift of the Spirit, for the sake
especially of Gods spirtuall Israell; not to be
read and preached only (as other parts of holy
writ) but to be sung also, they are therefore most
spirituall, and still to be sung of all the Israell of
God: and verily as their sin is exceeding great,
who will allow Davids psalmes (as other scriptures) to be read in churches (which is one end)
but not to be preached also,(which is another end
soe their sin is crying before God, who will allow them to be read and preached, but seeke to
deprive the Lord of the glory of the third end of
them, which is to sing them in christian churches.
obj. 1 If it be sayd that the Saints in the primitive Church did compile spirituall songs of their
owne inditing, and sing them before the Church.
1Cor. 14, 15, 16.
Ans. We answer first, that those Saints compiled
these spirituall songs by the extraordinary gifts of

* 3   the

Rev. Richard Mather's preface to the Psalms
contains the first few Hebrew words to appear in
North America in print. Since there was no
Hebrew type available in the colonies, the
printer himself carved these few words in wood,
therefore their large size.

28 Thou art my God, & I'le thee prayſe,
my God I'le ſet thee hye.

29 O prayſe the Lord, for he is good,
and aye laſts his mercy.

Pſalme 119.

א (1) Aleph

ALL-bleſt are men upright of way:
walk in Iehovahs law who do.

2 Bleſt ſuch as doe his records keepe:
with their whole heart him ſeek alſo.

3 And that work no iniquitie:
but in his wayes doe walke *indeed.*

4 Thou haſt giv'n charge, with diligence
unto thy precepts to give heed.

5 Ah that to keepe thy ſtatutes: *ſo*
my wayes addreſſed were by thee.

6 When I reſpect thy precepts all,
then ſhall I not aſhamed bee.

7 Whē I thy righteous judgements learne
with hearts uprightnes I'le thee prayſe.

8 Forſake thou mee not utterly:
I will obſerve thy ſtatute-wayes.

ב (2) Beth

9 By what may ' young man cleanſe his way?
by heeding it as thy word guides.

10 With my whole heart thee have I ſought:
thy lawes let mee not goe beſides.

11 I in my heart thy word have hid:
that I might not againſt thee ſin.

12 Thou o Iehovah, bleſſed art:
thine owne ſtatutes inſtruct mee in.

Psalm 119, which contains in the original He- 13 All
brew successive groups of eight verses beginning with each letter of the Hebrew alphabet,
was translated so that the first of the eight
followed the English alphabet. Also, in this
chapter, each section is preceded by the appropriate Hebrew letter as shown above.

The Hebrew Exercises
of
Governor William Bradford

by
ISIDORE S. MEYER
Editor Emeritus
American Jewish Historical Society

PILGRIM SOCIETY
1973
Plymouth, Massachusetts

William Bradford (1590–1657), second governor
of Plymouth colony, studied Hebrew late in his
life. In his history, *Of Plimouth Plantation*, he
includes the folios of a number of Hebrew pages.
Above is the title page from a recent reprint of
his *Exercises*.

185

Bradford provides on this page phrases and translations from the earlier and later prophets as well as from the Pentateuch. These pages were written in 1650 and 1652.

186

On this page Bradford wrote out some longer sentence fragments from Isaiah, Samuel, and Deuteronomy. He and others of his time frequently made numerous analogies between themselves and the ancient Israelites.

ARTE
HEBRAISPANO.

דִּקְדוּק לְשׁוֹן הַקֹּדֶשׁ בִּלְשׁוֹן סְפַרַדִּיתֿ

Dikduk leschon hakkodhefch bilfchon fipharadhith.

GRAMMATICA
DE LA LENGUA SANTA
EN IDIOMA CASTELLANO:

Por el R. P. F. MARTIN DEL CASTILLO, naturál de Búrgos : del Orden de N. P. S. Francifco, Lector Jubilado en Sánta Theología ; y Provinciál que à fido , en la Província del S. Evangélio de México.

Dedicafe a N. Rmo. P. F. IUAN LUENGO *, Lector Iubilado , Pádre de toda la Orden de N. P. S. Francifco, y Comiffário Generál de todas las Indias;*

Con todo lo neceffario y precifo , pára por fi fólo , quaiquiér afficionádo , podér leér , efcribir , entendér, y hablár la léngua fanta Hebréa.

&c.

EN LEON DE FRANCIA.
A Cofta de FLORIAN ANISSON, Mercader de Libros en Madrid.

M. DC. LXXVI.
Con Aprobacion y Licencia.

Title page of the first Hebrew book written in the New World. The author of this first grammar was a guardian of the Franciscan Convent in Mexico, New Spain. The various licenses in the book are given by authorities, signed and dated in Mexico, 1663. The manuscript was approved in 1656, but not printed till 1676, there being no printer in the Western Hemisphere who had available Hebrew type. The book was printed therefore in Lyons, France.

דִּקְדּוּק לְשׁוֹן הַקֹּדֶשׁ

Dickdook Lafhon Auk.defh

Grammar of the Holy Language the
Abilities. and I hope,

P R O P O S A L S

for Printing by SUBSCRIPTION,

A

Hebrew Grammar,

Being an ESSAY to bring the *Hebrew Grammar* into *Englifh*, with a Defign to facilitate the Inftruction of all thofe that are defirous to obtain a clear Idea of the primitive Language by their own Study, in order to their more diftinct Acquaintance with the Sacred Oracles of the *Old Teftament*, according to the Original. Whereto is annexed the *Lord's Prayer* and the *Apoftle's Creed*, Tranflated into H E B R E W, and an Alphabetical Catalogue of the Nouns & Verbs that confift of more than three *Radicals*, for finding the Roots of which, there is no Rule in any Grammar. Drawn for the fake of thofe that are willing to have a farther Knowledge in this ancient Language. A Work altogether New. Collected from the B I B L E with Care & Diligence. All

By

יְהוּדָה מוֹנִיש

J U D A H M O N I S, *M. A*

Teacher of the **Hebrew Tongue** at *Harvard College* in *Cambridge*, New-England.

THE Grammar will be confiderably larger than *Schickard's* ; with the Conjugations, Schemes of Tenfes & Moods of all denominations, and Quotations at large ; and will be Printed on the fame Paper with thefe Propofals, or thereabouts It will be afforded to Subfcribers (Bound) for *Eight Shillings per* Book, and they that Subfcribe for Six Books fhall have a Seventh *Gratis*.

N. B. IF a fufficient Number of Subfcribers appear, the Work will be forwarded with all convenient Expedition, the *Hebrew Types* being already arrived from *Great Britain*. A Specimen may be feen above.

Subfcriptions are taken in by faid *Monis* at his Houfe in *Cambridge*, and *Daniel Henchman* Bookfeller in *Bofton*.

Above is the prospectus Judah Monis published as a broadside in 1734 to solicit advance subscriptions to his *Grammar*. Note that he changed the title. Note also the inclusion of the Lord's Prayer and the Apostles' Creed.

189

דִּקְדּוּק

לְשׁוֹן עִבְרִית.

DICKDOOK LESHON GNEBREET.

A

G R A M M A R

OF THE

Hebrew Tongue,

BEING

An E S S A Y

To bring the Hebrew Grammar into. English,

to Facilitate the

I N S T R U C T I O N

Of all thofe who are defirous of acquiring a clear Idea of this

Primitive Tongue

by their own Studies ;

In order to their more diftinct Acquaintance with the SACRED ORACLES of the Old Teftament, according to the Original. And

Publifhed more efpecially for the Ufe of the STUDENTS of *HARVARD-COLLEGE* at *Cambridge*, in NEW-ENGLAND.

נֶחְבַּר וְהוּבַת בְּעִיּוּן נִמְרָץ עַל יְדֵי

יְהוּדָה מוֹנִשׁ

Compofed and accurately Corrected,

By J U D A H M O N I S, M. A.

B O S T O N, N. E.

Printed by JONAS GREEN, and are to be Sold by the AUTHOR at his Houfe in *Cambridge.* MDCCXXXV.

Title page of the Hebrew text by Monis, Harvard's first Hebrew Instructor, published in 1735. The transliterated title is given as *Dickdook Leshon Gneebreet*, the *Gn* illustrating the Sephardic pronunciation of the *ayin*.

190

PREFACE

SINCE through the good Hand of GOD upon me, he has not only taken Moses's Vail from me, but even has Placed me in his Service, i. e. to Teach and Promote the Knowledge of the Hebrew Tongue at HARVARD COLLEGE, in NEW-ENGLAND, especially for the advantage of those that will Dedicate themselves to the Service of the Sanctuary; and considering, that thro' the great & manifold Faults & Errors (at least of the Press) that are found in ALL the Hebrew Grammars extant, besides the shortness of them, my Expected Work could not be attained without farther Reformation; I thought therefore to facilitate said Instructions, it was necessary to Compose One more full and correct; But for want of Hebrew Types in these remote parts of the World, it could not be Accomplished till now: For altho' that Pious and Great Benefactor, Mr. THOMAS HOLLIS, Merchant of LONDON (among others of his great Donations to our COLLEGE, sent a Set of Hebrew Types to carry on said Work, yet that Set unhappily proving Imperfect, it could not go forward till the Reverend Corporation (who are true Lovers of Learning) sent for more Hebrew Types to Compleat such a good and desirable Design.

NOW the Rules herein contained, I think (with submission to the Learned) are the Best, Clearest, and most Necessary ones, to qualify any (tho' of mean Capacity) to understand the Word of GOD according to the Original, in a very short time, without being obliged to consult sundry Grammars, as many have said they have been forced to do.

I have likewise endeavoured, that the Examples should be the most Familiar, that so the Learner whilst he learns the Rules, might be acquainted with the Tongue by degrees.

I have in the first Chapter throughout, and in sundry other Places, turned the Pronunciation of the Hebrew Words in English Letters, as near as the difference of the Tongues would permit, with a design to lead (as it were) young Beginners into the way of Pronouncing this Tongue by their own Industry: I am very sensible that the way of my pronouncing it, will seem to be somewhat new; yet, I am prone to think, it is the Right and Genuine way, for, besides that all the Jewish Nation in all their Dispersions, do pronounce it as I do (which to me is not of small weight) I found in all my Travels, all the Learned in this Tongue that I conversed with, among the Europeans (English excepted) do pronounce it the same way also; and why the English differ from the rest, proceeds only (as I take it) from the various ways they have of pronouncing the Vowels, in which the other Nations are more conformed one to another, as it is well known to all observing Travellers and Linguists; and therefore in Conformity to the English Pronunciation ONLY, I have Spelt the Words in English Characters as I have done.

IN the Schemes you'll find the Verbs generally marked with this Mark ‾ under the Syllable which is to be Accented, to initiate the Learners in the way of Accenting the Hebrew Words where they should be.

AT the End I present you a Translation of the LORD's Prayer, and the Apostle's Creed, according (as I think) to the true Idiom of this Primitive Language.

I acknowledge my self chiefly beholden to the famous R. D. K. R. Arkivolty, and R. Templo, for the Rules herein explained.

A Significant, and a Plain Nomenclature, and the Short and Large Catechisms, in Hebrew and English, with some other Works that I have Prepared for the Use and Benefit of young Beginners, I propose to Publish as soon as Providence will permit.

THE whole of this ESSAY (such as it is) I offer to your candid Acceptance, hoping you'll overlook the defects in the English Phrase, and any other lesser Errors; and if you reap any Benefit by it, give the Glory to GOD, and Pray for the Prosperity of HARVARD-COLLEGE, and by so doing, you'll Oblige,

Yours &c.

Cambridge, Mar. 6. 1734, 5.

Judah Monis.

Though there had been works published earlier in the colonies containing Hebrew letters or a few Hebrew words, this was the first to contain lengthy Hebrew passages. In this preface, Monis describes how he arranged for the first set of Hebrew type fonts to be sent by ship from England specially for this book.

191

דִּקְדּוּק לְשׁוֹן עִבְרִית

Gnebreet Leſhon Dickdook.

A *Grammar* of the *Hebrew Tongue*.

CHAP. I.

Contains the Shape of all the Conſonants and Vowels, with their names and numeral Import, and what Engliſh Letters anſwer to them, and other things relating thereto.

Shape	Name	Anſwers to		Import	Shape	Name	Anſwers to	Impor
א	Auleph	A	1 or 1000		מ	Mem F	M	600
ב	Beth	B		2	נ	Noon	N	50
ג	Gimmell	G		3	ן	Noon F	N	700
ד	Dauleth	D		4	ס	Sſaumech	SS	60
ה	Ha	A or H		5	ע	Gnauine or Ng.	Gn or Ng	70
ו	Vaugh	V or W		6	פ	Pa	P or Ph	80
ז	Zauine	Z		7	ף	Pa F	Ph	800
ח	Heth	X or Ch		8	צ	Tſadde	Tſ	90
ט	Teth	T		9	ץ	Tſadde F	Tſ	900
י	Yode	Y or J		10	ק	Kuph	K	100
כ	Caugh	C or Q		20	ר	Reſh	R	200
ך	Caugh F	Ch		500	ש	Shin or Sin	Sh or S	300
ל	Laummedd	L		30	ת	Taugh or Tt.	T or Tt.	400
מ	Mem	M		40				

B

Alphabetical table from the opening pages of Monis's *Grammar*.

LANCASTER, October 15, 1763.

As the gentleman who teaches the grammar-school in this county has concluded to discontinue that employment next CHRISTMAS, I take this method of giving timely notice to the gentlemen who have their children or wards under his tuition, and to others who may be disposed to have their youth instructed in all, or in any one of the branches of education specified, that I design to continue it, at the same place, from the first of the new year.

The LATIN and GREEK languages, and HEBREW (if required) will be taught, agreeable to the most approved modern methods.

Instructions upon ENGLISH grammar will be given, in leisure hours, to the LATINISTS; which they will soon apprehend to be a pleasant, and very advantageous, amusement.

The rudiments of GEOMETRY AND SURVEYING, PLAIN TRIGO-NOMETRY, LOGICK, ONTOLOGY, ETHICKS, RHETORICK, GEO-GRAPHY, and the USE of the GLOBES, will be taught at reasonable prices.

I hope to introduce with success DECLAMATIONS and select pieces of dramatick compositions, for the improvement of my pupils in PRONUNCIATION, ACCENT, EMPHASIS, and GESTURE.

I expect a well qualified assistant from PENNSYLVANIA; and gentlemen may depend on having their children tutored with great care, and much I hope to their satisfaction, as my scholars shall be carefully proportioned to the number of their instructors.

And I can assure them that they need not fear the discontinuance of my school, which I am persuaded must not a little contribute to their encouragement.

JAMES WADDEL.

From Virginia Gazette, edited by Royle, Nov. 4, 1763, page 4, col. 1

Newspaper advertisement by a colonial teacher showing Hebrew as part of the standard educational offerings of the time.

193

עזרא שטילס לנופורט רהאד-אי לאעלאנד החלֶה לאמריכא
על החכם הרב ר'. חיים יצחק קאריגאל שבא מרחוק מירושלם
והמכפלה לחברון בארץ אשר עֵני יהוה בה : ברוך אתה לאל עליון
ולמשיח שהחֵי הֹוה צדקנו וגאל לנצירי ישראל אור גֹוים ןישֹועת
כל עֵמים לקצה הארץ : תמלֵא : ברוח הקדש ןשֵׁפֵע האור עולם
תכבֵדֵי בחכמה ובתבונה : עלֵין ועל עמֵן יעלה במהרה דרור וכבוד
עד מלאות כל נפלאות מֵדבר הבאות על עֵור ועם קדש
באחרית הֵמֵים וֵנֵמֵלכות הֵשֵר שלום : יראו עֵיניכם מֵלך צֵין
בֵתֵפֵארתן : אמֵן .

ראשֵנֵים הֵנֵוצֵרים שהֵון יהֵדֵים והם כהֵנֵים וחכמֵים יֹודעֵי בֵנֵה
וֵסֵרֵי רבֵותֵיכם יֵתֵנֵו דעת הֵזֵה לאנשֵים קֵדֵשֵים אחרֵיהם וֵמֵם
לֵאֵחֵרֵים אבותֵינו אֹוסֵבֵי וֵרֹום שחֵין שנה מֵאתֵים אחרֵי שֵמֵנֵת
העֵיר וֵנֵזרת הבֵית שֵנֵי ֵירֵושֵלֵמה וֵשֵכֵנֵים הֵיו עם רבֵותֵיכם בֵארן
צֵבֵי : לֹא מֵר שֵקֵבֵא כן אֵסֵרֵו אֵלֵה כֵמֵו עֵזֵרא הֵסֵופֵר הֵכֵהן שֵנֵה
וֵדֵעֵות וֵצֵורֵת הֵאֵותֵיות נֵתֵן סֵרֵים קֵדֵשֵים לֵאֵץ כֵמֵכֵתֵב עֵבֵלֵית
אבֵל לֵשֵן עֵבֵרֵית אֹו ֵיהֵדֵית וֵבֵכֵתֵב אשֵורֵית וֵכֵשֵדֵית : אֵן אֵלֵא
תֵחֵלֵך עֵזֵרא חשֵם אֵבֵבֵא : עֵורֵיגֵן שֵחֵיה בֵזֵמֵן ֵיהֵודֵה הֵקֵדֵ׳ֵט
וֵבֵֹום חֵכֵמֵים אשֵר כֵלֵלֵו תֵלֵמֵוד ֵירֵושֵלֵמֵי מֵצֵא הֵוא וֵראֵה
כֵסֵטֵרֵכֵם תֵורֵה עֵל ֵ׳ֵידֵיכם בֵֹומֵו הֵשֵם נֵכֵתֵב בֵאֵותֵ׳ֵית
הֵאֵלֵה אֵבֵבֵא אשֵר אֵתֵה ֵידֵעֵתֵה כֵֹ זֵאֵת שֵמֵרֵֹת הֵֹא׃
שֵלֵא נֵעֵשֵה כן טֵאֵלֵוֵלֵֹ קֵבֵל בֵגֵֹין מֵקֵדֵם : אֵיֵתֵֹת וֵלֵשֵֹ קֵדֵש
מֵאֵלֵהֵֹם לֵאֵדֵם וֵכֵֹדֵֹ חֵנֵוך נֵוח וֵאֵבֵרֵהֵם נֵתֵנֵו עֵד מֵשֵה
וֵאֵלֵה שֵֹתֵורֵה בֵתֵון ֵיֵשֵראֵל עֵד גֵֹירֵוֵ׳ֵט בֵבֵלֵֹ : חֵכֵמֵֹם
רבֵֹם הֵֹו הֵֹאֵמֵונֵֹם אֵת אשֵר מֵכֵתֵב מֵשֵה בֵלֵֹ שֵנֵו׳ֵֹ שֵמֵרֵה
בֵסֵפֵר תֵֹרֵה אֵֹשֵר עֵֹמֵכֵם עֵד הֵֹום הֵזֵה אֵבֵל הֵֹו ֵ׳ֵרֵבֵֹוֵתֵֹכֵם
הֵאֵמֵֹן. חֵלֵֹוֵך בֵעֵת עֵזֵרֵא הֵכֵהֵן וֵֹה חֵתֵֵֹף גֵֹודֵע מֵשֵֵקֵלֵֹם

Rev. Ezra Stiles who was president of Yale studied and taught
Hebrew. When Rabbi Karigal of Palestine came to visit the Jewish
settlements in the West Indies and the American Colonies, there
being no rabbi then in America, Stiles went to hear him preach in
Newport, R.I. Stiles stayed to study with and befriend the rabbi
during his stay. Thereafter, the two corresponded in Hebrew till
Karigal's death in 1777 in Barbados.

כתובים בשטרית אמאאד לקדש לאושל שיש ירושלם "

הקדישה אשר הש שקל ישראל : על

סקלי השמונים שמאנג לשאא ב שלאל שהוא שמעון

נשיא ישראל שלא אל# לדלל+ לשאאל שמל

אחת לגאלת ישראל : ר' בארטנורא ור' עזריה שראו שקלי

דוד בן ישי ומלכי ישראל בשטרית אבל אמרים אלה לא

בשטרית נכתב התורה : ר' משה לגירון אמר חליפת קדם

מאד מזמן עזרא ואת אשר על פלגת מלכות בימי ירבעם

בית דוד ויהודים יעזבו האותיות ישראל שנשארו כזעאות

לעשר שבטי ישראל. ובעת החיא יהודים לקחו חדשות

אותיות עד היום הזה : אנכי שמעש כמו ר' משה כך

סימון גאון והגדל חכם הוא האמין את עזרא ומיר מכתב

מעברית לכשדית ואת אשר תורה היום ביד עמו לא נכתב

באותיות משה :

בתלמוד חלק ב' תנאֹ סנדרין זויטרא וגד עוקבא

' אמר מר זוטרא ואי תימא מר עוקבא בתהילה ניתנה

• תורה לישראל בכתב עברי ולשן הקדש חזרה וניתנה

• להם בימי עזרא בכתב אשורית ולשן הקדש והניחו

• לִהֱדי וְטוֹת כתב עברית ולשן ארמית מאן הדיוטות

• אמר רב כסדא כותאי וגו:

ביפה עיר ניופורט לאמריכא שנת התקלג

לצרה סיון ג' :'רוזה יהוה יראין את ממחלים

לחסדו למאהבי שש צבאות ומשיחו שלום :

Ezra Stiles

24 May 1773.

הצעיר של התלמידי ישוש שורא שטילס דוריש שבע
נעימות ל.הנכבד היקר החכם הרב ר' חיים יצחק קארגאל
שהתנשא עיניו למרומים כל היום התמיד ונאור בטל אורים
מאת יהוה ומקובל בסתרי בינה ובדעת עליון ונשלם
בשכל נעלם הסוד מפי בעלי התורה ומשום החכמי כל
עולמים · בתוד ערפל לזמי הזה יאור עליך יהוה וינהל
בדרך תמים את הליכותיך עד תשקוט למעלה עם אצילי
קדש אל כתר הצבאות שנקבצו סביב כסא יהוה וכן
תטבע בסוד לחזות בנעם יהוה ותתבלע בנגהות הכ-
-בידו : אמן ·

יהיו לרצון מחשבות והגיון לבי על המשיח וגבורתי והדר מלכותו :
ישתחוו לו כל מלכים כל גוים יעבדוהו : תהלים עב ·

מי זה מלך הגדול : הוא דודי אשר לי ואני לו : אשירה לדודי
השירה · מה יפה אתה מה נעים בתענוגים : איה את אשר
אהבה נפשי : נבקש אתו בשושנים בתוד נפשות ונשמות
טהורות בגן עדן : גבור וגדול הוא מלבאות השרי צבאות
ובקרב עשר ספירות יושב הוא מלך מעולם וימלוך על בני
אלים ועל אראלים והשמלים ועל כל הוים הקדשים ולו
עליונים האלהים השתחוו כלם כאחד : אמן · אך מי המלך
זה הנכבד : הוא בן ליהוה כאמר יהוה בני אתה וגם נשקו
בר תהל' ב וגם מה שם בנו משלי ל' . כמו שם בר אלהין
כן שמו · היו בנים רבים לאדני ישנבראו ואלה כמתמול
אך משיח בן אחד ליהוה בכור ובחור הוא הגל פט אשר לא
נברא אף היה עם הה קודם מאד מאד להיות ההויות בכלל
אם

REVERSE.

OBVERSE.

The first design of the Seal of the United States, recommended by Franklin, Adams, and Jefferson, the Committee appointed immediately after the Declaration of Independence had been read, July 4, 1776. The drawing, though not adopted as our great seal for use on currency and elsewhere, depicts God as the pillar of fire based on Exodus 14:24, and the Children of Israel standing on dry land while the pursuing Egyptian charioteers drown in the Red Sea as depicted in Exodus 14: 28-29. The colonists of the Revolution were likened to the saved Israelites and His Majesty's British troops to the drowning legions of Pharoah. (From a drawing by Benj. J. Lossing in Straus's *Origin of Republican Form of Government*.)

197

Yale

Columbia

Emmanuel

Dartmouth

Many of the earliest founded colleges in the colonies adopted some Hebrew word or phrase as part of their official emblem or seal.

Olivet

Whitworth

Crozer Theological Seminary

Dropsie

Some later examples of college seals using Hebrew:

199

A
SERMON

PREACHED BEFORE HIS EXCELLENCY

JOHN HANCOCK, Esq;

GOVERNOUR;

HIS HONOR

THOMAS CUSHING, Esq;

LIEUTENANT-GOVERNOR;

THE HONORABLE THE

COUNCIL,

AND THE HONORABLE THE

SENATE,

AND

HOUSE of REPRESENTATIVES

OF THE

COMMONWEALTH

OF

MASSACHUSETTS,

MAY 29, 1782,

Being the Day of General Election.

By ZABDIEL ADAMS, A. M.

PASTOR OF THE CHURCH IN LUNENBURG.

COMMONWEALTH of MASSACHUSETTS:
PRINTED BY T. & J. FLEET AND J. GILL.

Title page and extract from the text illustrating how numerous ministers and government figures in colonial times looked to the Hebrew Bible for guidance and models in governing the colonies and the newly founded nation.

200

Judges have the fame appellation, Judges xvii ; to the four great Monarchies, the government of fome of which was democratic, viz. *Greece* and *Rome*, the fame title is given ; and in the new teftament, the feven kings, mentioned Rev. xvii. 10, are, by fome of the lateft and beft expofitors, underftood of feven particular emperors of *Rome*. So that by king in the text, without putting any force upon the words, may be underftood the ruling power of any nation, be it called in modern language by what name foever. Were this not the truth of fact, it would be neceffary for us, as we have changed our form of government, to omit a confiderable part of the fcripture as inapplicable to our condition. But interpreted in the manner above fuggefted, thofe paffages are as proper to be ufed by us, as by any people under heaven. The truth of the cafe feems to be this. At the time the text was penned, kingly rule was the moft prevalent. Thofe who were called by this name, were vefted with different degrees of power. *Some* governed by ftanding laws ; and *others* conducted the great affairs of ftates and kingdoms according to their own arbitrary pleafure. Amongft the Jews, the king was only the

fupreme

supreme executive magiftrate. He had little or nothing to do with matters of legiflation. Their code of laws was previoufly fettled by God himfelf, and given to Mofes for the rule of their conduct, in all the fubfequent ftages of their political exiftence. In the times of the *Judges* the adminiftration of their government was in the hands of God; and hence by the learned it is frequently called a *theocracy:* But the Jews, tired with having Jehovah for their fupreme ruler, and perceiving that the nations around them had a mortal man to ftand in this place, defired, as is too common at the prefent day, to be in the fafhion, and to have a king like others. The requeft, as being to their own difadvantage, was difpleafing to the God of heaven. But, as he would not rule them in a manner contrary to their own inclination, he confented to their petition, after pointing out to them the oppreffive manner of the king. Their kings for feveral generations ruled in righteoufnefs, and made the inftitutes of Mofes the meafure of their adminiftration. Concerning fuch, Solomon pronounces as in our text, *where the word of a king is, there is power.* Whilft they keep within conftitutional

limits

A
COMPENDIOUS
LEXICON
OF THE
Hebrew Language.

———•◇•———

IN TWO VOLUMES.

———•◇•———

VOLUME I. CONTAINING AN EXPLANA-
TION OF EVERY WORD WHICH OCCURS
IN THE PSALMS; WITH NOTES.

VOLUME II. BEING A LEXICON AND GRAM-
MAR OF THE WHOLE LANGUAGE.

———•———

By *CLEMENT C. MOORE*.

———•———

NEW-YORK :

PRINTED AND SOLD BY COLLINS & PERKINS.
NO. 189, PEARL-STREET.
• • • • • •
1809.

Clement Clarke Moore (1779–1863), who is most
remembered by the poem he wrote for his
children, " 'Twas the Night Before Christmas,"
was also a serious Hebrew Scholar. Above is the
title page of his Hebrew dictionary, the first
published in the United States.

203

UNIVERSITY OF THE CITY OF NEW-YORK

The Annual Course of Instruction in the Institution, will commence on Monday, the 3d of October, under the direction of the following Professors.

Rev. JAMES M. MATHEWS, D.D., Chancellor.

DAVID B. DOUGLASS, Professor of Civil Engineering and Architecture.

S. F. B. MORSE, Professor of the Literature of the Arts of Design.

Rev. HENRY P. TAPPAN, Professor of Intellectual and Moral Philosophy and Belles-Lettres.

ROBERT B. PATTON, Professor of Greek Lanuage and Literature.

Rev. JOHN PROUDFIT, Professor of Latin Language and Literature.

CHARLES L. PARMENTIER, Professor of French Language and Literature.

LORENZO L. DA PONTE, Professor of Italian Language and Literature.

MIGUEL CABRERA DE NEVARES, Professor of Spanish Language and Literature.

CHARLES RABADAN, Associate Professor of do.

ISAAC NORDHEIMER Acting Professor of German Language and Literature.

Rev. GEORGE BUSH, Professor of Hebrew, and Oriental Languages and Literature.

CHARLES W. HACKLEY, Professor of Mathematics.

WILLIAM A. NORTON, Acting Professor of Natural Philosophy and Astronomy.

LEWIS C. BECK, M.D., Professor of Chemistry and Botany.

Hon. B. F. BUTLER, Professor of Law, and Principal of the Law Faculty.*

L. D. GALE, M.D., Professor of Geology and Mineralogy.

ISAAC NORDHEIMER, Professor of Arabic, Syriac, Persian, and Ethiopic.

Rev. CYRUS MASON, Professor of the Evidences of Revealed Religion.

* The other Professors in the Law Faculty will be appointed within a few weeks; and the course of legal instruction will be commenced simultaneously by Mr. Butler and the other Professors early in May, 1837.

SCHEDULE OF THE RECITATIONS, AND OTHER EXERCISES, DURING THE WEEK.—(Prayers in the Chapel at half past nine o'clock A.M.)

HOURS.	MONDAY.	TUESDAY.	WEDNESDAY.	THURSDAY.	FRIDAY.	SAT.
10 to 11 A.M.	Latin. Belles-lettres. Natural Philosophy. Architecture and Civil Engineering. *Geology and Mineralogy	Latin. Belles-lettres. Natural Philosophy. Greek. Architecture and Civil Engineering. Geology & Mineralogy	Latin. Belles-lettres. Natural Philosophy. Chemistry. Architecture and Civil Engineering. Geology & Mineralogy	Latin. Belles-lettres. Natural Philosophy. Chemistry. Architecture and Civil Engineering. Geology & Mineralogy	Latin. Belles-lettres. Natural Philosophy. Chemistry. Architecture and Civil Engineering. Geology & Mineralogy	
11 to 12 A.M.	Mathematics. Latin. Greek. Psychology and Moral Philosophy.	Mathematics. Greek. Latin. Psychology and Moral Philosophy.	Mathematics. Greek. Latin. Psychology and Moral Philosophy.	Mathematics. Greek. Psychology and Moral Philosophy.	Mathematics. Greek. Latin. Psychology and Moral Philosophy.	
12 to 1 P.M.	Greek. Mathematics. Logic. Philosophy of Rhetoric and Criticism. Natural Philosophy.	Greek. Mathematics. Philosophy of Rhetoric and Criticism. Chemistry.	Greek. Mathematics. Logic. Philosophy of Rhetoric and Criticism. Natural Philosophy.	Greek. Mathematics. Logic. Philosophy of Rhetoric and Criticism. Chemistry.	Greek. Mathematics. Logic. Philosophy of Rhetoric and Criticism. Latin.	
1 to 2 P.M.	Evidences of Revealed Religion. Hebrew. New Testament as a Classic. Elementary Drawing.	Belles-lettres. Chaldaic and Syriac.	Evidences of Revealed Religion. Hebrew. Elementary Drawing.	Belles-lettres. Chaldaic and Syriac.	Evidences of Revealed Religion. Hebrew. Elementary Drawing.	
2 to 3 P.M.	Rabinical Hebrew.				Rabinical Hebrew.	
4 to 5 P.M.	Arabic.	Hebrew.	Hebrew.	Hebrew.	Arabic.	
7 to 8 P.M.	Persian.		Sanscrit.	Persian.	Sanscrit.	

(Declaration in the Chapel.)

* The class in Geology will commence in April.

NOTE.—There are also classes in French, Spanish, Italian and German, taught at such hours as will be found most convenient to the students and professors.

University of the City of New York was the original name of what is now New York University (NYU). Above is the first Bulletin of classes, showing the study of Hebrew as an integral part of the curriculum.

THE

NEW ENGLAND

PRIMER;

OR,

AN EASY AND PLEASANT GUIDE

TO

THE ART OF READING.

Adorned with Cuts.

TO WHICH IS ADDED

THE CATECHISM.

MASSACHUSETTS SABBATH SCHOOL SOCIETY

Depository No. 13 Cornhill, Boston.

In colonial times, "primers" were used in teaching the alphabet and reading to primary school children. Above is the title page of a later edition based on the famous Kneeland and Green *New England Primer* of 1727.

THE TEN COMMANDMENTS,

PUT INTO SHORT AND EASY RHYMES FOR
CHILDREN.

1. Thou shalt have no more gods but me.
2. Before no idol bend thy knee.
3. Take not the name of God in vain.
4. Dare not the Sabbath day profane.
5. Give both thy parents hor o due.
6. Take heed that thou no murder do.
7. Abstain from words and creeds unclean.
8. Steal not, though thou be poor and mean.
9. Make not a wilful lie, nor love it.
10. What is thy neignbor's, dare not covet.

Above is a rhymed version, for children, of the Biblical verses
in Exodus 20:3-17 and Deuteronomy 5:7-18. It was common at
that time to mix religious with secular instruction even in public
schools.

In Adam's fall
We sinned all.

Thy life to mend,
God's Book attend.

The Cat doth play,
And after slay.

A Dog will bite
A thief at night.

The Eagle's flight
Is out of sight.

The idle Fool
Is whipped at school.

A B C D E F

In learning the alphabet, children were required to memorize brief couplets featuring each letter of the alphabet.

As runs the Glass,
Man's life doth pass

My book and Heart
Shall never part.

Job feels the rod,
Yet blesses God.

Proud Korah's troop
Was swallowed up

The Lion bold
The Lamb doth hold.

The Moon gives light
In time of night.

G H I J K L M

While the basic format of the primers remained the same, some of the woodcuts and couplets were changed according to the times. Following the Revolution, the symbol for the letter K was changed from the King to Korah.

Nightingales sing
In time of spring.

The royal Oak, it
was the tree
That saved his royal
majesty.

Peter denies
His Lord, and cries.

Queen Esther comes
in royal state,
To save the Jews
from dismal fate.

Rachel doth mourn
For her first born.

Samuel anoints
Whom God appoints.

N O P Q R S

Some of the references were to animals, nature, or ethical lessons, but the largest part were to Hebrew Bible figures.

Time cuts down all
Both great and small

Uriah's   beauteous
   wife
Made David seek his
   life.

Whales in the sea
God's voice obey.

Xerxes the Great did
   die,
And so must you
   and I.

Youth forward slips,
Death soonest nips.

Zaccheus, he
Did climb the tree,
His Lord to see.

T U V W X Y Z

Department of State
Washington, October 20, 1902.

Rev. Marcus H. Dalon,
619 Bond St,
Evansville, Indiana

לְכתבך קבלתי, איש האלהים
ושלחתי כי מצא חן בעיניך מעשה
ידי אם בעד אחך הנורדפים
במלכות רומעניע. שלום לך ולעדתך
בני משה.

הוי שאל מן ה' אלהים כי יברך
יברך את אנשי בריתך אשרבעוואסויל
בכל אשר תעשו הן בדבר שפתים
או במעשה ידים. ואלהי השלום יהיה
עמכם לעלם. ואני אוהבך.

John Hay

The above Hebrew letter was written by then Secretary of State John Hay in response to a rabbi's letter thanking him for helping the persecuted Jews of Rumania. It reads: Your letter I have received Man of God and I was happy that my efforts have found favor in your eyes if they are for your persecuted brethren in the kingdom of Rumania. Peace unto you and your congregation the Sons of Moses. I hereby request of the Lord God that he bless bless [sic] the people of your covenant that are in Evansville in all their endeavors whether words or deeds. And may the God of peace be with you forever. And I am your beloved. (From the *Chicago Tribune*.)

211

האוניברסיטה של ייל

בעו היכן במדיעת קוענקטייקוט שולחים ברכות
נאמנות לכל מקבלי המסמך הזה
אנחנו, הדייקן וחברי האוניברסיטה הזאת מקבלים את

שילא מרים לוין

מועמדה לכבוד אקדמאי ומדרגה שעה לתואר

דוקטור למשפט

ומעניקים עליה את כל הזכויות, היתרונות, והסמל הנוגעים
לכבוד זה. לראיה הוטבע חותם האוניברסיטה על מסמך
זה ואנחנו, הדייקן וחברי האוניברסיטה באנו על החתום
בחודש ניסן תשל״א 372 שנה לקיום האוניברסיטה של ייל.

In 1971, when Yale Law School, as many other
law schools, changed its degree from a Bachelor
of Laws to Juris Doctor and offered the new
degree to its alumni retroactively, one alumnus,
Selma M. Levine '47, asked the Dean, "how
come the diploma was not available in Hebrew
in view of Yale's early tradition?" She received
the above Hebrew diploma signed by Yale Law
School Dean Abraham Goldstein and by former
trustee and Master of Branford College, William
Horowitz. (From the *Yale Law Report*, vol. 18 nos.
1 and 2, Fall-Winter 1971-72.)

Bibliography

Abbott, Lyman. *The Life and Literature of the Ancient Hebrews.* Boston: Houghton, 1901.

Abbott, Robert. *A Trial of Our Church-Forsakers.* London: Thomas Payne, 1639.

Abrahams, I.; E. R. Bevan; and C. Singer, eds. *The Legacy of Israel.* Oxford: Clarendon Press, 1927.

Adams, Hannah. *An Abridgement of the History of New England.* Boston: R. and J. Homans and John West, 1805.

Adams, James Truslow. *The Founding of New England.* Boston: Atlantic Monthly Press, 1921.

Adams, Mary Newbury. "The Discovery of America." In *Papers of the Jewish Women's Congress.*

Addison, Joseph, and Sir Richard Steele. *Critical Essays from the "Spectator,"* ed. Donald F. Bond. London: Oxford University Press, 1970.

Alexander, Hartley Burr. "The Hebrew Contribution to the Americanism of the Future." *Menorah Journal* 6, no. 2 (April 1920): 65–66.

American Jewish Historical Society Publications. Vols. 1, 2, 3, 5, 9, 11, 20, 25.

Arnold, Matthew. *Literature and Dogma.* New York: Macmillan Co., 1889.

Ashton, Thomas L. *Byron's Hebrew Melodies.* Austin: University of Texas Press, 1972.

Atkinson, Robert. *The Italian Language.* Dublin: Hodges, Smith & Co., 1868.

Atwater, E. E. *History of the Colony of New Haven to Its Absorption in Connecticut.* Connecticut, 1902.

213

Auerbach, Joseph S. *The Bible and Modern Life.* New York: Harper & Brothers, 1914.

Bacon, Leonard. *The Genesis of the New England Churches.* New York: Harper & Brothers, 1874.

Band, A. J. "Jewish Studies in American Liberal Arts Colleges and Universities." In *American Jewish Year Book, 1964.*

Banvard, Joseph. *Plymouth and the Pilgrims.* Boston: Gould & Lincoln, 1856.

Baron, Salo W. *A Social and Religious History of the Jews.* 15 vols., to date. New York: Columbia University Press, 1973.

————. *Steeled by Adversity.* Philadelphia: Jewish Publication Society, 1971.

Bates, E. S. *The Bible as Living Literature.* New York: Simon & Schuster, 1936.

Baugh, A. C. *A History of the English Language.* New York: D. Appleton and Co., 1935.

Becker, Carl. L. *The Declaration of I Independence.* New York: Alfred A. Knopf, 1942.

Belknap, Jeremy. *American Biography.* Boston: Isaiah Thomas & Ebenezer J. Andrews, 1794–98.

Bell, James. *Biblical and Shakespearean Characters Compared.* London: Hull Press, 1894.

Bentwich, Norman. *Philo-Judaeus.* Philadelphia: Jewish Publication Society, 1910.

Berdoe, E. *Browning's Message to His Time.* London: S. Sonnenschein & Co., 1890.

Berlin-Lieberman, Judith. *Robert Browning and Hebraism.* Jerusalem: Azriel Press, 1934.

Bertholet, Alfred. *History of Hebrew Civilization.* Translated by A. K. Dallas. New York: Brentano's, 1926.

Bewer, J. A. *The Literature of the Old Testament in Its Historical Development.* New York: Columbia University Press, 1926.

Bigelow, John. *Franklin.* Philadelphia: J. B. Lippincott & Co., 1889.

Booth, Henry Kendall. *The Background of the Bible.* New York: Charles Scribner's Sons, 1929.

Bradford, William. *History of Plimouth Plantation.* Boston: Houghton Mifflin Co., 1896.

Bradley, H. *Making of English.* London: Macmillan Co., 1904.

Breasted, James H. *Ancient Times.* Boston: Ginn & Co., 1944.

Broches, S. *Jews in New England.* New York: Bloch Publishing Co., 1942.

Brooke, S. A. *The Poetry of Robert Browning.* New York: Thomas Y. Crowell & Co., 1902.

Browne, Henry. *Triglot Dictionary of Scriptural Representative Words.* London, 1901.

Butterfield, Lyman H., ed. *The Letters of Benjamin Rush.* Princeton: Princeton University Press, 1951.

Byington, Ezra Hoyt. *The Puritan as a Colonist and Reformer*. Boston: Little, Brown & Co., 1899.

Calder, I. M., ed. *Letters of John Davenport*. New Haven: Yale University Press, 1937.

Calef, Robert. *More Wonders of the Invisible World*. London: N. Hillar & J. Collyer, 1700.

Calisch, Edward. *The Jew in English Literature*. Richmond: Bell Book and Stationery Co., 1909.

Cambridge History of American Literature. New York: G. P. Putnam's Sons, 1922.

Cambridge Platform of Church Discipline. Boston, 1653

Capitall Lawes. London: Ben. Allen, 1643.

Cardozo, J. L. *The Contemporary Jew in Elizabethan Drama*. Amsterdam: H. J. Paris, 1925.

Chadwick, H. Munro. *The Growth of Literature*. 3 vols. Cambridge: Cambridge University Press, 1932–40.

Champion, S. G. *Racial Proverbs*. London: George Routledge & Son, 1938.

Chiel, Arthur A. "Ezra Stiles and Rabbi Karigal." *Yale Alumni Magazine*, March 1974, pp. 16–19.

———. "Ezra Stiles' Rabbi Tobiah." *American Jewish Historical Quarterly* 59, no. 2 (December 1969): 228–29.

———. "Ezra Stiles: The Education of an Hebraician." *American Jewish Historical Quarterly*, March 1971, pp. 235–41.

———. "The Rabbis and Ezra Stiles." *American Jewish Historical Quarterly*, 61, no. 4 (June 1972): 294–312.

Chomsky, William. *Hebrew: The Eternal Language*. Philadelphia: Jewish Publication Society, 1957.

Cockayne, T. O. *Spoon and Sparrow*. Parker, Son & Bourn, 1861.

Cohn, J. R. *The Bible and Modern Thought*. London: John Murray, 1921.

Coit, Thomas W. *Puritanism*. New York: D. Appleton & Co., 1845.

Coleman, Edward D. *The Bible in English Drama*. New York: New York Public Library, 1931.

Coolidge, Calvin. "Jewish Contributions to American Democracy." Reprint from the *Jewish Center*, March 1940.

Corban, Alan G. *The King's Hall*. Cambridge: At the University Press, 1969.

Corhill, Carl H. *The Culture of Ancient Israel*. Chicago: Open Court, 1914.

Cotton, John. *A Meet Help*. Boston: B. Green & J. Allen, 1699.

———. *A Practical Commentary*. London: R. I. & E. C. for Thomas Parkhurst, 1656.

———. *The Way of Congregational Churches Cleared*. London: M. Simmons, 1648.

Davis, John, ed. *New England's Memorial*. Cambridge: Corcker & Brewster, 1826.

Dexter, Franklin B., ed. *The Literary Diary of Ezra Stiles*. New York: Scribner, 1901.

Dictionary of American Biography. New York: Charles Scribner's Sons, 1928.

D'Irsay, Stephan. *Histoire des Universités*. Paris: A. Picard, 1933–35.

Dobschütz, Ernst von. *The Influence of the Bible on Civilization*. New York: Charles Scribner's Sons, 1914. Reprint. New York: Frederick Ungar Publishing Co., 1959.

Drake, J. A. *A Book of New England Legends and Folklore*. Boston: Roberts Brothers, 1884.

Driver, S. R. *An Introduction to the Literature of the Old Testament*. New York: Charles Scribner's Sons, 1913.

Drucker, Aaron P. *The Culture of Ancient Israel*. New York: Bloch Publishing Co., 1911.

Eliot, J. *Biographical Dictionary of First Settlers and Other Eminent Characters in New England*. Salem: Cushing & Appleton, 1809.

Ellis, G. E. *The Puritan Age and Rule in the Colony of Massachusetts Bay. 1629-1685*. Boston, 1888. Reprint, New York: B. Franklin, 1970.

Elton, Romeo. *Life of Roger Williams*. Providence: George H. Whitney, 1853.

Emerson, O. F. *The History of the English Language*. New York: Macmillan Co., 1935.

Ernst, James. *Roger Williams*. New York: Macmillan Co., 1932.

Farbridge, M. H. *Judaism and the Modern Mind*. New York: Macmillan Co., 1927.

———. *English Literature and the Hebrew Renaissance*. London: Luzac & Co., 1953.

Feinstone, S. & Kelley, J. *Courage and Candlelight*. H'burg: Stockpole, 1974.

Fennel, C. *Stanford Dictionary of Anglicized Words and Phrases*, Cambridge, 1892.

Finkelstein, Louis, ed. *The Jews: Their History, Culture and Religion*. Philadelphia: Jewish Publication Society, 1949.

———; J. Elliot Ross; and William A. Brown. *The Religions of Democracy*. New York: Devin-Adair Co., 1941.

Fisch, Harold. *Jerusalem and Albion*. London: Routledge & Keegan Paul, 1964; New York: Schocken Books, 1964.

Fletcher, H. F. *The Use of the Bible in Milton's Prose*. Urbana: University of Illinois, 1929.

Ford, P. L., ed. *The Writings of Thomas Jefferson*. New York: G. Putnam's Sons, 1892–99.

Ford, Worthington Chauncey. "Moses, His Judicials." In *Proceedings of Massachusetts Historical Society*, 2d Series, xvi.

Friedlander, Gerald. *Shakespeare and the Jew*. New York: E. P. Dutton & Co., 1921.

Friedman, Lee M. *Jewish Pioneers and Patriots*. Philadelphia: Jewish Publication Society, 1942.

———. *Rabbi Haim Isaac Carigal,* Boston: Merrymount Press, 1940.

Froude, J. A. *Short Studies on Great Subjects.* London: Longman's, Green & Co., 1867–83.

Fuerst, Julius. *A Hebrew and Chaldee Lexicon to the Old Testament.* London: Williams & Norgate, 1867.

Furneaux, Philip. *Letters to Honorable Justice Mr. Blackstone.* London: T. Cadell, 1770.

Gardiner, J. H. *The Bible as English Literature.* New York: Charles Scribner's Sons, 1907.

Garnett, Richard, and Edmund Gosse. *English Literature: An Illustrated Record.* New York: Macmillan Co., 1926.

Gaster, Moses. "The Romance of the Hebrew Alphabet." In *Jewish Library,* edited by Dr. Leo Jung. New York: Bloch Publishing Co., 1930.

General Laws of the Massachusetts Colony. 1658.

Genung, J. F. *The Hebrew Literature of Wisdom in the Light of Today.* Boston: Houghton Mifflin Co., 1906.

Gilbert, Dan. *The Biblical Basis of the Constitution.* San Diego: Danielle Publishers, 1936.

Gipson, L. H. *The British Empire Before the American Revolution.* New York: Alfred A. Knopf, 1936–56.

Goitein, S. D. *Studies in Islamic History and Institutions.* Leiden: E. J. Brill, 1966.

Goldberg, I. *The Wonder of Words.* New York: Appleton-Century Co., 1938.

Goodenough, E. R. *The Jurisprudence of the Jewish Courts in Egypt.* Oxford: At the University Press, 1929.

Graetz, H. *History of the Jews.* Philadelphia: Jewish Publication Society, 1891–98.

Gray, F. C. *Remarks of Early Laws of Massachusetts Bay.* Massachusetts Historical Society Collections, 3rd series, vol. 8, pp. 191–237. Boston, 1843.

Greenough, J. B., and G. L. Kittredge. *Words and Their Ways in English Speech.* New York: Macmillan Co., 1926.

Gregory, J. *Puritanism in the Old and in the New World.* London: James Clarke & Co., 1895.

Gutstein, M. A. *The Story of the Jews of Newport.* New York: Bloch Publishing Co., 1936.

Hadley, J. A. *A Brief History of the English Language* (Revised by G. L. Kittredge) in *Webster's New International Dictionary of the English Language.* Springfield, Mass. G. & C. Merriam, 1940.

Hailperin, Herman. *Rashi and the Christian Scholars.* Pittsburgh: University of Pittsburgh Press, 1963.

Haraszti, Zoltan. *The Enigma of the Bay Psalm Book.* Chicago: University of Chicago Press, 1956.

Hargrave, Basil. *Origins and Meanings of Popular Phrases and Names.* London: T. W. Laurie Ltd., 1932.

Harvard Classics, Vol. 43. New York: P. Collier & Son, 1909–10.

Hastings, I. *Dictionary of the Bible.* New York: Charles Scribner's Sons, 1898–1904.

Hertz, J. H., ed. *A Book of Jewish Thoughts.* New York: Bloch Publishing Co., 1945.

Hoadley, C. J. *Records of the Colony and Plantation of New Haven from 1638–49.* Hartford: Case, Tiffany & Co., 1857.

———. *Records of the Colony; or, Jurisdiction of New Haven from May 1653 to the Union.* Hartford: Case, Tiffany & Co., 1858.

Holmes, Oliver Wendell. *The Breakfast-Table Series.* Boston: Fireside edition, 1890, 1891.

Holy Scriptures. Philadelphia: Jewish Publication Society, 1940.

Horowitz, Edward. "Hebrew Words Used in English." Mimeographed. 1939.

———. *How the Hebrew Language Grew.* New York: Ktav Publishing House, 1960.

Houghton, Louise S. *Hebrew Life and Thought.* Chicago: University of Chicago Press, 1907.

Howe, D. W. *The Puritan Republic of the Massachusetts Bay in New England.* Indianapolis, 1899.

Hutchinson, Thomas. *A Collection of Original Papers Relative to the History of Massachusetts Bay.* Boston: Thomas & John Fleet.

———. *The History of the Colony and Province of Massachusetts Bay.* Cambridge: Harvard University Press, 1936.

Jacobs, Joseph. *Jewish Contributions to Civilization.* Philadelphia: Jewish Publication Society, 1919.

Jameson, J. Franklin. *The American Revolution Considered as a Social Movement.* Princeton: Princeton University Press, 1926.

Jerome. *Contra Rufinium.*

Johnson, Charles F. *English Words.* New York: Harper & Brothers, 1891.

Josselyn, John. *New England's Rarities.* Boston: William Veazie, 1865.

Jowett, B. *The Interpretation of Scriptures.* London: Routledge & Sons, 1911.

Jung, Leo, ed. *Judaism in a Changing World.* New York: Oxford University Press, 1939.

Kallen, Horace M. *Culture and Democracy in the United States.* New York: Boni & Liveright, 1970.

Karp, Abraham J. *The Jewish Experience in America.* 5 vols. Waltham and New York: American Jewish Historical Society and Ktav, 1969.

Karpeles, Gustav. *Jewish Literature and Other Essays.* Philadelphia: Jewish Publication Society, 1895.

Katsh, Abraham I. "Biblical and Hebraic Mortar in American Structure." *Horizon* 2, no. 9 (March 1939).

———. Articles in *Hadoar,* 1940 (891); *Hadoar,* 21, no. 2 (January 17, 1941): 189 ff.; 54, 41 (October 31, 1975: 2405); 55, 1 (November 7, 1975:

2406); *Hatzofeh,* July 28, 1939; *Jewish Outlook* 4, no. 10 (1940); *New Palestine,* July 15, 1938.

———. "Current Trends in the Study of Hebrew in Colleges and Universities." *Modern Language Journal* 44, no. 2 (February 2, 1960).

———. "Hebraic Foundations of American Democracy." In *The Hebrew Impact on Western Civilization,* edited by Dagobert D. Runes, pp. 181–236. New York: Citadel Press, 1965.

———. "Hebraic Studies in American Higher Education." *Jewish World* 2, no. 9 (July 1964): 35, 70.

———. *Hebrew in American Higher Education.* New York: New York University, 1941.

———. *Hebrew Language, Literature and Culture in American Institutions of Higher Learning.* New York: Payne Educational Sociology Foundation, 1950.

———. *Judaism in Islam.* New York: New York University Press, 1954.

King James Version of the Holy Bible. London: Oxford University Press, n.d.

Knappen, M. N. *Tudor Puritanism.* Chicago: University of Chicago Press, 1939.

Knowles, J. D. *Memoir of Roger Williams.* London: Lincoln Edmands & Co., 1834.

Kohut, George Alexander. *A Hebrew Anthology.* Cincinnati: S. Bacharach, 1913.

———. *Ezra Stiles and the Jews.* New York: P. Cowen, 1902.

———. "Hebraic Learning in Puritan New England." *Menorah Journal* 2, no. 4 (October 1916).

Konvitz, Milton R. *Judaism and Human Rights.* New York: W. W. Norton & Co., 1972.

Korn, Bertram Wallace. *American Jewry and the Civil War.* Philadelphia: Jewish Publication Society, 1951.

———. *Eventful Years and Experiences.* Cincinnati: American Jewish Archives, 1954.

———. "Jews and the Revolutionary Struggle for American Freedom." Annual Sol Feinstone Lecture. Philadelphia: Gratz College, 1975.

———. *The Early Jews of New Orleans.* Waltham, Mass.: American Jewish Historical Society, 1969.

Kunitz, Joshua. *Russian Literature and the Jew.* New York: Columbia University Press, 1929.

Landa, M. J. *The Jew in Drama.* New York: William Morrow & Co., 1927.

Landau, J. L. *Short Lectures on Modern Hebrew Literature.* London: Edward Goldston, 1938.

Lapson, Judah. "A Decade of Hebrew in the High Schools of New York City." Reprinted from *Jewish Education* 16, no. 1.

Lasker, Bruno. *Jewish Experiences in America.* New York: The Inquiry, 1930.

Lebeson, Anita L. *Pilgrim People.* New York: Harper & Brothers, 1950.

Lecky, W. E. H. *Rationalism in Europe.* London: Longman's, Green & Co., 1910.

Lectures of Lowell Institute on Early History of Massachusetts. Boston, 1869.

Leshonenu. Jerusalem: Vaad Halashon, 1923–40.

Levinger, Lee J. *A History of the Jews in the United States.* Cincinnati: Union of American Hebrew Congregations, 1935.

Levison, Nahum. *The Jewish Background of Christianity.* Edinburgh, T. & T. Clarke, 1932.

Lewittes, Mordecai H. "Hebrew Enters New York High Schools." *Menorah Journal* 26 (April–June 1938).

Love, W. De Loss, Jr. *The Fast and Thanksgiving Days of New England.* Boston: Houghton Mifflin Co., 1895.

Lowe, H., ed. *Judaism and Christianity.* London: Sheldon Press, 1937.

MacDonald, D. B. *The Hebrew Literary Genius.* Princeton: Princeton University Press, 1933.

Madariaga, S. de. *Christopher Columbus.* New York: Macmillan Co., 1940.

Magnus, Laurie. *The Jews in the Christian Era from the First to the Eighteenth Century and Their Contribution to its Civilization.* London: E. Benn, 1929.

Malone, Dumas. *Jefferson the Virginian.* Boston: Little, Brown and Co., 1948.

Mandelkern, Solomon. *Concordantiae Hebraicae Atque Chaldaica.* Berlin: Apud Schocken, 1937.

Manly, John M., and Edith Rickert. *Contemporary American Literature.* New York: Harcourt, 1929.

March, F. A., and F. March, Jr. *March's Thesaurus Dictionary.* Philadelphia: Philadelphia Historical Publishing Co., 1930.

Marcus, Jacob Rader. *Early American Jewry.* Vol. 1. *The Jews of New York, New England and Canada, 1649–1794.* Philadelphia: Jewish Publication Society, 1955. Vol. 2. *The Jews of Pennsylvania and the South, 1665–1790.* Philadelphia: Jewish Publication Society, 1955.

Massachusetts Colonial Records.

Masserman, Paul, and Max Baker. *The Jews Come to America.* New York: Bloch Publishing Co., 1932.

Mather, Cotton. *Magnalia Christi Americana.* London: T. Parkhurst, 1702. New York: Russell & Russell, 1967.

Mather, Increase. *The Order of the Gospels.* Boston: B. Green & J. Allen, 1700.

Mather, Richard. *Journal of Richard Mather. 1635. His Life and Death. 1670.* Boston: David Clapp & Son, 1850 (2d ed., 1874).

Mawson, C. *Dictionary of Foreign Terms in English.* New York: Thomas Y. Crowell Co., 1934.

Mayhew, Jonathan. *Sermons.* Boston: Arno Press, 1766 and 1969.

McKnight, G. H. *English Words and Their Background.* New York: Appleton and Co., 1923.

Mencken, Henry L. *The American Language.* New York: Alfred A. Knopf, 1938; Supplement I, 1945; Supplement II, 1948.

Meyer, Isidore S. "Hebrew at Harvard, 1636–1760." *Publications of the American Jewish Historical Society* 35 (1939): 145–70.

———. "The Hebrew Preface to Bradford's *History of the Plymouth Plantation.*" *Publications of the American Jewish Historical Society* 38 (June 1969).

Miller, Perry. *The New England Mind.* New York: Macmillan Co., 1939.

———, and Thomas Johnson. *The Puritans.* New York: American Book Co., 1938.

Mitchell, P. Chalmers. *Thomas Henry Huxley.* New York: Putnam Press, 1900.

Modder, M. F. *The Jew in the Literature of England.* Philadelphia: Jewish Publication Society, 1939.

Moore, George Foot. "Judah Monis." *Proceedings of the Massachusetts Historical Society* 52 (1919): 4.

Moore, J. B. *Memoirs of American Governors.* New York: Gates & Stedman, 1846.

Morgan, Edmund S. "Puritan Love and Marriage (Part I)." *More Books: The Bulletin of the Boston Public Library* 17, no. 2 (February 1942): 43–64.

———. "Responsibilities of a Puritan Parent (Part II)." *More Books: The Bulletin of the Boston Public Library* 17, no. 4 (April 1942): 141–59.

———. *Roger Williams: The Church and the State.* New York: Harcourt, Brace & World, 1967.

Morison, S. E. *Founding of Harvard College.* Cambridge: Harvard University Press, 1935.

———. *Harvard in the Seventeenth Century.* Cambridge: Harvard University Press, 1932.

———. *The Intellectual Life of Colonial New England.* New York: New York University Press, 1956.

———. *The Puritan Pronaos.* New York: New York University Press, 1936.

Morris, Richard B. "Civil Liberties and the Jewish Tradition in Early America." *Publication of the American Jewish Historical Society* (September 1956).

———. "Essay of 'Body of Liberties'." *Publications of the American Jewish Historical Society,* 1922.

———. "Jewish Interests of Roger Williams." *American Hebrew,* December 9, 1921.

Moulton, Richard G. *The Literary Study of the Bible.* Boston: D. C. Heath and Co., 1899.

Muller, E. M. *The Science of Languages.* New York: Charles Scribner's Sons, 1876.

Murdock, Kenneth B. *Increase Mather: The Foremost American Puritan.* Cambridge: Harvard University Press, 1925.

Neuman, A. A. *Landmarks and Goals.* Philadelphia: Dropsie College Press, 1953.

New England Primer. Boston: Sabbath School Society, 1837.

New England's First Fruits with Divers Other Special Matters Concerning that Country. Reprinted for J. Sobin, New York, 1865.

New Haven Colony Records.

Newman, L. I. *Jewish Influence on Christian Reform Movements.* New York: Columbia University Press, 1925.

Noble, Richmond. *Shakespeare's Biblical Knowledge.* London: Macmillan Co., 1935.

Novak, William. "The Hebrew Language and Spirit in Early American Life." Unpublished Paper. April, 1969.

Oakes, Uriah. *New England Pleaded With* (Sermon: Boston, May 7, 1673). Cambridge: Samuel Green, 1673.

Orlinsky, Harry M. "Jewish Biblical Scholarship in America." *Jewish Quarterly Review* 45, no. 4 (April 1955): 374–414.

Osgood, H. L. *The American Colonies in the Seventeenth Century.* New York: Macmillan Co., 1904–7.

Palfrey, John Gorham. *The History of New England.* Boston: H. Shepard, 1873.

Parker, J. W. *The Jew and His Neighbor.* New York: Smith Inc., 1931.

Perry, Ralph Barton. *Puritanism and Democracy.* New York: Vanguard Press, 1944.

Pfeiffer, R. H. "The Teaching of Hebrew in Colonial America." *Jewish Quarterly Review,* April 1955, pp. 363–73.

Pitkin, W. *A Political and Civil History of the United States of America.* New Haven: H. Howe and Durrie & Peake, 1828.

Pool, David de Sola. "Hebrew Learning Among Puritans of New England Prior to 1700." *American Jewish Historical Society Publications* 20 (1911).

Pound, Roscoe. *Readings on the History and System of the Common Law.* Boston: Chipman Law Publication Co., 1925.

Powys, John Cowper. *Enjoyment of Literature.* New York: Simon & Schuster, 1938.

Prince, Nathan. *The Constitutions and Government of Harvard College: From Its Foundation in 1636 to 1742.* Boston: Rogers & Fowle, 1742.

Proceedings of the Massachusetts Historical Society. Vol. 44, pp. 529–42 (J. de Normandie); Vol. 50, pp. 123–32 (G. Hodges); Vol. 51, pp. 229–302 (G. F. Moore); Vol. 52, pp. 285–312; Vol. 53, pp. 80–82 (Letters of White Kennett to Benjamin Colman).

Publications of the American Jewish Historical Society. Nos. 3, pp. 112–14; 11, pp. 75–99; 12, 102–4; 19, pp. 107–10; 20, pp. 31–83; 22, pp. 1–24; 26, pp. 201–10; 28, pp. 242–45; 46, pp. 20–39.

Quincy, Josiah. *History of Harvard University.* 2 vols. Cambridge: J. Owen, 1840.

Rack, H. Th. *A History of Classical Philology.* New York: Macmillan Co., 1911.

Reed, John F. and Feinstone, Sol. *Pen for Freedom.* Philadelphia, 1971.

Ridgely, Frank H. *Jewish Ethical Idealism*. Boston: Gorham Press, 1918.

Roback, A. A. *Jewish Influence in Modern Thought*. Cambridge: Sci-Art Publishers, 1929.

Robertson, Stuart. *The Development of Modern English*. New York: Prentice-Hall, 1934.

Roseneau, William. *Semitic Studies in American Colleges*. Chicago, 1896 (Reprint).

Rosenthal, E. I. J. "Rashi and the English Bible." *Bulletin of the John Rylands Library* 24 (April 1940).

Rosenthal, Frank. "The Rise of Christian Hebraism in the Sixteenth Century." *Historia Judaica* 7 (1945): 167–91.

Rosenthal, S. "The Bible and the English Language." *Jewish Outlook* 1, no. 9 (May 1940).

Roth, Cecil. *The Jewish Contribution to Civilization*. London: Macmillan Co., 1938.

Roy, W. L. *A Complete Hebrew and English Critical and Pronouncing Dictionary*. New York: Collins Keese & Co., 1837.

Rudavsky, David. "Hebraic Studies in American Colleges and Universities with Special Reference to New York University." In *Doron (Hebraic Studies): Essays in Honor of Abraham I. Katsh*, edited by I. T. Naamani, D. Rudavsky, and C. F. Ehle, Jr. Reprint ed., New York University, 1965.

Runes, Dagobert D. *The Hebrew Impact on Western Civilization*. New York: Citadel Press, 1965.

Ruppin, Arthur. *The Jews in the Modern World*. New York: Macmillan Co., 1934.

Sarton, George. *Introduction to the History of Science*. 2 vols. Baltimore, 1927–28.

Savelle, Max. *Seeds of Liberty*. New York: Alfred A. Knopf, 1948.

Schechter, H. "The Influence of Talmudic and Midrashic Literature on Shakespeare." *Areshet* (Hebrew), Jerusalem, 1943.

Schiaparelli, G. *Astronomy in the Old Testament*. Oxford University, 1906.

Schlauch, Margaret. "General Values of the Study of Hebrew." In *Seventh Annual Foreign Language Conference, Proceedings of the Hebrew Panel*, edited by Abraham I. Katsh and H. Alpern, pp. 7–9. New York University, November 16, 1940.

Schleiden, M. I. *The Importance of the Jews for the Preservation and Revival of Learning during the Middle Ages*. London: Siegle, Hill & Co., 1911.

Second Part of a Reply to the Vindication of the Subscribing Ministers, by a Committee of the Non-Subscribing Ministers. London, Clark & Co.

Serjeantson, M. S. *A History of Foreign Words in English*. New York: Dutton Co., 1936.

Sermons on Important Subjects collected from a number of Ministers, in some of the northern states of America. Hartford: Hudson & Goodwin, 1797.

Seybolt, R. F. "Hebrew in the Schools of Colonial America." *Publications of the American Jewish Historical Society.* Baltimore, 1931.

Seymour, Charles. "Hebrew at Yale University." *Hadoar* 21, no. 12 (January 17, 1941).

————. "Yale University President Traces Influence of Hebrew Culture." *Jewish Review,* February 24, 1949, p. 9.

Sidney, Algernon. *Discourses Concerning Government.* London: J. Darby, 1704.

Silberschlag, Eisig. "Origin and Primacy of Hebrew Studies in America." In *Hagut Ivrit Be' Amerika,* edited by Menahem Zohori, vol. 1, pp. 15–41. Jerusalem, 1972.

Silliman, Benjamin. *Oration in Celebration of American Independence.* Hartford: Hudson & Goodwin, 1802.

Silverman, Hirsch L., ed. *Annals of the Jewish Academy of Arts and Sciences.* New York: MSS Information Corporation, 1974.

Simms, P. Marion. *The Bible in America.* New York: Wilson-Erickson, 1936.

Simon, Leon. *Aspects of the Hebrew Genius.* London: G. Routledge & Sons, 1910.

Skeat, W. W. *An Etymological Dictionary of the English Language.* Oxford: Clarendon Press, 1910.

Smalley, Beryl. *Hebrew Scholarship among Christians in XIIIth Century England As Illustrated by Some Hebrew-Latin Psalters.* London: Shapiro, Vallentine & Co., 1939.

————. *The Study of the Bible in the Middle Ages.* New York: Philosophical Library, 1952.

Smith, Bernard, ed. *The Democratic Spirit.* New York: Alfred A. Knopf, 1941.

Smith, L. P. *English Idioms.* Oxford: Clarendon Press, 1923.

Spitz, Leon. *The Bible, Jews and Judaism in America Poetry.* New York: Behrman's Jewish Book Shop, 1923.

Sterling, Ada. *The Jew and Civilization.* New York: Aetco Publishing Co., 1924.

Stewart, George R. *Names on the Land.* New York: Random House, 1945.

Stiles, Ezra. *A History of Three of the Judges of King Charles I.* Hartford: Elisha Babcock, 1794.

Stonehill, C. A. *The Jewish Contributions to Civilization.* Birmingham: F. Juckes, 1940.

Storrs, R. S. *The Puritan Spirit.* Boston: Congregational Sunday School and Publishing Society, 1890.

Straus, Oscar S. *Roger Williams: The Pioneer of Religious Liberty.* New York: D. Appleton-Century Co., 1936.

————. *Origin of Republican Form of Government,* New York: G. P. Putnam's Sons, 1885.

————. "The Pilgrims and the Hebrew Spirit." *Menorah Journal* 6, no. 6 (December 1920).

Streeter, B. H. *The Buddha and the Christ.* London: Macmillan & Co., 1932.

Strong, Herbert Augustus; William S. Logeman; and Benjamin Ide Wheeler. *Introduction to the Study of the History of Language.* London: Longman's, Green, 1891. New York: AMS Press, 1973.

Sulzberger, Mayer. *The Polity of the Ancient Hebrews.* Philadelphia: Julius H. Greenstone, 1912.

Sweet, William. *Religion in Colonial America.* New York: Scribner, 1942.

Taine, H. A. *History of English Literature.* London: Chatto, 1907.

Tawney, R. H. *Religion and the Rise of Capitalism.* New York: Harcourt, 1938.

Thorndike, Lynn. *University Records and Life in the Middle Ages.* New York: Columbia University Press, 1944.

Thornton, John Wingate. *Historical Relation of New England to the English Commonwealth.* Boston: Alfred Mudge & Sons, 1874.

————. *The Pulpit of the American Revolution.* Boston: Gould & Lincoln, 1860.

Tocqueville, Alexis de. *Democracy in America.* 2 vols. New York: Alfred A. Knopf, 1942.

Tolkien, J. R. R. *Beowulf: The Monsters and the Critics.* Sir Israel Gollancz Memorial Lecture. London: Oxford University Press, 1937.

Trumbull, John H. *True Blue Laws of Connecticut and New Haven.* Hartford: American Publishing Co., 1876.

Tuchman, Barbara W. *Bible and Sword.* New York: New York University Press, 1956.

Turner, F. J. *The Frontier in American History.* New York: Henry Holt & Co., 1920.

Wadsworth, Benjamin. *The Well-Ordered Family.* Boston, 1712.

Walker, Williston. *A History of the Congregational Churches in the United States.* New York: Charles Scribner's Sons, 1900.

Ward, Anna L. *A Dictionary of Quotations.* New York: Thomas Y. Crowell Co., 1883.

Washburne, Emory. *Sketches of the Judicial History of Massachusetts.* Boston: Little & Brown, 1840.

Weaver, B. *Toward the Understanding of Shelley.* Ann Arbor: University of Michigan Press, 1932.

Weekley, Ernest. *A Concise Etymological Dictionary of Modern English.* London: John Murray, 1924.

————. *Words and Names.* New York: E. P. Dutton & Co., 1929.

Wertenbaker, Thomas Jefferson. *The Puritan Oligarchy.* New York: Charles Scribner's Sons, 1947.

Whiting, C. E. *Studies in English Puritanism from the Restoration to the Revolu-*

tion, 1660–1688. New York: Macmillan Co., 1931.

Whitney, A. *Language and the Study of Languages.* London: N. Truber & Son, 1876.

Wiernik, Peter. *A History of the Jews in America.* New York: Jewish History Publishing Co., 1931.

Williams, Roger. *The Bloudy Tenent of Persecution.* London, 1644.

Wilson, Edmund. *A Piece of My Mind.* New York: Farrar, Straus & Cudahy, 1956.

Winslow, E. *Hypocrisie Unmasked: A True Relation.* Providence: Club of Colonial Prints, 1916.

Winslow, O. E. *Jonathan Edwards.* New York: Macmillan Co., 1940.

Winsor, Justin. *The Memorial History of Boston.* Boston: J. R. Osgood & Co., 1880–81.

Winter, Nathan W. *Jewish Education in a Pluralistic Society.* New York: New York University Press, 1966.

Winthrop, John. *A Journal.* Hartford: Elisha Babcock, 1790.

Wolf, Edwin II. "Ezra Stiles Writes a Letter." In *Studies and Essays in Honor of Abraham I. Neuman,* pp. 516–46. Philadelphia: Dropsie College, 1962.

———, and Maxwell Whiteman. *The History of the Jews of Philadelphia from Colonial Times to the Age of Jackson.* Philadelphia: Jewish Publication Society, 1975.

Wolf, L. *Menasseh ben Israel's Mission to Oliver Cromwell.* London: Jewish Historical Society of England, 1901.

Wood, K. B. *Quotations for Occasions.* New York: Century Co., 1896.

Woodhouse, A. S. P. *Puritanism and Liberty.* London: J. M. Dent & Sons, 1938. Chicago: University of Chicago Press, 1951.

Work, W. W. *The Bible in English Literature.* New York: Fleming & Revell Co., 1917.

Zangwill, Israel. *Selected Works.* Philadelphia: Jewish Publication Society, 1938.

Notes

INTRODUCTION

1. Joseph Addison and Sir Richard Steele, *Critical Essays from the "Spectator,"* ed. Donald F. Bond (London: Oxford University Press, 1970), No. 405 (Saturday, June 14, 1712).

2. P. Marion Simms, *The Bible in America* (New York: Wilson-Erickson, 1936), p. 203.

3. W. L. Roy, *A Complete Hebrew and English Critical and Pronouncing Dictionary* (New York: Collins Keese and Co., 1837), introduction.

4. Frank Rosenthal, "The Rise of Christian Hebraism in the Sixteenth Century," *Historia Judaica* 7 (1945): 167–91.

CHAPTER 1

1. Matthew Arnold, *Literature and Dogma* (New York: Macmillan Co., 1889), p. 308.

2. Jerome, *Contra Rufinium,* ii, p. 476.

3. Beryl Smalley, *The Study of the Bible in the Middle Ages* (New York: Philosophical Library, 1952), pp. 361–62.

4. For a detailed study of Rashi's influence, see E. I. J. Rosenthal, "Rashi and the English Bible," *Bulletin of the John Rylands Library* 24 (April 1940).

5. I. Abrahams, E. R. Bevan, and C. Singer, eds., *The Legacy of Israel* (Oxford: Clarendon Press, 1927), p. 307.

6. Cecil Roth, *The Jewish Contribution to Civilization* (London: Macmillan

Co., 1938), p. 61; cf. A. I. Katsh, *Hebraic Foundations of American Democracy* (reprint ed.; New York: New York University Press, 1952).

7. Abrahams, Bevan, and Singer, *Legacy of Israel*, p. 310.

8. M. I. Schleiden, *The Importance of the Jews for the Preservation and Revival of Learning during the Middle Ages* (London: Siegle, Hill & Co., 1911), p. 54.

9. For a fuller treatment of this subject and period, see A. I. Katsh, *Judaism and the Koran* (New York: A. S. Barnes & Co., 1962), introduction; and Salo W. Baron, *A Social and Religious History of the Jews* (New York: Columbia University Press, 1965), vols. 3–8; S. D. Goitein, *Studies in Islamic History and Institutions* (Leiden: S. J. Brill, 1966).

10. Richard Garnett and Edmund Gosse, *English Literature: An Illustrated Record* (New York: Macmillan Co., 1926), p. 204.

11. R. S. Storrs, *The Puritan Spirit* (Boston: Congregational Publishing Society, 1890), pp. 52–53.

12. J. A. Froude, *Short Studies on Great Subjects* (London: Longmans, Green & Co., 1867), vol. 2, p. 53.

13. Robert Abbot, *A Trial of Our Church-Forsakers* (London: Thomas Payne, 1639), pp. 127–28.

14. William Bradford, *History of Plimouth Plantation* (Boston: Houghton Mifflin Co., 1896), p. 110.

15. *Sermons on Important Subjects Collected from a Number of Ministers in Some of the Northern States of America* (Hartford: Hudson & Goodwin, 1797), p. 62.

16. Thomas Jefferson Wertenbaker, *The Puritan Oligarchy* (New York: Charles Scribner's Sons, 1947), p. 59.

17. John Cowper Powys, *Enjoyment of Literature* (New York: Simon & Schuster, 1938), introduction.

CHAPTER 2

1. Hartley Burr Alexander, "The Hebrew Contribution to the Americanism of the Future," *Menorah Journal* 6, no. 2 (April 1920): 65–66.

2. W. DeLoss Love, Jr., *The Fast and Thanksgiving Days* (Boston: Houghton Mifflin Co., 1895), pp. 61–62.

3. Cf. Edmund S. Morgan, "Responsibilities of a Puritan Parent," *More Books: The Bulletin of the Boston Public Library* 17, no. 4 (April 1942): 141–59.

4. S. Broches, *Jews in New England* (New York: Bloch Publishing Co., 1942), pp. 4–6.

5. John Davis, ed., *New England's Memorial* (Cambridge: Corcker & Brewster, 1826), p. 36.

6. Cotton Mather, *Magnalia Christi Americana* (London, 1702), 3:100.

7. Perry Miller, *The New England Mind* (New York: Macmillan Co., 1939), p. 475.

8. Ibid., p. 477.

9. Increase Mather, *The Order of the Gospel* (Boston: B. Green & J. Allen, 1700), p. 30.

10. Perry Miller and T. H. Johnson, *The Puritans* (New York: American Book Co., 1938), pp. 49, 54.

11. Joseph Banvard, *Plymouth and the Pilgrims* (Boston: Gould & Lincoln, 1856), pp. 204, 231–32.

12. Robert Calef, *More Wonders of the Invisible World* (London: N. Hillar, & J. Collyer, 1700), p. 152.

13. P. M. Simms, *The Bible in America* (New York: Wilson-Erickson, 1936), pp. 337–42.

14. L. I. Newman, *Jewish Influence on Christian Reform Movements* (New York: Columbia University Press, 1925), p. 641.

15. Paul Masserman and Max Baker, *The Jews Come to America* (New York: Bloch Publishing Co., 1932), p. 69.

16. Mather, *Magnalia Christi Americana*, 1:109–10.

17. Davis, *New England's Memorial*, p. 272.

18. G. R. Stewart, *Names on the Land* (New York: Random House, 1945), pp. 123 ff.

19. C. E. Whiting, *Studies in English Puritanism from the Restoration to the Revolution, 1600–1688* (New York: Macmillan Co., 1931), pp. 445 ff.

20. Mather, *Magnalia Christi Americana*, 1:63.

21. See Appendix B, "Place Names of Biblical or Hebrew Origin."

22. Stewart, *Names on the Land.*

23. Lee M. Friedman, *Jewish Pioneers and Patriots* (Philadelphia: Jewish Publication Society, 1942), p. 96.

CHAPTER 3

1. Cotton Mather, *Magnalia Christi Americana* (London, 1702), 2:183.

2. Perry Miller and T. H. Johnson, *The Puritans* (New York: American Book Co., 1938), p. 698.

3. Anita Liebman Lebeson, *Pilgrim People* (New York: Harper & Brothers, 1950), p. 85.

4. Cf. William Chomsky, *Hebrew: The Eternal Language* (Philadelphia: Jewish Publication Society, 1957), p. 18

5. Robert H. Pfeiffer, "The Teaching of Hebrew in Colonial America," *Jewish Quarterly Review,* April 1955, p. 365.

6. Ibid.

7. Perry Miller, *The New England Mind* (New York: Macmillan Co., 1939), p. 475.

8. Stephen D'Irsay, *Histoire des Universités* (Paris, 1933).

9. Pfeiffer, "Teaching of Hebrew," p. 366.

10. Frank Rosenthal, "The Rise of Christian Hebraism in the Sixteenth Century," *Historia Judaica* 7 (1945): 167–91.

11. Mather, *Magnalia Christi Americana*, 2:53.

12. Samuel Eliot Morison, *The Puritan Pronaos* (New York: New York University Press, 1936), pp. 4–42.

13. Mather, *Magnalia Christi Americana*, 2:7.

14. *New England's First Fruits with Divers other Special Matters Concerning that Country* (reprinted for J. Sobin, New York, 1865), pp. 29–35.

15. Pfeiffer, "Teaching of Hebrew," pp. 366–67.

16. Ibid.

17. Ibid.

18. S. E. Morison, *Founding of Harvard College,* (Cambridge: Harvard University Press, 1935), pp. 74–91.

19. S. E. Morison, *Harvard in the Seventeenth Century* (Cambridge, Harvard University Press, 1932, 1:203–4.

20. Charles Seymour, "Yale University President Traces Influence of Hebrew Culture," *Jewish Review,* February 24, 1949, p. 9.

21. Arthur A. Chiel, "The Rabbis and Ezra Stiles," *American Jewish Historical Quarterly* 61, no. 4 (June 1972): 294 ff.

22. Ibid. See appendix for Hebrew letter by Stiles, *Yale Alumni Magazine,* March 1974, p. 19.

23. Ibid.; cf. Edwin Wolf II, "Ezra Stiles Writes a Letter," in *Studies and Essays in Honor of Abraham A. Neuman* (Philadelphia: Dropsie College, 1962), pp. 516–46.

24. Franklin B. Dexter, ed., *The Literary Diary of Ezra Stiles* (New York, 1901), 2:397; cf. William Novak, "The Hebrew Language and Spirit in Early American Life" (unpublished paper April 1969).

25. "Hebraic Studies in American Colleges and Universities," in *Doron (Hebraic Studies): Essays in Honor of Professor Abraham I. Katsh,* ed. I. T. Naamani, David Rudavsky, and Carl F. Ehle, Jr. (reprint, 1965), pp. 3–25.

26. Abraham I. Katsh, *Hebrew Language, Literature and Culture in American Institutions of Higher Learning* (New York: Payne Educational Sociology Foundation, 1950), p. 4.

27. Abraham I. Katsh, "Current Trends in the Study of Hebrew in Colleges and Universities," *Modern Language Journal* 44, no. 2 (February 2, 1960).

28. A. J. Band, "Jewish Studies in American Liberal Arts Colleges and Universities," *American Jewish Year Book, 1964.* According to Professor David Rudavsky ("Hebraic and Judaic Studies in American Higher Education," *Bulletin for the Council on the Study of Religion* 6, no. 2 [April 1975]):

The introduction of Black Study programs has stimulated the inauguration of Judaic courses in many colleges and universities. Jewish students are motivated to pursue these studies by an aroused Jewish self-awareness, which prompts them to probe for meaning in their Jewish identity or to seek the spiritual dimension or sacred values to counter the prevailing secularism in the environment. On their part, college officials in recent years have become more democratic and more responsive to student pressures for the inclusion of Jewish and other accredited ethnic courses in their curricula. Some 375 institutions of higher learning now teach Judaic studies to an estimated 35,000–40,000 students. About 15 percent of this enrollment consists of non-Jews, desirous of learning about the parent religion of Christianity or the religious culture of their Jewish neighbors, which has been presently recognized as being on a par with Catholicism and Protestantism.

Accordingly, advanced academic institutions in America now provide Hebraic and Judaic studies for some 55,000–60,000 registrants. These impressive statistics point to the vast potentialities of the American college in combating the widespread ignorance among our college youth, both Christian and Jewish, of the Jewish factor in Western culture. This area of study could help the Jewish student achieve an appreciation of himself as a Jew, as well as foster an understanding of Judaism among non-Jews, thereby nurturing better Christian-Jewish relations. The qualitative improvement of the instructional effort is, however, hampered by the dearth of suitable textbooks in Judaic studies. The problem is not as pronounced in the area of the Hebrew language and literature as in the Judaic courses, for in the former it is possible to adapt existing textbooks produced in America or in Israel. In some of the Judaic studies, however, practically no texts are available. This is particularly true of the American, Russian, and other phases of Jewish history and philosophy, or of subjects such as Jewish mysticism, Hassidism, and others. To remedy the situation it is essential to launch a planned effort on the part of a representative and qualified professional textbook commission, to be provided with sufficient funds to initiate and operate a number of textbook projects.

There are presently some twenty endowed chairs of Hebrew or of various branches of Jewish studies in as many universities, notably Brandeis, Columbia, Denver, Dropsie, Harvard, Iowa State, Ohio, Pennsylvania, New York (School of Education), Vanderbilt, Wayne, and Wisconsin. . . In some instances they are subsidized by a national Jewish cultural body, or the local Jewish community, or by individuals. Close to a hundred full-time professors, and in addition a large number of part-time instructors consisting of Hillel directors, local rabbis, and academicians, are employed to teach these courses. There is yet a need for well prepared, competent scholars and able teachers for the diverse areas of the Hebraic and Judaic programs, which represent a unique venture in American higher education.

CHAPTER 4

1. Frank H. Ridgely, *Jewish Ethical Idealism* (Boston: Gorham Press, 1918), p. 88

2. A. A. Neuman, *Landmarks and Goals* (Philadelphia: Dropsie College Press, 1953), pp. 258, 264. Cf. Newman, *Jewish Influences. . .,* p. 638.

3. Cf. Neuman, *Science, Philosophy and Religion,* Second Symposium, p. 400.

4. Edmund S. Morgan, "Puritan Love and Marriage," *More Books: The Bulletin of the Boston Public Library 17,* no. 2 (February 1942): 45.

5. Benjamin Wadsworth, *The Well-Ordered Family* (Boston, 1712), pp. 25–36 (quoted in Morgan, "Puritan Love and Marriage," p. 49).

6. John Cotton, *A Meet Help* (Boston, 1699), p. 16 (quoted in Morgan, "Puritan Love and Marriage," p. 61).

7. John Cotton, *A Practical Commentary* (London, 1656), pp. 126, 200 (quoted in Morgan, "Puritan Love and Marriage," p. 49).

8. A. A. Neuman, *Landmarks and Goals,* p. 258.

9. I. Abrahams, E. R. Bevan, and C. Singer, eds., *The Legacy of Israel* (Oxford University Press, 1927), p. 241.

10. *General Laws of the Massachusetts Colony* (1658), pp. 67–70.

11. Joseph Banvard, *Plymouth and the Pilgrims* (Boston: Gould & Lincoln, 1856), pp. 318–26.

12. *Massachusetts Colonial Records,* 1:126.

13. P. Marion Simms, *The Bible in America* (New York: Wilson-Erickson, 1936), p. 222.

CHAPTER 5

1. Harold Fisch, *Jerusalem and Albion* (London: Routledge & Keegan Paul, 1964), p. 107.

2. Thomas Jefferson Wertenbaker, *The Puritan Oligarchy* (New York, Charles Scribner's Sons, 1947), p. 26.

3. Mather, *Magnalia Christi Americana* (London, 1702), 1:131.

4. Roger Williams, *The Bloudy Tenent of Persecution* (London, 1644), 3:496.

5. Ralph Barton Perry, *Puritanism and Democracy* (New York: Vanguard Press, 1944), pp. 195–96.

6. Hannah Adams, *An Abridgement of the History of New England* (Boston: R. and J. Homans & John West, 1805), pp. 21–22.

7. *Cambridge Platforme of Church Discipline* (Boston, 1653), p. 32.
8. Thomas Hutchinson, *History of Massachusetts* (1764), 1:26.
9. John Gorham Palfrey, *The History of New England* (Boston: H. Shepard, 1873), 1:279.
10. Mather, *Magnalia Christi Americana*, 5:57.
11. Richard B. Morris, "Civil Liberties and the Jewish Tradition in Early America," *PAJHS*, 46 (September 1956): 23.
12. E. Dobschütz, *The Influence of the Bible on Civilization* (New York: Charles Scribner's Sons, 1914), pp. 158–59.

CHAPTER 6
1. Oscar S. Straus, *Origin of Republican Form of Government* (New York: G. P. Putnam's Sons, 1885), p. 77.
2. Oscar S. Straus, "The Pilgrims and the Hebrew Spirit," *Menorah Journal* 6, no. 6 (December 1920): 308.
3. George E. Ellis, *The Puritan Age and Rule in the Colony of Massachusetts* (Boston, 1888), p. 147; quoted in Straus, ibid., p. 307.
4. Straus, "Pilgrims and Hebrew Spirit," p. 309 (no. 2).
5. Thomas Jefferson Wertenbaker, *The Puritan Oligarchy* (New York, 1947), pp. 7–8.
6. A. A. Neuman, *Landmarks and Goals* (Philadelphia, 1953), pp. 256–57.
7. W. Pitkin, *A Political and Civil History of the United States of America* (New Haven: H. Howe, Durrie & Peake, 1828), 1:57.
8. Neuman, *Landmarks and Goals*, p. 263. cf. Mayer Sulzberger, *The Polity of the Ancient Hebrews* (Philadelphia: Julius H. Greenstone, 1912).
9. John Winthrop, *A Journal* (Hartford, 1790), p. 137.
10. Mather, *Magnalia Christi Americana* (London, 1702), 2:7.
11. Neuman, *Landmarks and Goals*, p. 270.
12. O. S. Straus, *Roger Williams: The Pioneer of Religious Liberty* (New York: D. Appleton-Century Co., 1936), p. 38.
13. James Ernst, *Roger Williams* (New York: Macmillan Co., 1937), p. 350.
14. Ibid., p. 351.
15. John D. Knowles, *Memoir of Roger Williams* (London: Edmonds & Co., 1834), p. 145.
16. Straus, *Roger Williams*, p. 80.
17. W. E. H. Lecky, *Rationalism in Europe* (London: Longman's Green & Co., 1910), 2:168.
18. J. W. Thornton, ed., *The Pulpit of the American Revolution* (Boston, 1860), pp. 86–87.
19. Straus, *Republican Form of Government*, p. 110.
20. Lawrence Henry Gipson, *The British Empire Before the American Revolution*, vol. 1 (New York: Alfred A. Knopf, 1936), p. 32.
21. Louis Witt, *Judaism and Democracy*, p. 7; cf. Milton R. Konvitz,

"Judaism and the Democratic Ideal," in *The Jews: Their History, Culture and Religion,* ed. Louis Finkelstein (Philadelphia: Jewish Publication Society, 1949), pp. 1092–1113. In this connection I would also point out the probable influence of Deuteronomy 16:15 on the policy of permitting only native-born Americans to seek the highest office in the land: "one from among thy brethren shalt thou set as king over thee; thou mayst not set a stranger over thee, who is not thy brother."

CHAPTER 7

1. H. Thomas Rack, *A History of Classical Philology* (New York: Macmillan Co., 1911), p. 398; cf. Lynn Thorndike, *University Records and Life in the Middle Ages* (New York: Columbia University Press, 1944), pp. 297–98; cf. Alan B. Corban, *The Kings Hall* (Cambridge: At the University Press, 1969), pp. 81–85.

2. William L. Roy, *A Complete Hebrew and English Critical and Pronouncing Dictionary* (New York: Collins, Keese & Co., 1837), introduction.

3. Ibid.

4. J. R. R. Tolkien, *Beowulf: The Monsters and the Critics,* Sir Israel Gollancz Memorial Lecture (London: Oxford University Press, 1936).

5. Cf. David Daiches, "The Influence of the Bible in English Literature," in *The Jews: Their History, Culture and Religion,* ed. L. Finkelstein (Philadelphia: Jewish Publication Society, 1949), 3:1117.

6. J. L. Cardozo, *The Contemporary Jew in Elizabethan Drama* (Amsterdam: H. J. Paris, 1925), pp. 69–70.

7. Daiches, "Bible in English Literature," pp. 1114–15. Cf. Appendix A "Hebrew Words and Phrases in English."

8. James Bell, *Biblical and Shakespearean Characters Compared* (London: Hull Press, 1894), p. 11.

9. Haim Schechter, "The Influence of Talmudic and Midrashic Literature on Shakespeare." *Areshet* (Hebrew, Jerusalem, 1943), pp. 394–99.

10. Ibid.

11. C. E. Whiting, *Studies in English Puritanism from the Restoration to the Revolution, 1660–1688* (New York: Macmillan Co., 1931), p. 442.

12. S. A. Brooke, *The Poetry of Robert Browning* (New York: Thomas Y. Crowell & Co., 1902).

13. Judith Berlin-Lieberman, *Robert Browning and Hebraism* (Jerusalem: Azriel Press, 1934), p. 85.

14. Henry Kendall Booth, *The Background of the Bible* (New York: Charles Scribner's Sons, 1929), p. 260; cf. Daiches, "Bible in English Literature," passim.

15. S. E. Morison, *The Intellectual Life of Colonial New England* (New York: New York University Press, 1956), pp. 177–78.

16. S. E. Morison, *Puritan Pronaos* (New York: New York University Press, 1936), pp. 41–42.

17. Bernard Smith, ed., *The Democratic Spirit* (New York: Alfred A. Knopf, 1941), p. 15.

18. Dumas Malone, *Jefferson the Virginian* (Boston: Little, Brown, 1948), p. 172.

19. Leon Spitz, *The Bible, Jews, and Judaism in American Poetry* (New York: Behrman's Jewish Bookshop, 1923), p. 6.

20. *The Cambridge History of American Literature* (New York: G. P. Putnam's Sons, 1922), 1:266; cf. Increase Mather, *Magnalia Christi Americana* (London, 1702).

21. Cf. Edmund Wilson, *A Piece of My Mind* (New York: Farrar, Straus & Cudahy, 1956), pp. 92–94. See also Perry Miller, *The New Englad Mind* (New York: Macmillan Co., 1939).

22. Spitz, loc cit.

23. Margaret Schlauch, "General Values of the Study of Hebrew," in *Seventh Annual Foreign Language Conference, Proceedings of the Hebrew Panel,* ed. A. I. Katsh (New York University, November 16, 1940), pp. 7–8. Cf. Abraham I. Katsh, *Hebraic Foundation of American Democracy* (New York: New York University, 1952), pp. 1–65.

24. Cf. Salo W. Baron, *A Social and Religious History of the Jews* (New York: Columbia University Press, 1973); Oscar S. Straus, *The Origin of the Republican Form of Government in the United States of America* (New York: G. P. Putnam's Sons, 1885), pp. 77 ff.; A. A. Neuman, *Relations of the Hebrew Scriptures to American Institutions* (New York, 1956), pp. 6–12; D. de Sola Pool, "Hebrew Learning Among Puritans of New England Prior to 1700," *AJHS* 20 (1911).

Index of Names and Subjects

Saul, 148–50 passim
Schickard, Wilhelm, 58, 59
Schlauch, Margaret, 163
Schleiden, M. I., 19
Scriptures. *See* Bible
Scrooby Congregation, 30
Second Congregational Church (Newport), 63
Secretum Secretorum (medieval treatise), 19
Sefardi, Isaac Leon ben Eliezer Zur, 60
Sefer ha-Mitzvot (Maimonides), 60
Sefer Shaarey Orah, 64
Sefer Shaarey Tziyon (Hanover), 64
Selden, John 51, 57, 103, 136
Selling of Joseph, The (Sewall), 157
Sennacherib (Assyrian king), 25
Servetus, Michael, 17
Sewall, Samuel, 156, 157
Sewall, Stephen, 61
Seymour, Charles, 63
Shakespeare, William, 3, 103
　　Coriolanus, 151
　　Hamlet, 147, 151
　　Henry VIII, 151
　　Macbeth, 148–50
　　Richard II, 3
Shelley, Percy Bysshe, 153
Shepard, Thomas, 43, 53
Shulchan Aruch (Caro), 60
Sidney, Algernon, 135, 136
Simms, P. Marion, 4, 89
Slave Singing at Midnight, The (Longfellow), 161
Smalley, Beryl, 16
Smith, Eli, 72
Smith, John, 67
Smith College, 74, 76
"Snare Broken, a Thanksgiving Discourse, The" (Mayhew), 132, 135
Solomon; or, a Treàtise Declaring the State of the Kingdom of Israel (pamphlet), 24
Southern California, University of, 76
Southey, Robert, 155
Spanish Armada, 22
Spenser, Edmund, 151–52
Spitz, Leon, 159, 162
Stamp Act, 132
Sternhold, Thomas, 69
Stevens, John, 26
Stiles, Ezra, 63, 64, 65, 129
Stowe, Harriet Beecher, 162
Straus, Oscar S. 129

Supreme Court, U.S., 7
Survey of the Summe of Church Discipline (Hooker), 156
Susannah, 20
Suzanne (play), 146
Syracuse University, 73

Talmud, 54, 59, 63, 69, 154
Tawney, R. H., 81
Taylor, Jeremy, 155
Tea Act, 115
Tel el-Amarna documents, 141
Temple University, 74, 76
Ten Commandments. *See* Decalogue
Tennyson, Alfred, 153, 155
Texas (Whittier), 162
Texas, University of, 76
Thanatopsis (Bryant), 160
Thanksgiving Day, 84
Theodore of Mopsuestia, 14
Thesaurus Grammaticus Linguae Sanctae Hebraeae (Buxdorf the elder), 59
Thornton, J. W., 131
Throwgood, Thomas, 33
Touro, Isaac, 63
Tragedy of Mariam (and Herod), The, 146
Treatise of the Sabbath (Bound), 85
Tremellius, Emanuel, 51
Trinity College, 74
Tübingen, University of, 58
Tulane University, 74
Turner, Frederick Jackson, 27
Two Sins of King David (play), 146
Tyndale, William, 17, 36, 146

Udall, John, 59, 69
Union Theological Seminary, 72
University of the City of New York, 72. *See also* New York University

Vanderbilt University, 72, 76
Vaughan, Henry, 152
Versichorists, 17
"Visit from Saint Nicholas, A" (Moore), 66
Vulgate, 5, 50

Wadsworth, Benjamin, 82
Wakefield, Thomas, 56
Walton, Brian, 51
War of Independence. *See* American Revolution
Ward, Nathaniel, 53, 107, 155

Index of Passages

I. Hebrew Bible

246 *Index of Passages*